THE EMPTY THRONE

*The Quest for an Imperial Heir in
the People's Republic of China*

TONY SCOTLAND

VIKING

VIKING

Published by the Penguin Group
Penguin Books Ltd, 27 Wrights Lane, London w8 5TZ, England
Penguin Books USA Inc., 375 Hudson Street, New York, New York 10014, USA
Penguin Books Australia Ltd, Ringwood, Victoria, Australia
Penguin Books Canada Ltd, 10 Alcorn Avenue, Toronto, Ontario, Canada M4V 3B2
Penguin Books (NZ) Ltd, 182–190 Wairau Road, Auckland 10, New Zealand

Penguin Books Ltd, Registered Offices: Harmondsworth, Middlesex, England

First published 1993

1 3 5 7 9 10 8 6 4 2
First edition

Copyright © Tony Scotland, 1993

Typeset by Datix International Ltd, Bungay, Suffolk
Set in 11/13 pt Monophoto Sabon
Printed in England by Clays Ltd, St Ives plc

A CIP catalogue record for this book is available from the British Library

ISBN 0-670-849804

For Julian

CONTENTS

THE EMPTY THRONE
page 1

ILLUSTRATIONS

20. Duke Aisin-Gioro Yü-yan, great-great-grandson of the Emperor Glory of Right Principle and special aide to P'u-yi in Manchukuo in the 1950s. (Drawing by Sarah Godsill.)
21. Duke Yü-yan's mother Ching-kuei and her sister in the Palace of his great-grandfather, the first Prince Tun in Peking in the last years of the Manchu dynasty.
22. P'u-chieh, brother of P'u-yi, with his Japanese wife, Saga Hiro, and their first child, Hui-sheng in 1940.
23. P'u-chieh's bungalow in Ch'ang-ch'un is now a kindergarten.
24. The kitchen of the kindergarten, with the original tiled floor.
25. The Emperor's brother's bath has been redundant since the fall of Manchukuo in 1945.
26. P'u-chieh in the uniform of a Japanese officer cadet with his Japanese bride, Saga Hiro, on their wedding day in Ch'ang-ch'un in 1938.
27. Aisin-Gioro Hui-Sheng, the elder of two daughters of P'u-chieh and Saga Hiro.
28. A Japanese propaganda poster of P'u-yi as Emperor of the puppet state of Manchukuo.
29. As a protest against the Japanese, Beauty in Flower continued to wear the court dress of the Manchus for her rare appearances in public as Empress of Manchukuo.
30. Duke Yü-yan, favourite 'nephew' of the Emperor P'u-yi during the Manchukuo period with his Manchu bride, Ma-chia Ching-lan, on their wedding day in Ch'ang-ch'un in 1943.
31. The Tatala concubine, Jade Years, P'u-yi's favourite Secondary Consort, in her bedroom in the Imperial Palace in Ch'ang-ch'un in 1938.
32. The Han concubine, Jade Lute, P'u-yi's third Secondary Consort, in 1943.
33. Jade Lute divorced P'u-yi in 1956.
34. In 1987 Jade Lute returned to the Imperial Palace in Ch'ang-ch'un to relive her memories of the Manchukuo period.
35. The 'new' Imperial Palace in Ch'ang-ch'un, which the Japanese built for P'u-yi.
36. The author and Mr Interpreter Wang outside the 'old' Imperial Palace in Ch'ang-ch'un, known as the Salt Tax Palace because of its pre-Manchukuo incarnation.
37. Self-help in the War Criminals' Prison in Fu-shun.
38. Ex-Emperor P'u-yi receiving the news of his Special Pardon Order on December 8th, 1959.
39. Duke Yü-ts'ung, son of Beitzu P'u-lun, wearing a coat of Japanese armour made in 1351.
40. Duke Yü-ts'ung with his elder son Hêng-ming outside their house in Pei-hai Park in Peking, in about 1964.

Illustrations Acknowledgements

The author and publishers are grateful to the following for permission to reproduce photographs and line illustrations:

Aixinzhueluo Li Shuxian, 43, 44, 45, 46, 47
Professor Wang Qingxiang, 6, 21, 22, 26, 27, 28, 29, 30, 32, 33, 34
Sun Zhengzheng, 62
Sarah Godsill, 20, 41

All the other photographs either were taken by the author or are in his possession.

FOREWORD

by Patrick Leigh Fermor

Monarchs, dislodged by political change from most of the world's thrones, are beginning to stir restlessly in their places of exile, and some of them – at any rate in Europe – are dreaming of return. But what about Asia? Tony Scotland's sudden longing to find out what has happened to the Manchu dynasty propelled him last year [1991] on a solitary flight to Peking. He was in search of the heir of P'u-yi, the last Emperor of China, and the ensuing quest for dispersed princes and princesses is recounted in a fluent, racy and informal style that makes his narrative impossible to put down. One by one he tracks down the survivors of the dynasty that history has scattered about their evaporated empire, and the resulting conversations are recorded with insight, compassion and humour. The vigour, the intrigues and the wickedness of the Empress Dowager are related; ancient scandals surface; dark deeds abound and Manchu dynasts, revolutionary warlords, rival concubines and palace eunuchs crowd the stage. The author's quest is beset by delays, misunderstandings, lucky encounters, dashes across rainy Peking, frustrations, dead-ends and, finally, crowned by triumphant success. Language difficulties are hilariously overcome and the author's flair for capturing characters, moods and atmospheres, his eye for faces and scenery and the pace of his search turn this reconstruction and its conclusion into a stimulating, revealing and altogether unusual achievement. His susceptible friend and interpreter is called Loud Report, whose alternating passion for two beautiful girls – Morning Mist and Winter Stone – weaves a modern, picaresque and light-hearted strand into the intricate, sometimes threadbare but always shimmering fabric of the Manchu past.

ACKNOWLEDGEMENTS

This book could not have been written without Sun Zhengzheng – the irrepressible Loud Report – my guide, interpreter and companion in China, and friend ever since. His loyalty, courage, enterprise, tenacity and sheer bravura charm helped me complete a quest which he himself held in good-humoured, and healthy, disdain; to him I owe the greatest debt of gratitude.

I should also like to thank Zhengzheng's parents, Professor Sun Xuechen and Associate Professor Cao Guilan, his girlfriend Zeng Xi (Morning Mist) and her sister Zeng Qing (Sunshine), for their assistance and hospitality; Zhang Hongyu (Red Universe) for her cool negotiating skills and warm friendship; her Taiwanese-American employers, Joseph and Sophia Wang, for generously allowing me the use of their office in Peking, for advice and assistance, and for so many personal introductions – without which China would have been impenetrable; and their London-based niece, Dai-chi Chiu and her husband Valentin Schiedermair, as much for their Chinese connections – and unsurpassed Chinese cuisine – as for their expert and elegant translations of the less than elegant *Putonghua*, the Peking dialect which is now the official language of the People's Republic.

I must also thank Mme Aixinzhueluo Li Shuxian, widow of Mr Aixinzhueluo Puyi (formerly the Emperor Proclamation of Fundamental Principles, the last Emperor of the Qing dynasty), for her enthusiastic co-operation and her hospitality in Peking; Mr Aixinzhueluo Yuyan for his kind help and for his beautiful calligraphic poem; Jim Nason (formerly of the Chinese Section, BBC World Service), the first and invaluable link in a chain of introductions, which led via Carole Murray, a barrister and sinologist in London, and Xu Mingqiang, a publisher at the Foreign Languages Press in Peking, to the fount of all imperial knowledge in China: Associate Professor Wang Qingxiang, Head of the Pu-Yi Study Section at the Jilin Academy of Social Sciences in Changchun. I am deeply indebted to Professor Wang for answering all my questions so openly and for putting his unequalled store of late Manchu material – including photographs, documents, research notes and genealogical pedigrees – at my disposal, both during and after my visit to China; to his charming wife for her hospitality; and to Dr Wang Xueliang for translating our many conversations in Changchun, and for his special expertise in transliterating the antiquated Manchu given names of the imperial pedigree.

I am also specially grateful to Patrick Leigh Fermor, for his great generosity in writing the Foreword; to John Holmstrom, who read and corrected the manuscript so meticulously (though any remaining errors or omissions are entirely mine), and gave me good advice and kind encouragement; to Christopher Potter, for criticism and guidance; to Freda Berkeley, the staunchest of friends, for supporting the cause in all manner of ways from the beginning; to my editor Eleo Gordon, Clare Harington, Claire Péligry, Suzanne Dean, Dinah Benson and their colleagues at Penguin Books, and to my agent, Deborah Rogers, for their commitment to the book; and to Sarah Godsill, for her line drawings.

The following friends answered questions, provided leads, offered expert assistance or contacts or hospitality, or were simply encouraging, and I am extremely grateful to them all: Anne and Alastair Aberdeen, Anne Acland, the late Michael Annals, Stefan Artner, Adam Bager, Anthony Besch, Thomas Blaikie, Jane Brown, Julian and Clare Calder, Harvey Chalmers, Ginette Darwin, Sheila de Morales, Patric Dickinson (Richmond Herald of Arms), Ariane Goodman, Paul Guinery, Coote Heber-Percy, Father Michael Hollings, Patricia Hughes, the late Colin Keer, Jim and Alvilde Lees-Milne, Jill Day Lewis, Annie McCaffry, Sheila MacCrindle, Michael and Caroline Mitchell, Francesca Moffatt, Patrick O'Connor, Geoffrey Parsons, Joe Pataki, Burnet Pavitt, Thomas Ponsonby, Oliver and Meredith Ramsbotham, Douglas Reith, Paul Reynolds (BBC Radio foreign affairs and diplomatic correspondent), Father Cormac Rigby, Rupert Robertson, David Scotland, Susan Sharp, Sue Townsend, Petroc Trelawny, Christopher Walker, David Williamson (co-editor, *Debrett's Peerage*), and Trevor Wood.

I also want to thank: Mr David Clifton (CBC News, London), Sir Alan Donald (formerly H.M. Ambassador, Peking), Mr David Evans and his colleagues in the BBC Research Library, Mr Franco Giovale, Mr David Helliwell (Bodleian Library, Oxford), Mr Jim Hoare (Head of Chancery, H.M. Embassy, Peking), Mr Paul Kramer (editor, *The Last Manchu*), the Hon Sarah Lawson, Mr Geoffrey Lewis, Mr Donald Macleod (presentation editor, Radio 3), Mr James Miles (Peking correspondent, *BBC Radio News*), Mr Koyama Noboru (Japanese Books Department, Cambridge University Library), Mr Janos Paludan (formerly Danish Ambassador, Peking) and Mrs Ann Paludan (author, *The Chinese Spirit Road*), Mr Mark Peploe (scriptwriter, *The Last Emperor*), Mr Graham Pointon and Mrs Sharon Fairman and their colleagues in the BBC Pronunciation Research Unit, Miss Xu Dongyan (Winter Stone) and Miss Zhou Huiming (chief receptionist, Bamboo Garden Hotel, Peking).

Lastly I want to thank my friend Julian Berkeley, who read each page of the manuscript as it was written, and provided constant encouragement. Without his support and faith and patience the book would never have been finished; or started. To him, with love, it is dedicated.

Tony Scotland, Ramsdell, Hampshire, December 1992

A NOTE ON THE SPELLING OF CHINESE NAMES

The Pinyin system of conveying the sounds of Modern Standard Chinese in roman letters – devised in 1956, but not introduced till as recently as 1979 – has now generally replaced the old Wade–Giles system, both inside and outside the People's Republic of China. However, no system of romanization is free of ambiguities – none can accurately capture the sound of the Chinese original – and Pinyin, though intended to be simpler, often seems wilfully unpronounceable, with its *u*-less *q*s, its misleading *x*s and its absence of any breath or stress marks.

The family name of the Manchu imperial dynasty, for instance, is contorted into the almost incomprehensible *Aixinzhueluo* in Pinyin, but Wade–Giles renders it quite simply as *Aisin-Gioro*. Perhaps this is an unfair example, because the name is Manchu in the first place, not Chinese. But what about the dynastic title of the Manchus? Pinyin transliterates it as *Da Qing*, which is unfathomable without a knowledge of the pronunciation rules, but Wade–Giles goes for *Ta Ch'ing*, which sounds as it looks. Or take the name of the much-maligned Empress Dowager who ruled China for the second half of the nineteenth century: Pinyin reduces her to *Cixi*, which is too unfamiliar to trigger an immediate phonetic response, but Wade–Giles offers *Tz'ü-hsi*, which may look alien but is at least pronounceable, with an effort. However, the two versions are visually so different as to pose a serious identity problem, so I have settled on the English translation of her given name, *Beneficent Indulgence* – romantic, perversely inappropriate, but memorable.

I have taken refuge in this same recourse, for the same reasons, in as many other cases as possible – specially the Manchu Emperors. Following established practice I have identified Emperors by their reign titles, rather than their personal or given names, which are taboo, or their posthumously awarded temple names, which are, strictly speaking, the only correct form of identifying deceased Emperors; and where they recur in the text I have translated the reign titles into English, except in the case of the last Emperor who, having abdicated, committed treason, been re-educated, pardoned and converted into a Communist citizen, has always been identified by his personal name, P'u-yi.

Where Chinese names are unavoidable in the book itself, I have adopted the Wade–Giles transliteration, for reasons of ease of pronunciation, period flavour and historical verisimilitude. But in the Acknowledgements and the Bibliography, out of respect for Chinese friends and consideration for Western readers in search of wider reading of recent vintage, I have given the Pinyin of current usage. Thus, my guide appears in the text as Sun Cheng-cheng (Wade–Giles) and in the Acknowledgements as Sun Zhengzheng (Pinyin), and the professor who gave me so much help in Manchuria is Wang Ch'ing-hsiang (Wade–Giles) in the text and Wang Qingxiang (Pinyin) in the Acknowledgements and Bibliography.

Finally I should explain some of Wade–Giles' oddities: the pervasive apostrophe is designed to soften an otherwise hard initial consonant or group of consonants, so that *Chun* is sounded *joon* but *Ch'un* is *choon*, and *Pei* is *bay* but *P'ei* is *pay*; *hs* approximates to the sound of a thin and sibilant *sh*, as in *Hsin*, pronounced *shin*; and initial *js* are sounded as *rs*, e.g. *Jui* (*ray*) and *Jung* (*roong*).

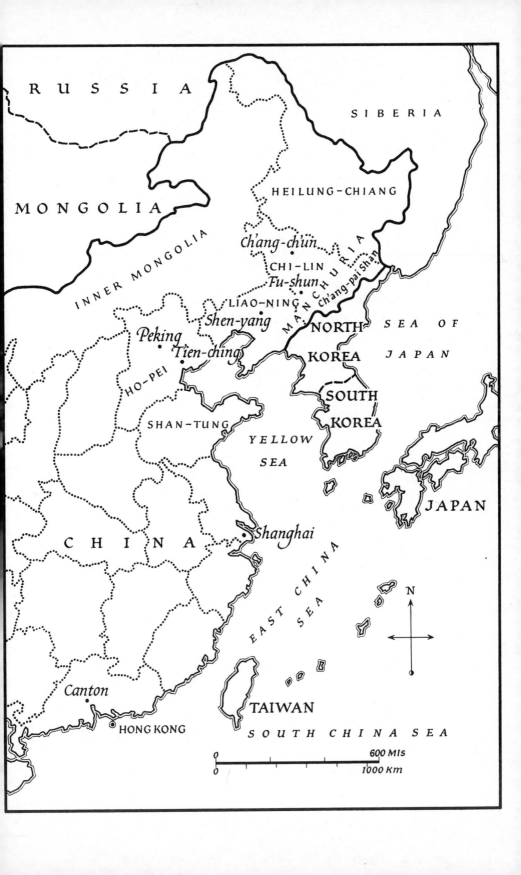

DRAMATIS PERSONAE

An Alphabetical List of the Principal Characters

Beauty in Flower (Wan-jung of the Kuo-po-lo clan), first wife of P'u-yi and last Empress of China, died 1946.

Beneficent Indulgence (Tz'ü-hsi of the Yehonala clan), ruled China as Empress Dowager for nearly half a century till her death in 1908, wife of Emperor Universal Plenty, mother of Emperor United Rule, aunt of Emperor Brilliant Succession and great-aunt of P'u-yi.

Brilliant Succession (Kuang-hsü), Emperor 1871–1908.

Chang, Principal: head of the Peking Institute of Calligraphy, director of Yü-yan's work unit.

Ch'un, Prince (Tsai-fêng), father of P'u-yi, P'u-chieh, P'u-chi and P'u-jen, Regent of China 1908–12, died Peking 1951.

Elegant Ornament (Wen-hsiu), first successive concubine of P'u-yi, divorced 1931, died 1950.

Enduring Glory (Ch'ien-lung), Emperor 1736–95.

Favourable Sway (Shun-chih), Emperor 1644–61.

Glory of Right Principle (Tao-kuang), Emperor 1821–50.

Harmonious Rectitude (Yung-chêng), Emperor 1723–35.

High Felicity (Chia-ch'ing), Emperor 1796–1820.

Honorific Abundance (Lung-yü), Empress of China by right of marriage to Emperor Brilliant Succession, as Empress Dowager signed the abdication of P'u-yi 1912, died without issue Forbidden City 1913.

Hsü, Mr (Hsü Ming-ch'iang), publisher, Book Section, Foreign Languages Press, Peking.

Jade Lute (Li Yü-chin), third successive concubine of P'u-yi, divorced 1956, lives in the North-East.

Jade Years (Tan Yü-ling), second successive concubine of P'u-yi, died Ch'ang-ch'un 1942, aged twenty-one.

Lasting Prosperity (K'ang-hsi), Emperor 1662–1722.

Li, Aunt (Li Shu-hsien), widow of P'u-yi, the last Emperor of China, lives in Peking.

Loud Report (Sun Cheng-cheng), a student in Peking, the author's guide and interpreter.

Morning Mist (Tseng-hsi), Loud Report's girlfriend in Peking.

Nurhachu (T'ien-ming) 1559–1626, founder of the Manchu House of Aisin-Gioro, ruler of Manchuria 1616–26.

P'u-ch'eng, Beitzu, son of Beileh Tsai-lien and grandson of Prince Tun (Yi-tsung, fifth son of the Emperor Glory of Right Principle), one of the claimants of the vacant throne in 1908, died 1932.

P'u-chieh, third Prince Ch'un, brother of P'u-yi, lives in Peking.

P'u-cho, Beitzu, eighth son of Beileh Tsai-ing, a favourite of Emperor P'u-yi at the court of Manchukuo, later a distinguished painter of the traditionalist school, who became vice-director of the T'ien-ching Academy after Liberation.

P'u-chün, Beileh, son of Prince Tuan (Tsai-i) and grandson of Prince Tun (Yi-tsung, fifth son of the Emperor Glory of Right Principle), appointed heir apparent with the title Ta-a-ko in 1900, appointment rescinded 1901, exiled to Ürümch'i, one of the claimants of the vacant throne in 1908, died Peking 1930s.

P'u-hsiu, Beitzu, second son of Beileh Tsai-lien, tenant of P'u-yi's house in T'ien-ching, died Peking 1950s.

P'u-jen, Beileh, half-brother of P'u-yi, lives in Peking.

P'u-lun, Beitzu, son of Beileh Tsai-chih and grandson by adoption of Prince Yin-ch'ieh (Yi-wei, eldest son of the Emperor Glory of Right Principle), one of the claimants of the vacant throne in 1908, died before 1934.

P'u-wei, second Prince Kung, son of Beileh Tsai-ying (adopted son of Yi-ch'ia, first Prince Chung) and grandson of the first Prince Kung (Yi-hsin, sixth son of the Emperor Glory of Right Principle), one of the claimants of the vacant throne in 1908, died 1937.

P'u-yi, last Emperor of China (succeeded 1909, abdicated 1912) and first and only Emperor of Manchukuo (1934–45), died without issue Peking 1967. His reign title was Proclamation of Fundamental Principles (Hsüang-t'ung) As the last Emperor of his dynasty, he received no posthumous temple title.

Red Universe (Chang Hung-yü), a secretary in Peking, the pivot of the author's investigations and the valuable intermediary in his conversations with the Pretender's work unit.

Saga Hiro, Japanese wife of P'u-chieh, died Peking 1986.

Tung-tung (Hêng-chün), born in 1966, third son of Yü-yan, works in a bank in Peking.

United Rule (T'ung-chih), Emperor 1862–74.

Universal Plenty (Hsien-fêng), Emperor 1851–61.

Wang, Mr Interpreter (Wang Hsüeh-liang), research fellow in Sino-American Relations, Chi-lin Academy of Social Sciences, Ch'ang-ch'un, Professor Wang's interpreter.

Wang, Professor (Wang Ch'ing-hsiang), head of the P'u-yi Study Section, Chi-lin Academy of Social Sciences, Ch'ang-ch'un, the foremost authority in China on the life and times of the last Emperor.

Winter Stone (Hsü Tung-yan), hotel chambermaid in Ch'ang-ch'un.

Yü-chan, third Prince Kung, seventh son of P'u-wei and great-grandson of Yi-hsin, first Prince Kung, calligrapher, lives in Peking.

Yü-yan, Duke, born 1918, younger son of Beitzu P'u-ch'eng and great-grandson of the second Prince Tun, favourite 'nephew' of P'u-yi at the Manchukuo court, where he was known as Little Jui; imprisoned in Russia with P'u-yi, 1945–50, 're-educated' at Fu-shun War Criminals' Detention Centre in Manchuria, 1950–57; retired road sweeper, calligrapher, lives in Peking with his second wife and third son.

GENEALOGY OF THE MANCHU HOUSE OF AISIN-GIORO
SHOWING THE EMPERORS OF THE CH'ING DYNASTY
FROM THE FOUNDER, NURHACHU, TO P'U-YI
AND HIS COLLATERAL DESCENDANTS.

All names given in Wade – Giles transliterations
Emperors identified by reign titles and shown in bold
Roman numerals in brackets indicate brother order

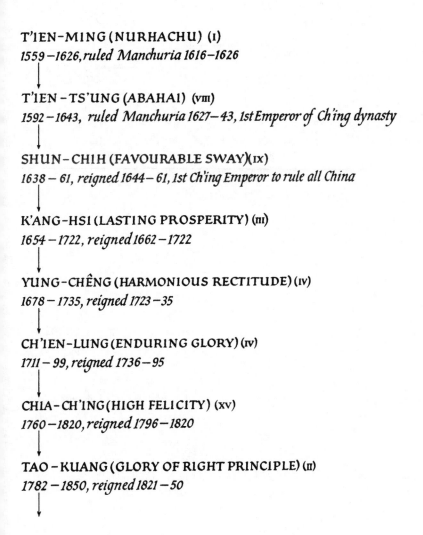

T'IEN-MING (NURHACHU) (I)
1559 –1626, ruled Manchuria 1616–1626

T'IEN –TS'UNG (ABAHAI) (VIII)
1592 – 1643, ruled Manchuria 1627– 43, 1st Emperor of Ch'ing dynasty

SHUN-CHIH (FAVOURABLE SWAY)(IX)
1638 – 61, reigned 1644– 61, 1st Ch'ing Emperor to rule all China

K'ANG-HSI (LASTING PROSPERITY) (III)
1654 – 1722, reigned 1662 –1722

YUNG-CHÊNG (HARMONIOUS RECTITUDE) (IV)
1678 – 1735, reigned 1723 –35

CH'IEN-LUNG (ENDURING GLORY) (IV)
1711 – 99, reigned 1736 –95

CHIA-CH'ING (HIGH FELICITY) (XV)
1760 –1820, reigned 1796 –1820

TAO –KUANG (GLORY OF RIGHT PRINCIPLE) (II)
1782 – 1850, reigned 1821 –50

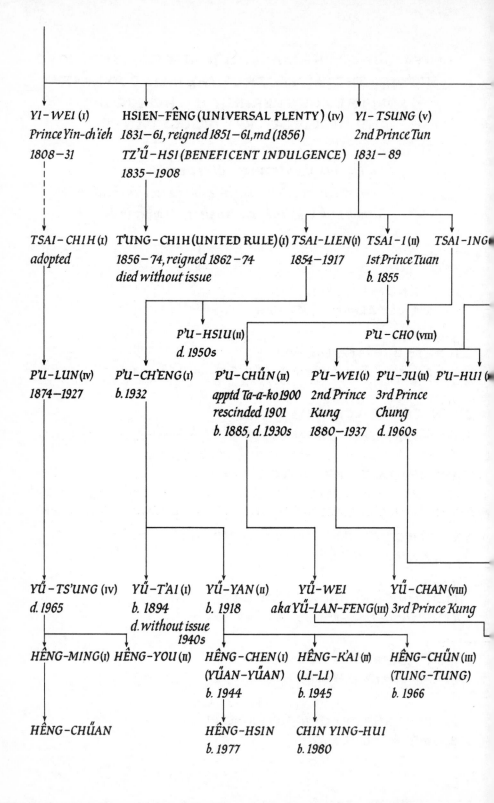

YI–WEI (I)
Prince Yin-ch'ieh
1808–31

HSIEN–FÊNG (UNIVERSAL PLENTY) (IV)
1831–61, reigned 1851–61, md (1856)
TZ'Ŭ–HSI (BENEFICENT INDULGENCE)
1835–1908

YI–TSUNG (V)
2nd Prince Tun
1831–89

TSAI–CHIH (I)
adopted

T'UNG–CHIH (UNITED RULE) (I)
1856–74, reigned 1862–74
died without issue

TSAI–LIEN (I)
1854–1917

TSAI–I (II)
1st Prince Tuan
b. 1855

TSAI–ING

P'U–HSIU (II)
d. 1950s

P'U–CHO (VIII)

P'U–LUN (IV)
1874–1927

P'U–CH'ENG (I)
b. 1932

P'U–CHŬN (II)
apptd Ta-a-ko 1900
rescinded 1901
b. 1885, d. 1930s

P'U–WEI (I)
2nd Prince
Kung
1880–1937

P'U–JU (II)
3rd Prince
Chung
d. 1960s

P'U–HUI

YŬ–TS'UNG (IV)
d. 1965

YŬ–T'AI (I)
b. 1894
d. without issue
1940s

YŬ–YAN (II)
b. 1918

YŬ–WEI
aka YŬ–LAN-FENG (III) 3rd Prince Kung

YŬ–CHAN (VIII)

HÊNG–MING (I)

HÊNG–YOU (II)

HÊNG–CHEN (I)
(YŬAN–YŬAN)
b. 1944

HÊNG–K'AI (II)
(LI–LI)
b. 1945

HÊNG–CHŬN (III)
(TUNG–TUNG)
b. 1966

HÊNG–CHŬAN

HÊNG–HSIN
b. 1977

CHIN YING-HUI
b. 1980

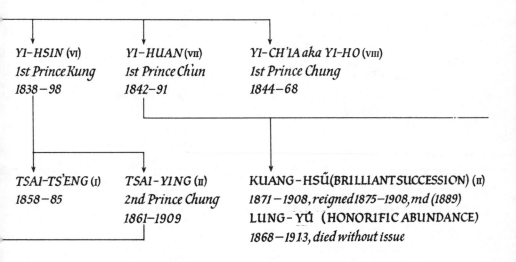

YI-HSIN (VI)
1st Prince Kung
1838 – 98

YI-HUAN (VII)
1st Prince Ch'un
1842–91

YI-CH'IA aka YI-HO (VIII)
1st Prince Chung
1844–68

TSAI-TS'ENG (I)
1858 – 85

TSAI-YING (II)
2nd Prince Chung
1861–1909

KUANG-HSŬ (BRILLIANT SUCCESSION) (II)
1871–1908, reigned 1875–1908, md (1889)
LUNG-YŬ (HONORIFIC ABUNDANCE)
1868–1913, died without issue

HSŬAN-T'UNG (PROCLAMATION OF FUNDAMENTAL PRIN-
CIPLES) (I) b. P'U-YI 7 Feb. 1906, enthroned Emperor 1909, abdicated
1912, restored for a fortnight 1917, expelled from Forbidden City 1924,
puppet Emperor Japanese state Manchukuo 1934–45, imprisoned
USSR 1945–50 and Communist China 1950–59, md 1st (1922)
EMPRESS WAN-JUNG (BEAUTY IN FLOWER), 1906–46, 2nd
(1922) SECONDARY CONSORT WEN-HSIU (ELEGANT ORNAMENT),
1909–50, divorced 1931, 3rd (1937) TAN YŬ-LING (JADE YEARS),
1921–42, 4th (1943) LI YŬ-CHIN (JADE LUTE), b. 1928, divorced 1956,
5th (1962) LI SHU-HSIEN (AUNT LI), b. 1925; died without issue 17 Oct. 1967.

P'U-CHIEH (II)
3rd Prince Ch'un
b. 1907, md 1st
(1924) T'UNG
SHIH-HSIA,
divorced 1936,
2nd (1938) SAGA
HIRO 1911–87

YŬ-HUAN (I)

HUI-SHENG
1939–57

YŬN-SHENG
b. 1941

YŬ-CH'ŬAN (I)

CHIN TZU-CHUNG (II)

LO HÊNG-LU (I)

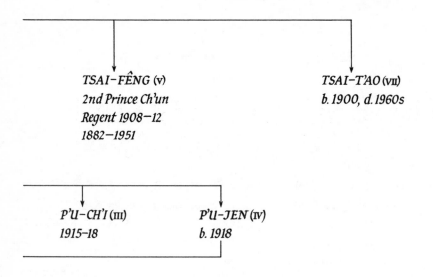

TSAI-FÊNG (v)
2nd Prince Ch'un
Regent 1908–12
1882–1951

TSAI-T'AO (vii)
b. 1900, d. 1960s

P'U-CH'I (iii)
1915–18

P'U-JEN (iv)
b. 1918

NOTE

Compiled from the JADE REGISTER of 1937,
translated for the author by Dr Wang Hsüeh-liang,
together with additional information supplied by
Prof. Wang Ching-hsiang (head of the P'u-yi Study
Unit at the Chi-lin Academy of Social Sciences, Ch'ang-
ch'un), the 1936 ALMANACH DE GOTHA and Hummel,
Arthur W. (ed.): EMINENT CHINESE OF THE
CH'ING PERIOD.

THE EMPTY THRONE

R ED Universe was tapping figures into her Japanese calculator in a minimalist office at the top of a glass-and-steel tower near the Friendship Store. Five years earlier a Chinese secretary would have done her sums on a government-issue abacus, but, learning from the collapse of European Communism, and anticipating the return of Hong Kong, the pragmatic Party leader Teng Hsiao-p'ing had buffed up the Chinese economy with a crash course in free marketeering. Lucky Red Universe was now the chatelaine of the chic-est office in the newest building on the smartest block in central Peking; with an American air-cooling system, this was the right place to be on a torrid day in June.

It was my first day back in China and I was not yet used to the thick and sticky heat, the airlessness, the grime. Every simple step was as much of an effort as running up a down escalator: my heart was thudding, my trousers were clinging to my legs and my white shirt was wet and smeared with smuts.

Red Universe looked fresh and elegant in a trouser suit of coral silk, with fashionable box shoulders. Her long, sleek ink-black hair was teased up in a height-enhancing quiff at the front and brushed in a cascade down her back to the waist; a Madonna on a silver chain hung around her neck. Despite her carefully cultivated Western gloss, Red Universe was unmistakably, delightfully, Oriental in appearance: small-boned, graceful and charming – but a level look in her eye, a determined set to her jaw and a pert, almost sexless confidence stamped her as the product of two generations of Maoist equality.

Her Chinese name was Chang Hung-yü. In China proper names always start with the family name – Smith – and end with the given name – John. The family name is usually formed of one character, the given name of two. Sometimes they make sense in English transliteration, sometimes not. Aisin-Gioro, the family name of the Manchu dynasty, has a meaning associated with gold; P'u-yi, the given name of the last Emperor, doesn't mean anything at all. But Hung-yü does, and it seemed so exotic that for me Ms Chang was always Red Universe. (The name owes its origin to the prevailing mood in China at the time of her birth during the Cultural Revolution, when optimistic expansionism was the dream of all good Party members.)

With a firm handshake, and a perpetual smile that was disconcertingly warmer than the appraising look in her eye, she said in English tinged with American, 'Welcome to my country.' Then she waved me towards a black leather sofa, beside a bare desk with only a Cambridge aircraft manufacturer's calendar on it. 'Can I fix you some coffee?'

I had arrived in Peking the day before on a ten-hour, non-stop flight from Copenhagen, using a short, cheap route over the West Siberian Plain. Dazed by the time-leap and doped by the heat, I still hadn't adapted to the brave, new China of word processors and coffee. It was almost exactly ten years since my first visit. Then I'd been on duty, the Radio 3 announcer accompanying the BBC Symphony Orchestra, an honoured guest of the People's Republic, with twenty-two hands of an official reception committee to shake. Now a lone tourist on a private visit, I was to China what it has always been to me, an enigma.

Expecting that the capital of the most populous country in the world, recently converted to free enterprise, would have built itself a showy new airport, with a modish atrium sprinkled with trees and fountains, arcades of duty-free shops, lots of shiny moving walkways and perhaps a dragon or two on the roof as a reminder, for the tourists' benefit, of an imperial past stretching back further than Western civilization itself, I was shaken by the Third World reality: barefooted peasants in coolie hats sweeping the tarmac with besoms, a luggage trailer abandoned on a deserted runway with two uniformed handlers fast asleep on top and a self-proclaimed Courtesy Car with a flat tyre and a sign tied to the rear mudguard saying FOLLOW ME.

As we stumbled across the hot tarmac, my fellow passengers and I, stiff, tired, bewildered and choking on the heavy wet heat, three boy soldiers, shy and grubby, in shapeless polyester uniforms, rushed forward to help us with our baggage; their guns lunged dangerously, but their smiles were warmly reassuring.

In the baggage hall I saw the first modest sign of economic change: standing in the middle of the luggage carousel, at the rakish angle of a 1950s advertisement, was a man-size pack of Salem Menthol cigarettes bravely proclaiming China's capitalist experiment.

The long drive into the city revealed more changes. Although bicycles were still thick on the road, there were more cars and fewer army trucks. The people were more engaged than I remembered, and they moved more purposefully; their clothes were more varied, plain still but definitely Western, and their faces more open. In ten years there had been an explosion of new buildings, most of them hotels – and most of those, I was to learn, sadly empty in the aftermath of the T'ien-an-men Square massacre – and an explosion of consumer goods: the shop windows, once empty or non-existent, were now discreetly displaying bottles of Great Wall wine and Chinese TVs, bicycles, T-shirts and bras. Even my taxi-driver was a free marketeer with a London cabby's contempt for receipts. A new and optimistic pulse beat in the Peking air.

It was all so different from that first visit in 1981, when the country was still recovering from ten years of chaos and destruction during the Cultural Revolution. Then I'd been struck by the uniformity of dress – men and women indistinguishable in the same dreary blue or green Mao tunic suits; by the cautious friendliness of our hosts and the dead-eyed torpor of the people – except the young, who were almost desperate in their eagerness to make foreign contacts; by the empty shops, the long queues for dog-eared cabbages piled high on the pavements, bright red banners everywhere proclaiming the soul-destroying slogans of Socialism.

'American coffee,' said Red Universe proudly, as she handed me a cup. 'Sugar?'

Neither coffee nor sugar had existed in Peking in 1981. What had happened? How could a country as sleepy and backward as China was then have shaken itself into sophisticated viability in ten years without changing its politics, or even its leadership? Red Universe ought to know, for she personified the change: I asked her.

She smiled and deflected my question. 'I thought you come to China to find last Emperor's family?'

I had, and Red Universe was the starting point of my quest. Back home in London, while scouting around for suitable – that's to say, independent – China contacts, I'd been given her name and address by a young Taiwanese pianist whose American-based uncle owned the Sino-American engineering trading company for which she worked as secretary. And I'd have been lost without her, for her office was to provide a central base for my operations, and she herself prove an invaluable mediator: through her I was to meet my aide-de-camp.

'You wrote in last fax,' said Red Universe, sinking into an armchair near my sofa, and turning a lidded cup of green tea in her slender fingers, 'that you want translator-guide. I have friend who is suitable. He is student at Astronautics University in Peking.'

'A trainee spaceman?' I asked archly.

'No,' she said, laughing. 'A sophomore of foreign trade, twenty-three years, very nice boy.' And she added, like a friendly procuress, 'I think you will like.'

I didn't have long to wait. Footsteps came to a hesitant stop outside the door and a large figure appeared in silhouette on the frosted glass. A knuckle rapped gently but firmly, once, twice, pause, a third time. Red Universe ran forward to open the door. And in tumbled Loud Report, stubbing his toe on the leg of the coffee table, puffing like a pet dragon and fanning his face with yesterday's *China Daily*: a handsome youth, as solid as a wrestler, with thick shiny hair, round frank eyes and a grin of winning warmth. He was wearing a white T-shirt with SPORT CONCEPT emblazoned across it, and sweat poured down his face in rivulets. Mopping his forehead with a scented flannel whilst rolling his eyes and grimacing, he advanced towards me, with his hand outstretched.

'Phooff!' he spluttered. 'Terribly sorry. Heat so hot. Terribly late. Haw! Traffic very very bad, and crazy taxi hit my bus: daang! Stupid-man. Pwoo! Excuse me. How you do, Misiter Socotolan. My name Sun Cheng-cheng.'

Cheng-cheng means Clang Clang, as in the sound of metal striking metal. But I couldn't bring myself to call him Clang Clang, or Bong, or Big Bang. So Cheng-cheng became 'Loud Report'.

When he'd regained his equilibrium with a cup of strong sweet black coffee and had gobbled up three lumps of sugar, he lay back on the sofa, vigorously fanning his dripping face, while Red Universe explained in rapid Chinese what I required of him. After she'd finished he turned to me in mock agitation, his eyes revolving in their sockets: 'Terribly sorry, Misiter Socotolan,' he said, 'but my English not too good enough, I think.'

He was probably right, but I liked him instantly, sensed that everyone else would, too, and knew that I could trust him. He was quick, bright, fun and as open as a child. As for English, I felt sure that if his vocabulary ever let him down, his face would come to the rescue. I assured him that I was less interested in interpreting skills than in

4

reliability, initiative, perseverance and good humour; in short, I was convinced he was the right man for the job and I hoped he could start immediately. After further polite demurrals – a necessary part, I was later to learn, of the Chinese decision-making process – Loud Report said OK and beamed. But his pleasure evaporated when I outlined the terms. For a moment I was afraid I'd insulted him by offering too little, or too much.

'No,' said Loud Report firmly. 'Thank you very much say-so, Misiter Socotolan, but no. I am guide because you my friend. I like money, but money not good between friends. OK, please?'

We talked about this for a few minutes and finally, prompted by the more pragmatic Red Universe, Loud Report agreed to accept expenses but no payment. Anxious not to offend sensibilities which I didn't yet understand, I accepted this for the time being, but I was determined to have my way – and eventually, though not without the intervention of his father, a man as honourable as he was wise, I succeeded in paying Loud Report a fair wage.

Meanwhile, he felt the brush with Mammon had lost him face, and to regain it he invited me to lunch.

'You like noodles, Misiter Socotolan? Mmmm, I like.' And he rolled his eyes and licked his lips. Loud Report, it soon turned out, liked anything edible. 'We have lunch at my favourite restaurant. I take you. But first we find Bamboo Garden.'

I had emphasized that my visit to China was a private one, that although I worked for the BBC this trip was nothing to do with broadcasting; I was an individual on holiday. My means, therefore, were limited. Loud Report got the message and from that day on he fought tooth and nail to prevent my spending a *fen* more than was necessary; protecting Misiter Socotolan's wallet became Loud Report's clarion call.

It started with a change of hotel. Red Universe had assumed that all Westerners were businessmen, that all businessmen were rich and that the rich were too delicate to stay anywhere but the grand joint-venture hotel not far from her office. So that's where she booked me in. And I ought to have been grateful, for the hotel was as comfortable and reasonably priced as any traveller could wish for; furthermore, it offered a standard of service unmatched in the West.

But there were two drawbacks: even at the discounted rate which Red Universe had negotiated for a month, it would cost a little too much – no more than a cheap hotel back home, but still more than my budget would allow. The other disadvantage, from my point of view, was its primarily business clientele: dollar-dealing Orientals from Japan and Hong Kong, Singapore, Malaysia and Taiwan, with a few noisy pushy Europeans and Americans. In such an atmosphere it was difficult to feel the pulse of old Peking.

I wanted a small, clean, quiet, central hotel that was essentially Chinese, even though I had been warned by a Western Chinese lady, who called a spade a spade, that I was looking for a paradox: by definition, she'd said, if a hotel were Chinese, then it had to be dirty and inefficient. (And by and large her blunt logic turned out to be right.) I wanted, moreover, air-conditioning, my own bathroom, a balcony with a view and a direct-dial telephone. And I dared hope, in over-hotelled, under-touristed Peking, that I could secure all this for no more than the price of a good bed and breakfast in London. I was asking for the moon – and found it in the Bamboo Garden, a small Chinese establishment set in a traditional garden off a quiet lane near the Drum Tower in the Tartar City. And its provenance was impeccably *echt*. It had been built a century ago for Shen Hsüan-huai, Minister of Posts in one of the last governments of the Ch'ing dynasty, and in the Cultural Revolution, faced with demolition, it had been commandeered by Kang Sheng, the notorious boss of Public Security, who pimped for Chairman Mao and met his end in prison with the Gang of Four; now it was a state-run hotel in the 'moderate' category.

Loud Report piled my things into a taxi, having first, with a Scottish instinct for economy, fixed the price of the fare. Then we joined the bicycle armada heading westwards down Chien-kuo-men Avenue towards the ill-fated T'ien-an-men Square, where, exactly two years earlier, the Chinese army had massacred hundreds of unarmed civilians, most of them students, who were taking part in a peaceful demonstration in support of democracy in China.

There are said to be four million cycles in Peking, ranging from the standard sit-up-and-beg bicycle to the pedicab tricycle, the modern equivalent of the coolie-drawn rickshaw; in between are bicycles towing armchairs for Granny or elaborate curtained palanquin-cabins for the wife and children, tricycles pushing dog carts laden with scrap metal or water melons, bicycles fitted with baby baskets on the handlebars or girlfriend slings on the back mudguard. Bicycling gear in this conspicuously unselfconscious capital is equally varied and ranges from the Mao suit (or Sun Yat-sen suit, as it's known in China) for the old or the very poor, to picture-hat, veil and lace gloves for nice young ladies understandably squeamish about Peking's famous dirt.

From the safety of the back seat of a taxi the volume of Peking's cycle traffic is a delightful phenomenon; to the visiting pedestrian the relentless stream of cycles, a dozen thick and suicidally nose-to-tail, seems to pose a constant threat to life itself. But in the course of a month I never saw a single cycle accident, for the pace, though fast, is steady. So once you've gauged the traffic's speed, crossing the road isn't the nightmare you expect. The secret is determination and a fixed purposefulness. Relying on traffic lights is fatal. The successful road-crosser simply strides across as though the cycles weren't there, the cycles then weave around him as though he weren't there and, so long as all parties keep going, the roads are spared the spillage of blood. This everyday miracle is a tribute to one of the Chinese's greatest assets, cool common sense.

Passing that icon of modern China, the blown-up, air-brushed colour portrait of an ever-youthful Chairman Mao above T'ien-an-men Gate, we turned north towards the Tartar City, following the purple walls of the Forbidden City. On the map it looked as though the Bamboo Garden Hotel were no more than a block or two north of the Forbidden City, but blocks come bigger in Peking and even the simplest journey takes twice as long as expected. At last we could see the great triple-roofed pavilion of the Drum Tower, with its two-horned guardian dragons warding off evil spirits at either end of the upper roof ridge. (The Drum Tower is Peking's oldest building; it was built by the Mings nearly 600 years ago for the sounding of the night-watches: one of their original drums is still there.) And in a few minutes we turned down a narrow lane and into a network of alleyways leading to the Bamboo Garden.

My room was right at the back of the hotel grounds, across a courtyard, down a red-painted garden corridor, through a bamboo grove and past a fish-pond, in a building called the Listening-to-the-pines Tower. From the balcony I could see across the lawns and flower beds and bamboos to the Mandarin Duck Pavilion perched on a rocky outcrop, as picturesque as a Chinese classical painting – and a great deal more useful, too, for the paranoid Kang Sheng excavated his own nuclear fallout shelter underneath it. Opposite lay the pond, its fountain frothing with rutting frogs. Immediately below me was a beauty salon dominated by a sinister dentist's chair which remained empty throughout my stay and a large coffee bar which did open but only when I wasn't there. And at the other end of the garden were two restaurants: the Studio-of-the-tending-of-the-pines (which claimed to be Western but would have frightened most Westerners on to the next plane home) and the Drunken Beauty Verandah (which remained as mysteriously shut as the beauty parlour).

The names alone were intoxicating; this was the perfect base for my imperial forays. I rang room service for some beer for Loud Report, who was fanning himself furiously on my bed, and some mineral water to dilute my Heathrow whisky. There wasn't any room service. Beer? In the bar. Where was the bar? Closed. Was there anywhere else selling beer? The shop. Ah, where was that? Next door to the reception, but it was shut now. I'd been at the Bamboo Garden no more than five minutes and already my enthusiasm was waning. This was the tails side of the Communist coin: I knew it well from travelling in Eastern Europe, pre-1989. The difference was that in Romania, Bulgaria and particularly in East Germany the inefficiency had been arrant anti-foreigner bloody-mindedness, while here in China, I felt sure, it was simple ignorance.

Willing myself to turn a blind eye to these shortcomings, I walked through the garden to the Studio-of-the-tending-of-the-pines kitchens, hoping to find a fridge of drinks, and on the way the song of the birds and the screech of the crickets, the rustle of the breeze in the bamboos restored my sense of proportion.

Returning to Room 303, I discovered the Chinese Laoshan mineral water I had bought was too salty for the whisky, so I poured out two beers instead and, raising my glass, I drank a toast to the Manchus.

Loud Report nearly choked. 'To China!' he corrected, with a splutter. Then, in an ominously soft voice, he came in for the kill: 'Misiter Socotolan, why you interested in Manchu?' He spat out the 'Manchu' as though it were a gob of bile.

'Because,' I said, 'the last imperial dynasty happened to be Manchu, and because I'm interested in the last Emperor, P'u-yi, and his surviving family.'

'But why?' His voice leapt to falsetto in perplexity. 'Last Emperor so ugly.' And he screwed up his face.

'Why? Because he was a fascinating phenomenon.'

'Femon—? Excuse please. Dictionary.' He rifled through the Fs till I redirected him to the Ps. 'A "p-r-o-d-i-g-y"?' He tilted his head like a puzzled puppy.

'Sort of. But more of a freak, perhaps.'

'Ah!' said Loud Report, with satisfaction, when he'd looked that up. 'A monster.' And he nodded enthusiastically, as though we agreed at last. 'So you think he was bad man?'

'Less bad, perhaps,' I said, 'than weak – a helpless victim, a stool-pigeon.' Loud Report's eyes glazed over.

From the day he was born, P'u-yi was used as a political pawn, and the fascinating thing about him is that he should have survived for as long as he did. His great aunt, the Empress Dowager Beneficent Indulgence, put him on the throne in 1908 when he was two. Four years later, when the Nationalist leader Sun Yat-sen proclaimed China a republic, his aunt Honorific Abundance, widow of the Emperor Brilliant Succession, took him off it. He spent his teens as a prisoner in the Forbidden City, with a pair of child wives he was frightened of – the smouldering Empress Beauty in Flower and the dumpy but spirited Elegant Ornament – and a thousand eunuchs who believed he really was the Son of Heaven.

In 1917 his supporters staged a feeble coup, and P'u-yi returned to his throne. But only for a couple of weeks. For the next seven years he stayed on in the Forbidden City, the pampered prisoner of the National-ists. Corrupted and useless, a feudal anachronism, he was finally given the push in 1924 and the whole imperial system came crashing down.

The Japanese then took him in hand. He thought they were going to restore him to his lost throne; they thought he'd be a useful tool in their plan to conquer China – so they made him puppet Emperor of Manchukuo. Once again, he was a prisoner – with nothing to do but study ants, chant Buddhist mantras and flog his page-boys.

When the Russians defeated the Japanese in 1945, they captured the Emperor and sent him to Siberia. Four years later China became a Communist republic, and the Russians sent the Emperor home. He could have been executed for collaborating with the Japanese, but he wasn't: instead Chairman Mao packed him off to the War Criminals' Prison at Fu-shun in Manchuria for 're-education through labour'. After a decade there he was pardoned and released. Now a model Maoist citizen, he was rewarded with a job as a gardener and a wife – a nurse – who looked after him to the end. But even then he was caught up in a political game. It was the start of the Cultural

Revolution. Red Guards were rampaging through China, bullying, torturing, even killing, anyone suspected of 'revisionism'.

The last Emperor was dying of cancer in hospital in Peking. The Red Guards found him, called a public meeting in his ward. A concubine and a eunuch from the old Manchukuo days denounced him as 'an arch capitalist-roader' and shouted in his face: 'We will take you back to the North-East and smash you, dog's head!' A few days later he died.

'Noodles, Misiter Socotolan?' Loud Report chivvied.

Eleven o'clock: lunchtime in Peking. Loud Report's 'masses' restaurant was crammed with young working people, the men in open-necked light-coloured shirts and dark trousers, the women in fresh mute-toned blouses and skirts. It was nearly a hundred degrees in the street outside and only slightly cooler inside, despite the fans, yet no one else seemed as hot as we were. Loud Report was swabbing his forehead and neck with his sweet-smelling face flannel; I grinned and bore it.

We'd had to wait for space at a table. Then Loud Report arranged me on a stool beside a lissom youth with dark glasses and a Benetton T-shirt ('Hong Kong Chinese!' he hissed in my ear, disapprovingly), while he vanished in the crush to choose our lunch. Now we were admiring the dishes he'd selected: fat noodles in a hot soy sauce, a tiny teapot of vinegar, plain boiled rice, stewed rice with jujube berries, a salad of carrot chippings and cucumber chunks, and some transparent jelly sticks which looked horribly like grubs.

'Enough?' asked Loud Report, as he handed me a pair of chopsticks.

'More than.' I tried to sound appreciative, but in truth the combination of the heat, the unfamiliar food and, worst of all, the surroundings had destroyed my appetite. The Chinese aren't pretty eaters. Whilst they themselves are scrupulously clean – almost obsessively so, washing their hands and faces at the drop of a tap – their tables are hog-wallows, war zones littered with bones and gristle, slops, left-overs and tooth-pickings. And in the absence of napkins, a corner of the table-cloth will do just as well. The aural ambience is no less comforting than the visual, for hawking and burping and farting are par for the course at the Chinese table.

'Why you not eat?' asked Loud Report, hurt.

'I'm sorry, but I think it must be the heat. We're not used to it in England, you know.'

'You have this in England?' He pointed to the jelly grubs. My stomach recoiled. With the generosity typical of the Chinese host, Loud Report nipped an entire family of grubs between the tips of his chopsticks and swung them over to my little bowl. 'For you. Is good. Eat.'

Eager to delay this new taste sensation, I pretended I couldn't catch the little creatures in my chopsticks. The gallant Loud Report came to the rescue and, cupping his right hand over mine, pincered a long thin one. Closing my eyes, I drew it to my mouth. At first my lips were unwilling to receive it, so I forced my tongue out on a recce and I was so relieved to discover that it tasted of nothing that I boldly bit, but the jelly body was quite impenetrable. Opening my eyes for inspiration I discovered I was being watched with interest by most of the table, and, embarrassed at the thought of the jelly thing still dangling from my lips, I drew in my cheeks and sucked. With a slurp it shot into my mouth, but not before it had slapped my face with its wet tail. The small boy opposite winked.

'You like this place?' asked Loud Report anxiously.

'Love it,' I lied.

'Ice cream now?'

'Yes, please!' I said, adding, rather ungraciously, 'but somewhere else perhaps?' Loud Report was about to look hurt again. 'Somewhere quieter.'

Ten years ago ice cream didn't exist in China, now it's available everywhere – in makeshift freezer chests towed behind bicycles, on pavements, in shops and in at least one specialist ice-cream parlour in Peking. If Loud Report's weakness was food, his vice was ice cream – so he knew where to go.

'All is couples here,' he said, as we were going in. At first I thought he meant the ices were served in double scoops. Then I understood: each of the little tables was occupied by a boy and a girl. With Cupid himself presiding, the parlour should have been hot with love, but it was as chilly as the ices themselves. None of the couples were speaking to one another. Or smiling. Or even looking at each other. Perhaps it was simply because the ices were so good – and they certainly were. Unable to make up our minds which of fourteen flavours to go for, Loud Report threw caution to the wind and ordered one of each.

'Misiter Socotolan,' he said, when we'd both finished – and he'd had a bowl of yoghurt, for good measure – 'how you find last Emperor's family?' He always wore a bad-smell look when he spoke of the Aisin-Gioros, the former imperial family – the Windsors of China – but now he looked worried, too – perhaps because he thought it was a tall order to go looking for strangers in a country of one-and-a-quarter billion people, especially if they were disgraced members of the Manchu dynasty, and perhaps because he knew more than I did about the authorities' attitude to unofficial research of any kind.

I explained that I knew P'u-yi had a brother, several sisters, a half-brother and a widow still living, and I was sure that if I could get an introduction to one then access to the others would follow. Sir Alan Donald, who'd retired as British Ambassador in Peking a few days earlier, had kindly put me in touch with one of the Aisin-Gioro clan, Yü-chan, and I'd been promised an introduction to the head of the family, P'u-yi's brother, P'u-chieh. I had a long list of the Aisin-Gioros I wanted to meet, and an even longer list of people who might help me reach them. My objective was to find veterans of the Ch'ing dynasty, the last imperial house of China, and to discover how they'd survived the cataclysmic changes from feudal imperialism to warring republicanism, then to Maoist Communism and now to this capitalist socialism – all in the space of a single lifetime.

I had a further specific objective which I kept to myself, partly because I was shy, in the People's Republic, to admit to anything so apparently irrelevant, and partly because if word were to get out, then someone else, with fewer scruples and greater resources, might reach my goal before I did, or the authorities might try to obstruct me, or both. I wanted to find the man who would be Emperor, the *de jure* Lord of Ten Thousand Years and Grand Khan of Tartary, the Chinese Pretender.

I knew that the last legitimate Emperor, Aisin-Gioro P'u-yi, had died childless in 1967, but had he died without an heir? Even deposed Emperors in Communist republics need heirs to make the necessary ritual sacrifices at their tombs, to carry out the traditions of ancestor-worship in accordance with the Confucian precepts of filial piety and generally to honour their predecessors.

Furthermore, in the light of developments in post-Communist Eastern Europe, where fallen monarchs were clamouring for their former crowns, the question mightn't be entirely hypothetical: was it fanciful to suggest that a descendant of the Son of Heaven – who had ruled in China, in a variety of dynastic disguises, for nearly 4,000 years – might one day replace the Central Committee of the Chinese Communist Party, regain the Dragon Throne and unite the vast state of modern China, the largest and most populous country in the world?

'We start tomorrow,' I told Loud Report, 'with a visit to the Foreign Languages Press. I've got a letter of introduction to someone there who may be able to put me in touch with the Manchus.'

'Foreign Languages Press? I not know this place.' Loud Report had suddenly gone all negative; he'd lost his sparkle. What was the matter?

'Misiter Socotolan, I think we are friends. Can I speak truth?' I nodded encouragingly. 'I'm terribly sorry, but I don't like Manchus.' He looked as though he'd got a mouthful of lemons.

'Why ever not? What's wrong with them?'

'They are lazy and have not manners. Excuse me say so but Manchus are . . . waste.'

A LL that I knew of the Foreign Languages Press was that its name appeared as the publisher on the title page of my copy of the English-language edition of P'u-yi's remarkable autobiography, *From Emperor to Citizen* – one of the weirdest and most enthralling life stories of the twentieth century (and P'u-yi's ghost-written Life is far superior, not only in fact, but also in drama and colour, to any of the biographies it has spawned). I assumed that the Press was a vast state organization employing hundreds, if not thousands, of editors, writers and translators involved in the international exchange of books judged ideologically sound.

P'u-yi's Life must certainly carry the Party imprimatur, for it starts with an account of the decadence, corruption and vice of the last Manchu court, into which he was born in 1906, and ends with as convincing and effective a piece of propaganda as any Red Goebbels could dream up: the former Emperor 'remoulded through labour and study' and 'reborn' as an ordinary citizen of the People's Republic, proving, as the text never tires of telling, that a leopard can change its spots.

I hoped that this might be one of many books about the disintegra- tion of the Ch'ing dynasty published by the Foreign Languages Press and that my contact would be able to put me in touch with a Manchu scholar who could flesh out my skeletal pedigree of the Aisin-Gioro family, brief me about the surviving collaterals and perhaps point me in the direction of one or more of the imperial relics on my calling list.

I imagined myself being passed from Manchu princeling to Manchu princeling in much the same way as the teenage Patrick Leigh Fermor hopped from *Graf* to *Graf* in pre-war Germany.

My introduction at the FLP was to Hsü Ming-ch'iang in the Book Section. I didn't telephone first because I thought I would have a greater chance of success if I simply turned up in his office. I was determined to keep all my approaches unofficial. I dare say I could have gone along to the Chinese Embassy, up the road from Broadcasting House in London, and said, 'I'd like to go to China to talk to members of the former imperial family: please will you arrange the details?' and they'd have fixed me up with a dozen tame Aisin-Gioros – but in their time and on their terms. In other words, it would have taken months of negotiating, if it had been allowed to happen at all, and the Aisin-Gioros would have been hand-picked for their loyalty to the Communist textbook; I certainly shouldn't have been allowed to roam at random in search of any Pretender.

For these reasons I had declared, on the Chinese visa application form, that 'tourism' was the purpose of my visit and 'radio broadcasting' the nature of my regular employment (no mention of the BBC, which had been *persona non grata* since its reporting of the T'ien-an-men Square massacre two years before); in neither case was the statement untrue. And recalling the Oriental's weakness for business cards, I'd found, in London's Chinatown, a bilingual printer who had printed me some visiting cards on which I described myself as 'Su T'ou-ni, Genealogist'. I was rather pleased with my Chinese name, which had been abbreviated (to more or less Tony S) by my Taiwanese friend, who felt that the full, seven-character, phonetic transliteration of 'Su-k'o-t'e-lan An-t'ou-ni' might be confusing, even comical. I was equally proud of the 'Genealogist' solution to my identity problem. It was innocuous enough to avoid suspicion, yet interesting enough – in a society obsessed with family relationships – to provide an entrée, in the absence of any other credentials; and it came with an impressive, though safely non-committal, reference, on discreetly embossed paper, from Richmond Herald of Arms (formerly – and, alas, no longer, for I'd have been a wow with his emblem in China – Rouge Dragon Pursuivant).

But what was I to tell Mr Hsü? How much should I reveal of my imperial quest?

'Tell him everything,' advised the writer of my letter of introduction, an English lady barrister who knew and understood China and its ways.

'Everything?' I'd echoed nervously. 'What if . . .'

'Don't worry,' she had laughed. 'You'll find Peking very different from ten years ago. People talk much more freely, and they don't take much notice of the Government. In fact, there's a kind of freebooting anarchy, specially among the young.'

This freebootery manifests itself most violently on the Peking omnibus. Clutching the lady barrister's letter in one hand and a chocolate ice cream in the other, I tried to climb aboard the Number 5, behind the protective bulk of Loud Report, who was in charge of the camera, the dictionary, the map, his face flannel and a vanilla ice cream. We were heading westwards from the Bamboo Garden, across the top of the Forbidden City. It was rush hour.

Catching a bus in Peking isn't a Western matter of queueing politely at the stop, letting 'em off first, please, then climbing aboard in twos, the elderly, the pregnant and the otherwise incapacitated downstairs by the doors, smoking forbidden and only eight standing, thank you. It's jungle rules here: a crowd at the stop, a scramble for the doors, then heads down and push. And if the man, or woman, in front won't get out of the way, stamping, kicking, punching, hair-pulling and face-slapping aren't beyond the pale.

I didn't know the rules, so only the hand with the ice cream had got on the bus when the automatic doors began to close. Unable to pull it out, I thought the best thing would be to push me in. With all my weight I pressed against the closing doors which suddenly changed their mind and opened and I went flying against Loud Report's legs with the ice cream caught between us.

'Well done, Misiter Socotolan,' he said, his good manners, as usual, prevailing over his discomfort.

Despite the rough scrum of seconds before, the atmosphere aboard the bus was now as calm and seemly as a vicarage tea party: squashed toes, torn hair, bruised arms, winded stomachs were forgotten in the silent satisfaction of having demonstrated the right of individual existence. And even though the rush-hour bus was as chronically overcrowded as an African mammy-wagon, not one millimetre of person touched its neighbour, such is the Chinese sense of propriety. Dwelling on these apparent paradoxes, I was reminded of an observation in an evocative travel book of the 1930s called *Eastern Visas*, in which the author, Audrey Harris, records her 'first feeling of admiration for the weighty sense of vitality' in Peking: 'The lowest coolie has an inborn dignity, which everyone expects him to defend although they are all too absorbed with their own for altruistic concern.'

If the driver of the Peking bus is usually a man, the conductor is always a young woman. She sits, white-gloved and with a gold star pinned to her chest, in an enclosure running along the nearside of the bus so that she can roam freely in search of lurking fares even when the bus is packed to bursting. If, having reached the extremity of her pen, she still can't quite reach the outstretched banknote, then it's passed from hand to hand till it's safe in hers. Fares are astonishingly cheap: even for quite long excursions into the suburbs I never had to pay more than 2 *jiao* (about 2p). By comparison, taxi fares seem inflated – and taxis unnecessary anyway, because of the efficiency and regularity and speed of the buses. The only other form of public transport is the pedicab rickshaw, which has its charms, but at a price. A hired bicycle is probably the best way to get around the city, walking – because of the heat and the traffic and the huge distances involved – the worst.

The Foreign Languages Press lay within five minutes' walk of the stop where we got off the bus. But we made the mistake of asking the way – mistake because the Chinese will always invent an answer rather than admit they don't know the right one – and so we walked some miles in every direction of the compass before ending up where we'd started. Eventually a woman who said she lived next door to the Press led us there.

Inside it felt and looked and smelled like an institution, a school perhaps or a lunatic asylum: endless corridors with closed doors off them, bare walls, lino on the floors and concrete stairs. But no workers. 'They are sleeping,' said Loud Report, and I assumed he was joking till, finding one door ajar, I peeped around and saw two men stretched out on their desks with their eyes closed; one had his shirt-tails rolled up to his chest to cool his stomach. At last we heard some signs of life – shouting and laughter – and, following the sound, we stumbled on an inter-office ping-pong match at the junction of two corridors. 'Hsü Ming-ch'iang?' said a helpful young observer in a T-shirt. 'Down there on the left.'

Mr Hsü wasn't at home, but his neighbour, on the other side of the corridor, invited us to sit and wait in his office. Mr Hsü wouldn't be long, he said; would we like some tea?

Everyone in China drinks tea all day long. *Lü-ch'a*, green tea, on its own, with no milk or sugar. They carry it in jam jars which they sip contentedly even when the tea's gone quite cold. Our host poured some hot water from a large vacuum flask into two tall china cups; then he added a few leaves and put the lids on. I was thirsty and, after a few moments, I made as though to drink: 'No, no, Misiter Socotolan,' admonished Loud Report, in a scandalized whisper. 'Must wait seven minutes.' By then, I thought, Mr Hsü would be back and the tea would have stewed to its usual undrinkable bitterness; I'd found that the only way to drink green tea was quickly while it was both hot and young.

Loud Report explained in Chinese the purpose of our visit; as he spoke, he mopped his face, which streamed in the blazing sunshine by the open window; and the more he mopped, the more, it seemed, he had to mop, as though a sort of subcutaneous pressure mat had activated a spring. Exasperated, he started to puff and blow like a carthorse.

'Maybe you like to sit in Vice-Director's office,' suggested our host in English, adding, with delicate consideration, 'Not so hot on north side.' So we carried our teas across the corridor.

'Computer!' breathed Loud Report in awe as his eye fell on the machine on Mr Hsü's desk. There were plants growing up the windows, a large standard fan (which he soon switched on), a jacket on a hanger, a wall calendar with a picture of a panda and shelves of books in a dozen different languages: *Atlas of Therapeutic Motion for Health*; *La Quête de la Jeunesse*; *The Sayings of Confucius*, in Russian; and *P'u-yi – Der letzte Kaiser von China*.

Loud Report was feeding a sheet of paper into Mr Hsü's computer. 'Are you sure you should?' I warned, like a maiden aunt. Laughing excitedly, he ignored me and continued to play with the computer till he realized it was switched off. Unable to find the power switch, he lost interest and darted across the room towards an enamel wash-basin on a portable stand. The lure of the clean cold water was too much for him: bending down, he gently submerged his head.

It was at this moment that Mr Hsü arrived. Fearful of alienating my very first imperial contact, I leapt up to obscure Loud Report's ablutions.

'*Ni hao!*' I said, taking great care to sound the aitch, or I'd have turned 'hello' into something like 'piss off', for '*niao*', I'd discovered, by accident, means 'urine'.

'*Ni hao!*' returned Mr Hsü with a friendly smile, and no trace of irritation, or even surprise, at finding these unexpected visitors in his office.

'Ah! *Ni hao!*' called Loud Report, drying his face with Mr Hsü's towel.

And '*Ni hao!*' replied Mr Hsü, still smiling benignly, as though strangers were always dipping their heads in his wash-basin.

'Sorry about this,' said Loud Report, laughing.

'No problem,' said Mr Hsü with a dismissive wave.

Obviously it meant nothing to either of them. I couldn't help wondering what would have happened in Broadcasting House if the Controller of Radio 3 had walked into his office and found me having a lunchtime wash. If this was Communism, it was rather nice. But it was more likely to be ordinary Chinese pragmatism: 'Chinese very informal,' Loud Report was always telling me.

While Loud Report went out to change the water in the basin, Mr Hsü read the lady barrister's letter of introduction. 'She writes good Chinese,' he said. He specially enjoyed her description of me as 'a friend of a friend': 'So I am friend of friend of friend,' he chuckled.

'Well, Su T'ou-ni' – and he stressed the name, because that seemed to make him laugh, too – 'I think I can help you.'

It was a good thing, he said, that I'd come to see him first, because, although he himself didn't know any Manchus, he knew people who did and he understood that the Aisin-Gioros were riven with dispute: the old versus the young, the rich versus the poor, the former imperial family versus the rest. If I spoke to the wrong one, it might preclude my speaking to others. The best course of action was to take advice from an impartial specialist. He knew of an academic in the North-East of China who would be just the job if he was prepared to help: a professor of history at the Chi-lin Academy of Social Sciences in Ch'ang-ch'un; his name was Wang Ch'ing-hsiang.

IT was June 4th, two years to the day since the Peking massacre, and I was walking through T'ien-an-men Square, on my way to meet Loud Report in the city centre.

For the past two months the British press had been brooding on China's mounting sense of insecurity in a rapidly changing world. 'The one certainty in the political fog,' wrote Colina MacDougall in the *Financial Times* on April 24th, 1991, 'is the growing stress on security ... in the capital, police and video cameras are thick on the streets. Particularly monitored, by video cameras, bugs or simple tailing, are local Chinese contacts with foreigners.'

I'd read this before leaving for Peking and had been duly alarmed, but a week into my visit I still hadn't seen any sign of Public Security activity – and I thought I knew what to look for, after a month as an independent traveller in Ceauşescu's Romania. In fact, I hadn't really noticed any police at all, except the white-uniformed traffic controllers, whose balletic posturings on the two-tiered cake stands at busy intersections are one of the most delightful sights of Peking. There were, it's true, soldiers everywhere, but the People's Liberation Army troops – most of them unemployable peasants – were so young and dirty and hungry-looking, their uniforms so old and cheap and ill-fitting, their equipment so out of date and their practice of lolling around, giggling and holding hands so innocently childlike that it was difficult to take them seriously.

Now here I was in T'ien-an-men Square on the anniversary itself, and it didn't seem all that different from Trafalgar Square. Just hotter and hugely bigger, and lacking the pigeons. The grandiose buildings – of the empire, to the north and south, and of the Republic, to the east and west, were just as much of a tourist attraction as the National Gallery and Nelson's Monument, and served much the same purpose as backdrops for snapshots. As far as the eye could see there were ice-cream and soft-drink vendors, postcard stalls and street photographers hawking rolls of Chinese film and Polaroid instant snaps, and hordes of tourists, most of them in groups, easily identifiable by their baseball caps and video cameras as Japanese or Westernized Chinese from Hong Kong, Taiwan, Singapore and Malaysia.

But actually the eye couldn't see very far: the square was too enormous, the sun too bright. Looking north from the Fore Gate at the bottom end of T'ien-an-men the famous outlines of the Gate of Heavenly Peace, leading to the Forbidden City, were barely discernible in the shimmering heat. Besides, the no less famous air pollution of Peking – such an effective filter that it was almost impossible to get sunburned – muddied the long-distance visibility.

So it wasn't till I was within sight of the great state flagpole across Chang-an Boulevard from Mao's portrait on the purple walls of the main entrance to the Forbidden City that I noticed the road was lined with soldiers. A man in a suit and dark glasses held up a hand to prevent my getting any nearer: 'Road closed,' he said. 'Go back.'

I learned later that the authorities had sealed off the whole of the northern part of the square 'for a state visit', which conveniently prevented any public demonstrations in remembrance of the massacre. In what was perhaps a further ploy to distract attention from the anniversary the leadership chose that day to announce the death of Chiang Ch'ing, 'principal criminal in the case of the Lin Piao Chiang Ch'ing counter-revolutionary clique', better known as Chairman Mao's widow and ringleader of the Gang of Four. In fact, she had died three weeks earlier, after hanging herself in the suburban villa in Peking where she'd been living under house arrest since 1984. It was in 1981 that Chiang was convicted and sentenced to death for helping to carry out the Cultural Revolution. Execution was suspended for two years to give her time to repent, but she never did: instead she stuck to her defence that 'I was Chairman Mao's dog. If he said bite someone, I bit him.' In 1983 the death sentence was commuted to life imprisonment, and the following year she was allowed to live at home so that she could get treatment for cancer of the throat.

Although Chiang and her Cultural Revolution had long been recognized as enemies of the people, their influence survived in the Ministry of Public Security, which Chiang refined to a degree that would have won the admiration of Himmler himself. Chinese policing is based on the theory that public order begins at home. A visible police force isn't necessary when the people can be persuaded to police themselves with courtyard and apartment block committees which watch the minutiae of their daily lives and report to street committees, which report to suburb committees, and so on up the scale via city committees and provincial committees to the Central Committee of the Communist Party itself, the acme of power in the People's Republic.

Back in England the following month I told an old China hand how surprised I'd been by the absence of police. 'Don't you believe it,' he said, 'the place is bristling with them – and they're using all the latest high-tech surveillance equipment.'

'But I never saw anything,' I insisted. 'I wasn't followed, I wasn't bugged, and no one ever asked me any questions or tried to stop me doing anything I wanted. I was a free agent.'

My friend laughed. 'Oh, they wouldn't bother with you,' he said.

'They're only worried about their own people: no Chinese can draw breath without the permission of the Public Security.'

Once, having noticed that there weren't any beggars or vandals or loiterers to be seen in Peking, I asked Red Universe why. 'There are beggars,' she said. 'I sometimes see them on way home, but police chase them away.'

'Police? – but there aren't any.'

Red Universe smiled. 'They come when you need.'

I had been drinking my way across the square and now I needed a pee. Public lavatories are everywhere in China, because so many homes are without their own, but they are notoriously unsavoury and I was interested to investigate. Now that I had to use one, though, there wasn't one in sight. Turning south again towards the old Chinese city, I headed down a little lane which looked hopeful and found what I wanted on the next corner, a textbook example of the most primitive kind of Peking loo. Without any windows or electric lights it was quite difficult, at first, to see where to go. But when my eyes adjusted, I could pick out a gutter running along a wall which smelled as though it might be a urinal: that, anyway, is what I used it for. I'd assumed I was alone, so the sudden loud hawking sound behind me was rather a shock. Peeping over my shoulder, I saw a newspaper with a hand at either edge in a cubicle with sides no higher than a Chinese thigh. Zipping up, I continued to stare until the newspaper was suddenly thrust aside, a corner torn away and both the paper fragment and the right hand disappeared under a man crouched over a hole in the ground. 'Ni hao!' I said, feeling that some response was called for. Unimpressed, the man grunted, or I thought that's what I heard, till my nose delivered a strikingly more vivid message. Leaving hurriedly, I brushed past a basket of plastic flowers hanging on the back of the door. Their imaginary perfume did little to disguise the stench; but it was a gesture.

Loud Report was beside himself when I arrived in his girlfriend's office at the grand hotel where she worked as a secretary. Pumping my hand, rolling his eyes and whooping with delight, he could barely get the words out. 'Misiter Socotolan,' he gushed, 'all fine and dandy!'

Loud Report was a treasure. He had found Professor Wang's telephone number in Ch'ang-ch'un – no easy matter in China, where directories are rarer than telephones; he'd spoken to the professor and explained my requirements; and the professor – himself something of a treasure, it seemed – had said that if I could get myself to Ch'ang-ch'un, he would be delighted to tell me all he knew about P'u-yi and the Aisin-Gioro family, which was not inconsiderable as he'd been studying the subject for fifteen years and had written many books; all I had to do was to let him know when I was coming and how much of his time I would need, so that he could arrange to be free; and if I liked, he would also book me a hotel. 'Professor Wang very nice man, I think,' said Loud Report.

'So when do we leave?' I asked.

'We?'

'Well, you're coming too, I hope.'

'Only if Misiter Socotolan want me.'

'He does,' I said truthfully. 'He can't do without you.'

Loud Report beamed and puffed and mopped. 'I love to travel,' he said, 'and Ch'ang-ch'un really good. My father say so. In North-East people very straightforward. And they love to drink. We will drink all the times and get very drunken.'

A slim, good-looking girl in a smart navy suit appeared at Loud Report's side, smiling shyly. He put his arm around her. 'Misiter Socotolan, I want you meet my girlfriend, Haven't Wet.'

'Hallo,' purred Haven't Wet, in a deep, dark, soft voice. Then she giggled nervously and buried her face in Loud Report's shoulder.

'How do you do?' I said. 'What a charming name – what exactly does it mean?'

'Mean?' Loud Report looked puzzled and he repeated, loudly, as one does to stupid foreigners: 'Haven't Wet. Chinese name.'

'But it doesn't quite make sense,' I persisted. 'Do you mean "Dry"?'

'Not dry, not wet. Haven't Wet.'

'Damp, perhaps?'

Loud Report, blowing out his cheeks and popping his eyes with exasperation, consulted his dictionary. 'Fock.'

'Fock?' I repeated. 'Are you sure?'

He pointed to the word.

'Ah, Fog. But that's not a very nice name for a pretty girl.'

'Smog?' suggested Haven't Wet.

'That's worse,' I said. 'What about Dew? Or, better still, Morning Mist?'

So Haven't Wet became Morning Mist, and Loud Report kissed her on the forehead. 'My girlfriend,' he said protectively, his eyes swimming with romance.

22

'Misiter Socotolan, can I ask question?' His voice was soft and insinuating. 'Are you married?' He spoke the words caressingly and with a teasing smile, as though relishing some delicious mystery. I shook my head, and Loud Report looked sad.

O NE of the great pleasures of travelling alone – perhaps even its *raison d'être* – is chance encounters: unexpected meetings with strangers who may do no more than point you in the right direction, or may do as much as put you up for a few days, but the very gesture of friendship itself transcends the hospitality that follows, for with that initial smile or handshake or meeting of eyes an alien environment is suddenly, if only temporarily, turned into home. With Loud Report constantly at my side, and necessarily so, for he was my Chinese mouth and ears, there was neither the need nor the opportunity to strike up casual friendships; and with most of the day taken up with meetings and telephone calls on imperial business, there wasn't time anyway.

But I could have done with a chum at the Bamboo Garden Hotel, where the room was rather gloomy, with no sunlight and a smelly bathroom, and the service poor. All the staff were courteous, but only one – the senior receptionist, Miss Ch'ou – had any grasp of English, or urgency. Like the Irish, the Chinese have no sense of time and a fondness for talk. There wasn't an employee there who didn't want to please – it's part of the Chinese nature – but there was hardly one who knew how to. So the enticing bags of jasmine tea left in the room lay untouched because the flask of hot water tasted of swimming pool; laundry, if left in the morning, would be returned, done, in the evening – but the white shirt would be grey, the socks would have shrunk and the linen trousers would be mysteriously stained; the air-conditioning kept the temperature bearable but it smelled of old cigarettes, rattled like a steam engine and regularly conked out; the cleaning women, with their willow besoms, would ring the door bell with mounting impatience from 9.30 a.m. on, but when you let them in they'd never sweep the floor; the bed would be made with two feet of sheet tucked under the mattress and none left at the top so the blanket scratched your chin at night. Little things, which could have been put right so easily, but no one seemed to care: they would simply shrug and smile. Or if they did care, they didn't know what to do about it because they'd never been taught. One morning's tuition at any of Peking's joint-venture hotels would have taught them the basic lesson that the customer is always right, and one month's joint-venture wages might have provided the incentive to solve the customer's problems. The market-economy principle hadn't yet hit the Bamboo Garden.

My worst experiences – and, of course, the fault lay primarily with me for not speaking Chinese – occurred in the Studio-of-the-tending-of-the-pines Restaurant. Even without its kitchens, I would have had to avoid it for its aquarium. We all know the Chinese are unsentimental about animals, but this was systematic, if ignorant, torture. A new oxygenating system had been installed and no one knew how to regulate it properly, so, one day, half-a-dozen fat river trout, grossly overstimulated, would suddenly burst through the cloth cover and fling themselves to death on the floor, and, on another, the oxygenation having been drastically reduced, five replacements, keeling to one side like stroke victims, would lie on the bottom of the tank, gasping in the most piteous way and staring goggle-eyed at those diners Western enough to care. I begged the manager to do something, but he shrugged and smiled. Eventually, the sheer cost of repeated service charges forced him to drain the tank and buy his fish dead at the fishmonger's.

Dinner at the Tending-of-the-pines was not only expensive but a question of pot-luck, too. There was an abbreviated menu in English for Westerners, but it made little sense and no one showed any inclination to help. I stuck it for a night or two, then abandoned it in favour of the much cheaper and more interesting Ma-k'ai Restaurant, below the Drum Tower, which specialized in Hunan cuisine – brightly coloured, strongly flavoured, but rather overoiled.

My appetite wasn't enhanced by the sight of dog on the menu – two sorts, one plain braised, the other 'sour peppery' – and stewed shark's lip and steamed turtle. But I was hungry, so I chose spring chicken with mushrooms and bamboo shoots in a white sauce and pecked at it with my chopsticks, alone at a large circular table, its once-white cloth spattered with stains and food rejects, while I pondered on the fate of the dog in China.

I like dogs – in fact, I'm cuckoo about dogs. We have two at home, both labradors, an old black bitch and a teenage golden boy. To me it is as inconceivable to eat dogs as it would be to eat children. Presumably the Chinese used to feel the same, judging by the popularity of dogs – and birds and crickets – as household pets in old Peking. But that is to forget – and, to my cost, I kept forgetting – that the Chinese are simply not like anyone else, they are 'the most incomprehensible, unfathomable, inscrutable, contradictory and illogical people on earth', as Eliza Ruhamah Scidmore, an American traveller, wrote in 1900.

A more practical paradox is the popularity of dog meat in a city in which dogs are non-existent – though I did see a fat and breathless Pekinese in the arms of a smart Western woman in the embassy district. Has the table exhausted the supply? The answer is to be found in a book called *Peking, 1950–1953* by Peter Lum, wife of an English diplomat, who records that in 1950 the entire dog population of Peking was destroyed on the orders of Chairman Mao; Mrs Lum herself, however, managed to save her two – a 'goat-sized octoroon' called Barnaby, and Nigger, a black puppy 'the size of Barnaby's head' – by confining them to the British Embassy compound. Mrs Lum admits that something had to be done about the droves of wild dogs in Peking, but she was shocked by the manner and extent of the massacre: 'The dogs were clubbed to death or hanged. They were taken away in small carts, like garbage cars, closed tight and packed solid, and if you passed one, you could hear them thrashing inside and see blood on the sides.' The official reason given was that they were rabid. Two years later the Ministry of Health changed its story: the 'elimination' had been necessary, it said, because the United States had started bacteriological warfare in Korea. The people of Peking had a simpler explanation: the dogs were put down because their barking drew attention to the activities of the secret police at night.

The Chinese penchant for exotic meats doesn't stop at dogs: frogs, salamanders, monkeys, bears and scaly ant-eaters all feature in their cuisine. So do lions and dragons, which, when translated from hyperbole, turn out to be cat and snake. There is an old Chinese proverb which says that when a man sees birds and beasts alive he doesn't have the heart to kill them, and when he hears them cry in pain he doesn't have the heart to eat them; this, so the saying goes, is why man keeps out of the kitchen. Given the extent to which he does eat them nevertheless, the conclusion must be that the Chinaman consciously avoids any contact with living creatures. But he can't – the trees and bushes, even in crowded, polluted Peking, are full of birds and insects; the streets aren't devoid of horses and donkeys; and, even today, old men in Mao jackets, baggy cotton pants gathered at the ankle, cloth shoes and coolie hats, can be seen doing their T'ai-chi exercises in the city parks, while their pet birds, hooked by their cages to an overhead branch, take the air. I suppose, in the end, it's no more hypocritical than my eating chicken, knowing and choosing to ignore its likely provenance in some rural Belsen. But man's best friend?

Dog meat, slurpings and dirty tables aren't the only hazards in the poorer Chinese restaurants, the 'masses' restaurants as they're known: hepatitis and TB sometimes linger in the kitchens. While I was in Peking the English-language *China Daily* reported – honestly, but surely tactlessly, since its readers are exclusively Western visitors – that four people had died and 111 people had been, in its own words, 'laid low' as a result of food poisoning in the few weeks since the summer began. And it disclosed the disturbing results of a survey carried out by experts from the Food Hygiene Inspection Institute: of 124 Peking restaurants examined, only a third met the health standards required. The results were presented to demonstrate the poorer showing of the privately run restaurants – and indeed they did score dismally – but the really worrying revelation was that food hygiene generally was so substandard. That said, it's only fair to add that though I ate a wide variety of food in a wide variety of restaurants, I never once fell ill.

Chinese dinner ends with boiled rice – on its own, in a bowl held up to the mouth and shovelled straight in with a lot of unpleasant sucking noises – and clear soup, usually made from the bones of the main meat dish, with some edible fungus floating about. The Chinese don't go in for puddings, so I was surprised to find four sweet things on the menu at Ma-k'ai – 'Crispy, three-delicious-ingredient cake', 'Silver-thread roll', 'Roast egg tart' and 'Crisp haw cake'; less surprised to find they weren't available.

I plunged into the night for an ice cream. Although restaurants close at about 8 p.m. and most shops at 6 p.m., Peking bursts into life as darkness falls, and the people spill out of their homes and on to the pavements. There had been a storm, the air was now clear and it felt fresher but still very hot. By the pale light of a street lamp filtering through the leaves of a mimosa tree, a group of old men, all smoking, were concentrating on their game of *Wei-ch'i*, Chinese chess; one of them rested his arm on a wicker cage with a baby boy inside it, while the grandmother, squatting on her haunches, watched, silently, from her front door. Under an awning, half a dozen sweaty men, bare-topped, their trousers rolled up to the knee, sat at a table with their faces buried in rice bowls; in a lean-to behind them, their women, faces burning, stirred hot pots on a coal-fired range. In the dark, below a lofty ginkgo, a boy and his girl squatted, facing each other, the one embracing the other's knees, their eyes locked in intimate silence. Four youths, with their T-shirts rolled up to their chests, sat on a step, sharing a bottle of beer.

Up and down the street there was a steady stream of traffic – bicycles, tricycles, taxis and trucks – but it was strangely quiet, as though the night were sacred.

The little shops were open still, keen to exploit the new possibilities of the free market. In one, beneath shelves so thickly stocked that an East European's eyes would pop, the proprietor sat watching a Tampax ad on a flickering black-and-white television set. I bought an iced chocolate on a stick and a can of Sprite. I hadn't enough coins in my pocket so I drew out a note from the zip wallet I always wore strapped round my waist.

Back at the Bamboo Garden, I was getting ready for bed when I suddenly noticed my money belt had disappeared. I didn't believe it could have been snatched, for the Chinese, everyone knows, just don't steal. So I must have dropped it. The fastener, I'd noticed, wasn't very secure, and I'd been meaning to tie it to one of the loops on my trousers. This was the very disaster I'd been dreading, for the wallet contained my passport, my credit cards, my letter from Richmond Herald and the British Ambassador in Peking – and absolutely all my holiday money in dollar bills. It may seem recklessly unwise to have been carrying so much currency, but I knew from experience in Communist Europe that travellers' cheques and credit cards aren't always easily convertible, and that the merest peep at a nice fresh dollar can soften the pupil of the hardest-eyed *apparatchik*.

Replaying my movements since leaving the shop where I'd last seen the money belt, I was sure I hadn't felt it at my waist since then. So I fled back, knowing that my chances of finding it were pretty slim. I was wrong. There it was on the counter where I had removed the note; the shopkeeper hadn't touched it, even if he'd noticed it. I was so profuse in my thanks that he looked rather puzzled. The next morning I took Loud Report in to explain in Chinese just why I was so grateful. The man shrugged: 'It's normal.'

Perhaps it is. P'u-yi lost his watch once, just after he'd left Fu-shun War Criminals' Prison and he was working as a seedsman at the

Botanical Gardens in Peking. It was a very special watch, a gold French one he'd bought in a ploy to shake off his pursuers while fleeing from the Forbidden City in 1924. Subsequently it had played a significant part in his re-education as a Communist citizen when he presented it – and 468 pieces of imperial jewellery which he'd been hiding in the false bottom of his suitcase – to the prison governor.

On his release, he'd been allowed to take this watch with him. Now he'd dropped it, on a walk, and was convinced he would never find it, as he records in his autobiography:

When Old Liu, my room-mate, heard that I had lost it he asked me in detail about the route I had taken, and set off at once although he was off duty. To my great embarrassment many of the others . . . went out to look for the watch. In the end Old Liu found it in front of the dining hall of the Evergreen People's Commune and brought it back in the highest of spirits. I felt that I was being given back much more than just a watch . . . I was embarrassed by the amount of concern and support I received, but there is in fact nothing unusual about it in our country.

Thieving isn't, however, unknown: in a country of one-and-a-quarter billion people, most of them very poor indeed, it would be surprising if the Western visitor's wallet weren't sometimes an irresistible temptation. A BBC friend visiting Peking at this time had his wallet stolen in a crowd at the Summer Palace, while trying to buy some film with his bag not completely zipped up. It was his last day and he hadn't the time to pursue the matter with the police. If he had, he might have been surprised at their response. A French tourist whose bag was snatched outside another imperial palace, at Ch'eng-te, wrote to the *China Daily* to record her appreciation of the police, who had 'taken the situation very seriously and were very thorough in their investigation'. Eighteen members of the Ch'eng-te Public Security Bureau were assigned to the case and within twenty-four hours a witness had come forward with a description of the thief. Six days later the thief was arrested and the bag returned with its entire contents intact.

'PAH!' said Loud Report, as he put the telephone down after a long call to Professor Wang in Ch'ang-ch'un. 'There is problem.'

'But,' I said, bewildered, 'I thought it was all going so well. He seemed so keen to see me.'

'He is. Excuse me, so hot.' Loud Report blew down the top of his shirt. 'Professor Wang want you send cable to work unit for permission to speak with him.'

I was surprised, but shouldn't have been, that even a professor was answerable to his work unit. Every single citizen of the People's Republic belongs to a work unit. It looks after and watches over him, it guides and controls, rewards and punishes him, from the cradle to the grave; and, in general, he doesn't much complain, because submission to authority runs in his blood: in the old days Confucianism kept him in subservience to his father, now Communism keeps him in thrall to the work unit. If he's a student, his work unit is his school or university; if a car assembler or fruit picker, it's his factory or his agricultural commune; if a history professor, his department. His work unit governs the citizen's life: near it he has to live, through it he is usually married, to it he has to declare all payments and gifts, from it he has to seek permission for travel, days off, sick leave and meetings, especially with foreigners. Nothing can be done without the work unit's permission; the citizen doesn't exist without his work unit.

This was a problem, for I specially wanted to avoid official channels. Loud Report tried to look on the bright side: 'Professor say he make big reception for you if you mention BBC Corporation.'

'BBC? You told him I work for the BBC?'

'It won't be good for professor if you do not tell.'

'It won't be good for me if you do. I'm a tourist with a genealogical interest. My visit is nothing to do with the BBC.'

'But BBC is Big Corporation.' Loud Report stressed the capitals and rolled his eyes to demonstrate just how impressive this was. I was beginning, but only faintly, to realize that I might have miscalculated in my insistence on independence. Much later, by which time I had already learned the hard way, I was to appreciate that the Chinese have no conception of self-determination, that the individual exists only in so far as he is part of a whole; that, conversely, he doesn't exist, if he's not part of the whole. By insisting on my autonomy I was, in China, a non-person: I didn't exist because I didn't belong.

This attitude wasn't introduced by the Communists – though its pre-existence may have assisted the acceptance of Communism; it comes from 4,000 years of a civilization based on the ideals of family life – on those virtues which Confucius later formalized as filial piety and brotherly love. My business card described me as 'Genealogist', but genealogist working for whom? the Chinese wanted to know.

Loud Report had told Professor Wang that I was a British scholar interested in P'u-yi. Yes, the professor must have said, but where's he from, this Socotolan – who does he belong to, what are his bona fides? And Loud Report had resorted to the BBC. To him the problem was a bureaucratic technicality – the professor simply wanted a work unit reference; to me it seemed to pose a threat to my whole project. We were, though we didn't know it, at cross purposes.

'But what if the Ch'ang-ch'un Party people tell Peking to check me out?'

Loud Report laughed as though this only happened in spy films. 'Impossible,' he said.

I surrendered. Red Universe, on behalf of her American employer, vouched for me, Loud Report wrote the cable and Morning Mist sent it off. All that remained to be done was to book the tickets.

I had decided to travel by train because I like trains – the pace, the view, the noises and smells, the stations and the other passengers. But I nearly changed my mind when I discovered the journey was going to take eighteen-and-a-half hours. The distance as the crane flies is about 300 miles, but the line lollops down to the coast to take in T'ien-ching – and trains in China, though frequent and widespread, aren't fast.

If it weren't for the two-tier price system, they'd also be remarkably inexpensive, but one of the inequities of tourism in China is that Westerners have to pay nearly double for their tickets. Even at the inflated tourist rate, they're still cheap – mine in a first-class, or 'Soft', sleeper cost about £35 single – so I wasn't very sympathetic when a young English backpacker, his handsome face distorted with anger, pitched into the clerk at the ticket office, first in hesitant Chinese, then in flaming English.

'It's blatant racism,' he shouted, as an audience gathered. 'You wait till I get home and I'm running my own business, I'll charge you yellow buggers double, then you'll know what it's like.'

Loud Report, hurt on his country's behalf, and always anxious to smooth things over anyway, tried to mediate but the young man was in his stride.

'I hate these grasping yellow shits,' he said, with a froth of spittle at the corner of his mouth. Forced to join in, though I'd been pretending I wasn't there, I said I liked the Chinese and if they charged us a bit more well so did the Romanians and the Bulgarians, and it was still pretty cheap, wasn't it? And anyway nobody had forced us to come to China, had they?

'I bet you're new here, aren't you?' he snarled at me. 'Yes. Well, I've had three years in Taiwan and I know what they're like: dirty, deceitful and greedy. You wait.'

Later he returned, cool again, to apologize, but not before I'd given Loud Report a smug little lecture on the arrogance of the English, the importance of following St Augustine's advice about Rome and the Romans, and the virtue of self-control. Three times over the next three weeks I was to recall those words with shame.

There are four classes of rail travel in China: Soft and Hard Seats and Soft and Hard Sleepers. Loud Report had insisted that I travel by Soft Sleeper, while he, accustomed to roughing it, took the Hard Seat; I was equally insistent that if he went Hard Seat, then so should I.

'But Misiter Socotolan, you will be very uncomfortable for eighteen hours and one half.' Which was true. So I suggested we should both travel Hard Sleeper. Loud Report pulled his bad-smell face. 'No, no, no. Chinese in Hard Sleeper take off shoe – oooff!' There weren't any Soft Seats on the train we wanted to catch, so two Soft Sleepers it had to be. Which is probably what we both intended all along: I was learning the Chinese art of compromise.

Like everything else in China, organizing the tickets took far longer than I expected, or was necessary. First we had to queue for forms, then we had to fill them in and queue again to get them authorized and exchanged for a chit, and finally we had to join another queue to swap the chit for the tickets. Anxious not to have to repeat the process, Loud Report checked them with great care. 'Travelling on China railways is terrible business,' he said, like an old hand.

And like an old hand he warned of the horrors of Chinese restaurant cars – quite wrongly, as we later discovered. He suggested a picnic and wondered if I had any special requests. I had.

'Ah, cheethe,' he said, wrinkling his brow. 'I don't think we can buy cheethe in China. Cheethe is unusual. China hath not cheethe.'

IN a journey lasting a day and a half, the North-East Express follows the course of seven momentous years in the life of P'u-yi, from Peking to Ch'ang-ch'un via T'ien-ching and Shen-yang. As I gazed out of the window, on the first day of the storms which were to cause such havoc throughout China that summer, and watched the hail battering the rice and maize which had been so skilfully introduced to the former salt marshes of Liao-ning Province, I thought of that day in the winter of 1924, when P'u-yi was finally driven from the palace which had been home to twenty-four Emperors for 500 years.

It was breakfast time on Guy Fawkes' Day in 1924 and P'u-yi, then eighteen years old, was sitting in the Palace of Accumulated Elegance sharing an apple with his senior wife, the Empress Beauty in Flower. He'd been expecting trouble since receiving reports that the warlord Feng Yü-hsiang – the so-called Christian General – and his National Army had carried out an amazingly successful *coup d'état*. The Palace Guard had been disarmed and disbanded and Feng's troops were now occupying the imperial barracks at the Gate of Spiritual Valour on the north wall of the Forbidden City.

Just before breakfast P'u-yi had taken his telescope to the top of the rockery in the Imperial Garden and discovered to his alarm that Prospect Hill was swarming with Nationalist troops. He'd ordered the Household Department to send them up some tea and rice and, as the soldiers had accepted these gifts, he'd judged that the situation wasn't as critical as it seemed.

Yet here now was the Head of the Household Department, in a state of advanced excitement, pushing the boy Eunuch of the Presence out of the way as he slid across the floor on his knees, performing the nine kowtows.

'Your Majesty ... Your Majesty,' the mandarin panted, 'the Republic is going to abolish the Articles of Favourable Treatment. They have sent this document' – he waved it in the air – 'and they want you to sign it. We have three hours to pack up.'

Ever since the Revolution of 1911 and the creation of Sun Yat-sen's Republic the Emperor and his predecessors' widows – the Empress Dowager Honorific Abundance and the three High Consorts – and latterly his own newly acquired Empress and Primary Consort, had continued to act out the medieval rituals of imperial court life inside the Forbidden City, while outside the revolutionaries were systematically shearing the shackles of China's feudal past.

In many a Western society the old order would have been summarily executed, no questions asked; in China the revolutionaries not only spared the Emperor's life – as Chairman Mao was to spare it again, a quarter of a century later – but they even offered the most generous terms.

This remarkable compromise was engineered in 1912 by Honorific

1 Aisin-Gioro P'u-yi, the last of the Manchu Emperors (seated, centre), with his brother P'u-chieh and their seven sisters in exile in the Japanese Concession in T'ien-ching after being driven out of the Forbidden City by the Nationalists in 1924. The imperial spectacles and the decorated Christmas tree were innovations introduced by Sir Reginald Johnston, the ex-Emperor's tutor.

2 A traditional galleried walkway at the Bamboo Garden Hotel near the Drum Tower in the Tartar City: the author's Peking base.

3 Loud Report, the author's interpreter and guide, in the garden of the newly restored Palace of Prince Kung in Peking.

4 Loud Report, a republican, blowing soap bubbles beside a wax effigy of the Empress Dowager Beneficent Indulgence at the Summer Palace. Note the Empress Dowager's platform shoes, elaborate Manchu head-dress and lethal finger stalls.

Overleaf

5 His Majesty the Emperor Hsüan-t'ung (Proclamation of Fundamental Principles), Son of Heaven, Lord of Ten Thousand Years and Grand Khan of Tartary, aka P'u-yi (right), at the time of his accession to the Dragon Throne as a bewildered two-year-old in 1908, with his brother P'u-chieh (left) and their father, Tsai-fêng, second Prince Ch'un.

6 P'u-yi's mother, Kua-erh-chia-shih, Princess Ch'un (centre), with his eldest sister Yün-ying (left) and brother P'u-chieh, in the Northern Mansion, Peking, in about 1915.

7 Reginald Johnston with three of his imperial pupils – the ex-Emperor P'u-yi (right), his brother P'u-chieh (behind Johnston) and their half-brother P'u-jen (on the elephant's head) – in the garden of the Forbidden City in about 1924.

8 P'u-yi, aged sixteen, a prisoner of the Articles of Favourable Treatment, glimpsing freedom from a palace roof at the north end of the Forbidden City in 1922; behind him is the Pavilion of Ten Thousand Springs at the top of Coal Hill.

9 P'u-yi outside the Palace of the Nurture of the Mind in the Forbidden City in 1923.

10 A double self-portrait of the ex-Emperor, aged seventeen: P'u-yi was a keen and imaginative photographer.

5

8

6

9

7

10

1 12 13

14

11 P'u-yi after losing his pigtail, the badge of the Manchus, in 1922. When his eunuch-barber, in fear of his life, refused to cut it off for him, the ex-Emperor did the job himself – and within a month all 1,500 court eunuchs had followed suit.

12 Her Majesty the Empress Beauty in Flower at the time of her marriage to P'u-yi in 1922, aged sixteen.

13 Secondary Consort Elegant Ornament at the time of her marriage to P'u-yi in 1922, aged thirteen.

14 The Dragon-Phoenix Couch, the nuptial chamber in the Palace of Earthly Peace – where P'u-yi, overwhelmed by a profusion of reds, failed to perform on the night of his double wedding.

15 Westernized in exile in T'ien-tsing, in the late 1920s: the ex-Empress Beauty in Flower, her hair in marcel waves, and ex-Emperor P'u-yi, wearing the French wrist-watch he bought during his flight from the Forbidden City.

15

16 Chinese doctor dispensing *lü-ch'a* (green tea) on the North-East Express from Peking to the Manchurian city of Ch'ang-ch'un.

17 Professor Wang Ch'ing-hsiang (left), Mrs Professor Wang and Mr Interpreter Wang at dinner in the professor's flat in Ch'ang-ch'un.

18 Loud Report and the Circe of Manchuria, Winter Stone, a chambermaid in the Ch'ang-pai Shan Guest House in Ch'ang-ch'un.

19 Professor Wang with his book, *A Pictorial Biography of Aisin-Gioro P'u-yi*, in his study in Ch'ang-ch'un.

20 Duke Aisin-Gioro Yü-yan, great-great-grandson of the Emperor Glory of Right Principle and special aide to P'u-yi in Manchukuo, during his re-education programme in the War Criminals' Prison in Fushun, Manchuria, in the 1950s.

21 Duke Yü-yan's mother Ching-kuei (left), wife of Beitzu P'u-ch'eng, and her sister in the palace of his great-grandfather, the second Prince Tun, in Peking in the last years of the Manchu dynasty.

Abundance and Yüan Shih-k'ai, first President of the Republic of China. She wanted to consolidate her position as *éminence grise*; he – the sinister figure who was its real mastermind – wanted to prepare the way for his own presumptuous claim to the throne three years later.

Under the terms of the treaty, known as the 'Articles Providing for the Favourable Treatment of the Great Ch'ing Emperor after his Abdication', P'u-yi was allowed to retain his title and to receive from the Republic 'the courtesy due to a foreign sovereign'; he was permitted to remain in the Forbidden City and to retain his court in its entirety – so long as he didn't take on any more eunuchs; the Republic guaranteed that his ancestral temples and the imperial tombs would be maintained for ever, and his private property protected; the tomb of his uncle the Emperor Brilliant Succession was to be completed and his funeral fully observed, in accordance with the ancient rites, at the Republic's expense; and finally the Republic agreed to pay him an enormous annual subsidy of $4 million.

In addition, two subsidiary documents allowed the Manchu princes and nobles to retain their titles and property and guaranteed equal status for the Manchu, Mongol, Muslim and Tibetan minorities.

In return, all the Emperor had to do was to abdicate and lie low behind his purple walls, the pampered prisoner of an imperial system too ingrained in the Chinese psyche to be dismantled all at once.

For the past twelve years he'd played his part dutifully, and now he was heartily sick of it. In the memoir of his Scottish tutor Reginald Johnston, there's a touching photograph that conveys something of the caged bird which he must have felt at the time: in his 'National Health' spectacles, which Johnston had acquired for him, and wearing his usual day dress of high-necked jacket over a long silk robe, the boy Emperor is posing on a roof of the Imperial Palace, where he's scrambled up for a glimpse of the real world beyond his prison walls.

The High Consorts had tried to distract him with a glamorous marriage ceremony which took the best part of a year, but neither the Empress, Beauty in Flower, then aged sixteen, nor the Secondary Consort, Elegant Ornament, still only thirteen, held any interest for him. In fact, on his wedding night he had abandoned them both, because, as he explains in his autobiography, he felt stifled by all the red in the bridal chamber of the Palace of Earthly Peace: 'red bed-curtains, red pillows, a red dress, a red skirt, red flowers and a red face ... it all looked like a melted red wax candle. I did not know whether to stand or sit, decided that I preferred the Mind Nurture Palace and went back there.'

This was familiar territory – the gloomy, black-wooded, red-lacquered rooms that had been his home since he'd been removed from his parents as a baby in 1908. In here he could indulge his passion for ants and dogs and pebbles – and flogging young eunuchs, an interest he was to refine under the Japanese in Manchukuo. And in here he had his daily meeting with his beloved Johnston, the middle-aged Scots sinologist and colonial administrator who, as tutor, had such a powerful influence over him.

It was Johnston who introduced him to the world beyond the Forbidden City, beyond even China; Johnston who told him about the Great War and the defeat of the Kaiser; Johnston who brought him copies of the *Illustrated London News*, with exciting photographs of motor cars and film stars and the Prince of Wales playing golf; Johnston who discovered the Emperor was suffering from severe progressive myopia and fought the Household Department for a pair of imperial spectacles; it was under Johnston's influence that the Emperor had a telephone installed in the palace, cut off his pigtail, Westernized his menus, clothes and furnishings, and bought a bicycle and had all the ancient thresholds sawn off so he could ride in and out of his palaces; and it was at Johnston's express wish that he banished the bulk of the one-and-a-half thousand eunuchs, whose venality and greed had so emasculated the imperial system in the last half-century of the Ch'ing dynasty, and then, against great odds – and ultimately with no success – ordered the reform of the Household Department, 'the incompetent and corrupt organization' which 'controlled the finances and grossly mismanaged the property of the imperial family'.

Johnston's one great mistake – though it was forced on him by circumstances and he couldn't, perhaps, have anticipated its consequences – was to come in this first week of November 1924.

'Telephone Johnston,' ordered the Emperor, when the Head of the Household Department, shaking with fear, had handed him the Christian General's terms.

'The wires have been cut.'

'Then fetch His Highness my father.'

'But we can't get out, Your Majesty – there are soldiers guarding the gate.'

'Well, then, go and negotiate for me.'

Meanwhile the Emperor read the Christian General's document. It was a revision of the Articles of Favourable Treatment, under which the title of Emperor was to be abolished in perpetuity and the Forbidden City handed over to the Republic. 'The Hsüan-t'ung Emperor of the Ta Ch'ing [Hsüan-t'ung, meaning Proclamation of Fundamental Principles, was P'u-yi's reign title; Ta Ch'ing, meaning Great Pure, was the name of the Manchu dynasty] . . . shall henceforward enjoy the same legal rights as all the citizens of the Republic of the Five Races' – but with an annual allowance of $500,000. The Republic guaranteed to protect both him and his private property, and, as before, 'the sacrifices at the ancestral temples and mausolea of the Ch'ing House will be continued for ever'. In addition, the Republic promised to make a special payment of $2 million to set up a factory for the poor of Peking, which would give priority to any Manchu clansmen down on their uppers.

Like the original Articles of 1912, these were vastly more generous terms than the Emperor could have expected. But where was he to go? Time was running out, and the Christian General had threatened to open fire with artillery from Prospect Hill if he hadn't vacated the Forbidden City by midday. He decided to sign the document and to go straight to his father's house, the Pei Fu (Northern Mansion) on the shores of the Shih-ch'a Lake near the Drum Tower. The Empress Beauty in Flower and the Secondary Consort Elegant Ornament accompanied him. The two surviving High Consorts refused to leave the Forbidden City, for they were still in mourning for the third High Consort, who had recently died; they were finally persuaded to take up residence in a small palace on the east side of the city, after the funeral.

When the imperial family arrived at the Northern Mansion, in a procession of five cars provided by the National Army, they were met by an envoy of the Christian General, who stepped forward and addressed the Emperor:

'Mr P'u-yi, do you intend to be Emperor in future, or will you be an ordinary citizen?'

'From today I want to be an ordinary citizen. I have felt for a long time that I did not need the Articles of Favourable Treatment and I am pleased to see them annulled. I had no freedom as an Emperor; now I have found my freedom as a citizen.' The surrounding soldiers clapped politely.

'Good,' said the envoy, with a satisfied smile, 'then we shall protect you.'

Having abandoned the Forbidden City and signed the revised Articles, P'u-yi was faced with three possible courses of action: he could forget about restoring the old order and simply retire as an enormously rich teenage citizen; he could rally his sympathizers and fight; or he could do what he'd long set his heart on: go abroad, perhaps to Oxford, and acquire some learning, whilst drumming up foreign support for a restoration.

In the event, he did what the Manchu nobles always did when there was a political flutter, he fled to the Legation Quarter. It was Johnston's idea, the escape plan, and he recounts it authoritatively – and vividly – in *Twilight in the Forbidden City*.

Without telling anyone – not even his wife Beauty in Flower or his father Prince Ch'un – P'u-yi made his getaway in a car, accompanied by Johnston and a fourteen-year-old boy concubine, pretending they were going to view a house that was for sale. P'u-yi couldn't resist taking with him a bag of jewels, for he was almost pathologically addicted to precious stones, and used to scoop up handfuls of treasure from the imperial collections whenever he had a chance. After stopping off to buy a French wrist-watch – in an unsuccessful attempt to shake off one of Prince Ch'un's servants who'd leapt aboard at the last minute – they eventually arrived at the German Hospital, where the ex-Emperor was deposited with a Dr Dipper in an empty ward upstairs, while Johnston sped on to the Japanese Legation to arrange sanctuary.

This was the mistake which was to have such far-reaching implications. But it was made with the most honourable of intentions, as Johnston explains:

I went first to the Japanese Legation . . . because I felt that of all the foreign ministers the Japanese Minister was the one most likely to be both able and (I hoped) willing not only to receive the Emperor but also to give him effectual protection . . . He listened to what I had to say, and when I begged him to extend to the Emperor the hospitality of his Legation he did not answer immediately. He walked up and down the room considering the matter and then gave me his decision. He would receive the Emperor, but wished to arrange suitable accommodation for him and therefore asked me to return to the German Hospital and await a message. I discovered later on that the 'suitable accommodation' which Mr Yoshizawa and his wife prepared for the Emperor were their own private apartments – the best rooms that the Legation contained.

And what about the British Minister, who might have been expected to help, since Johnston was a British subject? Johnston reports that he called on Sir Ronald Macleay and told him briefly what had happened, but, he continues,

Knowing . . . that the British Legation attitude was strongly hostile to any action on the part of a British subject which might be construed as interference in Chinese internal politics, I referred as lightly as possible to my own share in the Emperor's escape, and merely remarked that acting on the Emperor's instructions I had driven with him into the Legation Quarter.

The Minister agreed with Johnston's opinion that 'if Mr Yoshizawa would consent to give him protection he could not be in better hands'.

And in this apparently haphazard way P'u-yi was delivered up to the Japanese, like a lamb to the slaughter – for, over the course of the next twenty-one years, the Japanese were to exploit his naïvety, his weaknesses and his hopes of a restoration to further their own plans for the conquest of China.

For three months the Emperor and his wives, with their dozens of attendants, concubines, eunuchs, ladies-in-waiting, maids and scullions, squatted at the Japanese Embassy, while arrangements were made to find them permanent accommodation in the Japanese Concession at T'ien-ching. Late one night in February 1925 P'u-yi boarded a train for T'ien-ching in the company of one of his Manchu advisers, a Japanese official and a posse of plain-clothes police. His family and court followed a few days later and they all moved into a vast Edwardian villa called the Chang Garden. The house belonged to a former Ch'ing general who refused to accept any rent and used to sweep the yard as a gesture of respect for his unseated Emperor. When the old general died and his son demanded rent, the imperial family moved to another house in the Japanese Concession, which P'u-yi called the Quiet Garden. 'The name . . . did not mean that I wanted peace and quiet,' he explains in his autobiography. 'It implied that I intended to wait quietly for my opportunity' (to regain the Dragon Throne).

'Waiting quietly' is an imperial euphemism for a carefully orchestrated and hugely expensive PR campaign, which involved wooing the foreign diplomatic, military and business community with lavish hospitality and buying promises of military and political assistance from a motley crew of warlords, politicians and foreign 'advisers'.

Although he was now thoroughly Westernized – wearing European clothes, eating European food and dancing to European music – P'u-yi still thought of himself as Emperor, and the expatriate community in T'ien-ching delighted in playing along with this delusion for the seven years he languished in exile there. Apart from the young eunuchs whom he ritually beat, the chief victims of his frustration were his two long-suffering wives, who had always been neglected and were now singled out as scapegoats. Beauty in Flower took to clairvoyancy in the hopes of finding the secret of winning her cold husband's love and later, when divination failed, she resorted to opium. Meanwhile she consoled herself with massive shopping sprees. Elegant Ornament, who was made of sterner stuff and anyway had less to lose, took a very modern and, in the circumstances, an extraordinarily bold, way out: she ran off, got herself a lawyer and sued for divorce. P'u-yi, still equipped with some of the tools of an autocrat, issued an edict demoting her from consort to commoner – but he had to pay $50,000 alimony all the same. Elegant Ornament later became a primary-school teacher and died in 1950.

P'u-yi admitted his neglect:

Even if I had only had one wife, she would not have found life with me at all pleasant as my only interest was in restoration. Frankly speaking, I did not know what love was, and where husband and wife were equal in other marriages, to me wife and concubine were both the slaves and tools of their master.

The violation, in 1928, of the Eastern Mausolea, one of the Manchus' holiest shrines, further concentrated P'u-yi's determination to regain his throne. Not only were the imperial tombs robbed of their priceless funerary ornaments but the remains of the two incumbents were barbarously hacked to pieces and their bones scattered. Such desecration would have offended any decent ancestor-worshipping Chinese; that the bodies were those of one of the greatest of all the Ch'ing Emperors, P'u-yi's great-great-great-grandfather Enduring Glory and of his notorious great-aunt, the Empress Dowager Beneficent Indulgence, moved him more profoundly, he tells us, than his expulsion from the Forbidden City. The perpetrator was one of Chiang Kai-shek's Kuomintang generals, and Madame Chiang was reported to have bagged the pearls from the Empress Dowager's phoenix crown to decorate the toes of her shoes.

'My heart smouldered with a hatred I had never known before,' records P'u-yi, 'and standing before the dark and gloomy funerary hall I made an oath before my weeping clansmen: "If I do not avenge this wrong I am not an Aisin-Gioro."'

In this mood, it is not surprising that he should have been so blind to the truth when the Japanese finally proposed his return to the North-East, to the ancestral home of the Manchus, as, he fondly imagined and was encouraged to believe, monarch once more of the great Ch'ing Empire.

In the middle of a November night in 1931, almost seven years since he'd fled to T'ien-ching, he escaped again – by boat this time. Disguised as a Japanese soldier, the 25-year-old fallen Emperor crept out of the Quiet Garden – leaving Beauty in Flower behind as usual – and joined Colonel Doihara, the charming Japanese spy who'd planned it all. Together they boarded a Japanese merchantman and steamed off up the Pai river, while paid decoys distracted the Nationalist Army's attention with a little organized diversion in the Chinese Concession.

Col. Doihara took P'u-yi to Port Arthur, which Japan had won from Russia in 1905, and held him there for three months, in isolation. At last he was told that the new state in the North-East that the Japanese had recently seized from Russian military control was to be not the great Ch'ing Empire but 'Manchukuo', and that he himself was to be not Emperor but Chief Executive. P'u-yi, 'almost faint with rage', refused to accept, whereupon the Japanese gave their last word: 'The demands of the Army cannot be altered in the least. We will regard their rejection as evidence of a hostile attitude and act accordingly.'

A few days later Beauty in Flower was fetched from T'ien-ching, and together the Chief Executive and his wife left for Ch'ang-ch'un, the capital of the new Japanese puppet state in what the West has always called Manchuria, but which the Chinese know, simply, as Tung-pei, or North-East. (Actually the name means East-North, but the Chinese, who do everything upside-down, believe that the magnetic needle points not to the north but to the south, so their compass nomenclature is reversed.) As they approached the tombs of the early Manchu rulers near Shen-yang, their ancient capital, the train stopped briefly, while the Emperor kowtowed to the spirits of his forefathers.

Having been rejected and thrown out by the Chinese people – 'spurned, insulted, robbed and denounced as an alien' in the 'dearly

loved land of his birth' – the Emperor was now, in the words of
Reginald Johnston, writing only two years later, 'resuming possession
of the "rightful heritage" which had been the dowry brought by his
Manchurian forefathers to the China–Manchuria union'. According to
P'u-yi himself, 'Trembling with fear . . . I shamelessly became a leading
traitor and the cover for a sanguinary regime which turned a large
part of my country into a colony and inflicted great sufferings on
thirty million of my compatriots.'

A N elderly Japanese couple sat opposite us in the Soft Sleeper on
the North-East Express. The wife, a slight, girlish woman in a
trouser suit, crouched in the corner with her feet curled beneath her; if
her hair hadn't been white, she could have been twelve. She never
spoke, nor ever stopped smiling. With her head inclined in a gesture of
passive happiness, she seemed to exist simply to serve her husband,
whose every need – tea, a pencil, a dab of cooling cologne, a dictionary
– was anticipated even before the need had occurred to him.

The old husband seemed almost worthy of this slavery, for his lively
warmth and intelligence filled the compartment with a buzz of energy.
He had a leathery face, the cheeks lined with laughter, the forehead
furrowed and high, and his eyes were so bright with curiosity that they
twinkled through several layers of lens in his gold-rimmed spectacles.
He sat on the edge of his seat, like an eager schoolboy, talking slowly
and carefully in Japanese to his wife, in Chinese to Loud Report and
the lady doctor sitting on my right, and in old-fashioned Oxford
English to me. He spoke a little German, too, he confided shyly, and
to prove it he sang – in a quavery treble – a setting of Schiller's 'Des
Mädchens Klage': 'Schubert wrote that music when he was thirteen,' he
said.

As he spoke, the old Japanese wrote it all down, in the language of
the moment, on a spiral-bound notepad which he handed round, for
(quite unnecessary) clarification, at the end of each speech.

'I don't like Japanese,' Loud Report whispered in my ear, 'but this
man very nice.' And in a friendly gesture, acknowledging, as it were,
Japan's technological supremacy, Loud Report produced his Hitachi
cassette-recorder and showed off its finer points. Following his lead, I
produced my Seiko watch and Fuji camera, and the Chinese doctor,
joining in the fun, pulled from her carpet bag a Japanese calculator.

The Japanese, thinking this would make some colourful footage, unpacked his hi-tech video camera and attempted to film us, but he couldn't get it to work. So he signalled to his wife to find the stills camera – a shiny nugget of Japanese micro-technology, with a subcompact body, dual-focal-length lens and full automatic focusing; alas, that wouldn't work either. His wife's smile showed signs of strain. The doctor, giggling behind her hand, got so hot that she had to flap her black-and-white polka-dot silk blouse to cool down. Loud Report, touched by the old man's loss of face, offered him a piece of our Toblerone.

Remembering the warning about railway meals, I felt quite superior when a waitress came in for dinner orders. 'No, thank you,' I said, unpacking our Peking Mother's Pride and precious processed cheese, fresh pineapples, crumbly biscuits and cans of Sprite. The Japanese, who ordered heartily, had the last laugh: their dinner was Chinese cuisine at its best. Loud Report struggled hard not to slaver and ogle as dish after dish was arranged on the little window table. The old man smiled and, patting Loud Report's knee, said there was far too much food for two – would we help them out? No amount of polite demurring had the least effect, nor was it meant to, and Loud Report and I tucked in.

The Japanese was, or had been, as I suspected, a schoolmaster, head of a school for orphaned Japanese refugees returning home from Manchukuo after the Russian victory in 1945. He himself had been brought up and educated in Ch'ang-ch'un, where his father had been an official in the Japanese administration. The father had been taken prisoner by the Russians and had never been heard of since. His son was returning now, for the first time, to try to find out what had happened to him.

I wondered what his line would be if I asked him how the Japanese had first got a foothold in Manchuria. It all started, he said, in the Depression. Japanese farmers, faced with economic ruin, had sailed west in search of a living, first in Korea, which Japan had taken fifty years earlier, and then in the richer territories of Chinese Manchuria, with its ideal grazing, its soya bean, sugar and rice production and vast natural resources of timber and minerals. Because the government of China was then in such disarray – this was the period of warlord rule, between the collapse of the Ch'ing dynasty and the establishment of Sun Yat-sen's Republic – the Japanese had been able to dig themselves in with so little opposition that the Tokyo government had adopted Manchurian migration as official overspill policy. In 1932 they 'dismissed' the Russian army of occupation and embarked on a huge investment programme – building new roads and railways, mining the coal, gold and oil, and establishing the motor industry – which still produces that behemoth of Chinese industry and agriculture, the Liberation truck. All of which had been to the lasting benefit of China.

So runs Japan's post-war version of the Manchurian 'adventure'. But her leaders made no bones about their aggressive intentions at the time. In 1927 Baron Tanaka, then Prime Minister of Japan, was unashamedly hawkish in outlining his Manchurian aspirations to the Emperor Hirohito: In an extract of the Tanaka Memorandum quoted in Tsui Chi's *A Short History of Chinese Civilisation*, he says:

Evidently Divine Providence wishes me to assist Your Majesty in ushering in a new era for the Far East and in developing a continental empire. If we succeed in conquering China ... we shall proceed to conquer India, the Archipelago, Asia Minor, Central Asia and even Europe. Our seizure of control in Manchuria ... is the first step.

The Japanese occupation of Manchuria was no cosy matter of expatriate Japanese bringing their expertise to a benighted Chinese populace. The programme, later claimed as a civilizing mission, was in fact as genocidally motivated as Hitler's Aryanism. Farmers were forced to grow the white poppy instead of the Manchurian staple of acorn meal and sorghum to feed a campaign of mass opium addiction, designed to subdue, if not actually to kill, the Chinese.

In the towns of the North-East Chinese children had to learn Japanese script and forged history, while their parents were encouraged to frequent newly established drug dens, to eat and smoke opium, to inject heroin – which was suddenly widely available – to gamble, drink, whore. 'The Chinese will be the victims of opium,' a Japanese official is quoted as saying, in Amleto Vespa's *Secret Agent of Japan*, 'the Koreans will be eaten by vice; the Russians will be ruined by vodka. They will all be annihilated.'

Opium wasn't Japan's only weapon in the subjugation and plunder of Manchuria. Having extracted record crop productions from the slaving Chinese farmers, they shipped it all back to Japan or diverted it to the kitchens of the occupying forces. The same thing happened with Manchurian coal. So the Chinese went both cold and hungry.

And if they were unwise enough to top up their subsistence-level diet with rice, they risked dire punishment. Rice was absolutely banned for the Chinese – one single grain found in a Chinese person's vomit would lead to arrest on grounds of 'economic criminality' and probably torture. This could take the form of a beating, or having peppered water forced down the nose, or branding with a red-hot poker, or being hung upside-down in a wicker cage. The Japanese have always been imaginative torturers.

Whole towns were evacuated and their inhabitants herded into compounds in a control programme as ruthlessly thorough as Ceauşescu's village-razing 'Systemization' in Romania in the 1980s. The dissident and the destitute were thrown into concentration camps called 'reformatories'. Thousands of farmers lost their land; thousands of conscripted labourers lost their lives – starved or frozen or beaten to death on construction projects. The massacres were on such a scale that the dead had to be buried in graves known as 'ten-thousand-people pits', which were publicly displayed before being covered over.

All this took place in the name of the puppet P'u-yi – first as Chief Executive of Manchukuo, later as Emperor – who sat in his palace prison in Ch'ang-ch'un signing edicts with such socially useful titles as the 1944 'Five-Year Plan for Developing Production'.

'I never knew or cared much about the calamities that the Japanese had inflicted on the people of the North-East,' P'u-yi wrote, after his release from Fu-shun Prison twenty years later, 'and I never thought they had anything to do with me.'

Under the Manchukuo constitution P'u-yi was supposed to have unlimited legislative, executive and judicial powers; his proclamations were law; he was supreme commander of the army, navy and air force. In practice, as he himself records, 'I did not even have the power to decide when I would go out of my own front gates.'

And these rare outings were carried out with all the pomp of Ruritania – and the paranoid security of the Gestapo. On the day of a scheduled public appearance 'undesirables' would be rounded up, police posted along the route, sand scattered over the road and the people ordered to stay indoors.

A typical imperial progression was the annual meeting of the Concordia Association, Manchukuo's only political party. Before the Emperor's car left the palace, the radio station would broadcast to the whole city in Chinese and Japanese that 'the carriage of his Majesty the Emperor is leaving the palace'. The officials of the Concordia Association would then gather at their headquarters and, when the car arrived, an army band struck up the national anthem and the Concordians executed the ninety-degree bow which represented to the Japanese the same level of respect as the Chinese kowtow, nine times in a row, forehead to floor. The Emperor would then read an address written for him by his Japanese army minders, while the entire assembly stood with their heads bowed. And the whole nonsense was repeated in reverse on the journey home to the palace.

The Japanese assiduously promoted the Emperor's majesty. P'u-yi believed that 'this was not only to make the Chinese accustomed to blind obedience and feudal, superstitious beliefs, but also to have the same effect on Japanese people'. And as with all good propaganda it began at an early age.

My old Japanese travelling companion had his own personal memories of imperial propaganda in Manchukuo. He recalled that in the headmaster's study at his school in Ch'ang-ch'un – and at all other Manchukuo schools, offices, public buildings and in many private homes, too – there was a curtained shrine with a photograph of P'u-yi in his Generalissimo's uniform – known reverently as the True Imperial Image – and a copy of his Imperial Rescripts (edicts). 'Every time we went in the headmaster's office,' the old man said, 'we had to bow to the photograph. And at morning assembly the whole school had to bow first to the Japanese Emperor's palace in Tokyo and then to the Manchukuo Emperor's palace in Ch'ang-ch'un.'

What he didn't tell me, perhaps didn't know, was that Chinese children, in their separate, impoverished schools, were no less subject to this same propaganda – only in their case, cold and undernourished, they were beaten into submission, the girls slapped on the face, the boys hit on the head with a wooden club. Jung Chang, in *Wild Swans*, recalls that when local Chinese children passed a Japanese, of whatever age, they had to bow and make way. And when they passed a Japanese teacher, the bow had to be specially elaborate and low: 'My mother joked to her friends that a Japanese teacher passing by was like a whirlwind sweeping through a field of grass – you just saw the grass bending as the wind blew by.'

P'u-yi was so dominated by his Japanese masters that he even added a wing to his palace to accommodate a Shinto shrine, dedicated to the Japanese Sun Goddess Ama-terasu-O-mi-Kami (Heaven-Shining-

Bright). Here, twice a month, he used to offer sacrifices to the divine ancestor of the Japanese imperial family. This betrayal of his own ancestors worried the young Emperor almost more than anything else. But he still believed that it was all in the cause of his eventual restoration as Emperor of the great Ch'ing dynasty. He went on kowtowing to his own ancestors in private and, whenever he had to pay homage at the Shinto shrine, he used to say to himself: 'I am bowing not to Ama-terasu-O-mi-Kami, but to the Palace of Tranquil Earth in Peking.' (This was the 'forbidden' palace which contained what Johnston called 'the sacrificial vessels, witches' cauldrons and musical instruments . . . reserved for . . . the invocation of spirits by means of the mystic rites and dances of . . . Shamanism . . . a cult with which the Manchus were familiar in the early days of their history'; it also housed the 'red' nuptial chamber of such uncomfortable memory.)

The old Japanese schoolmaster remembered that one day in 1935 the whole school had to put on their best dark green Concordian uniforms and troop off to the palace for the proclamation of an 'Admonitory Rescript on the Occasion of the Emperor's Return' – from Tokyo, after his first state visit to Japan. The Emperor was sitting on a red throne at the end of a long hall lined with tall windows hung with bright yellow curtains. He must have cut a sinister figure in his military jacket covered with medals and gold braid, khaki breeches and black leather boots with spurs, a plumed hat and dark glasses; beside him sat the Empress Beauty in Flower in the full regalia of a Manchu queen: a high-necked, long-sleeved robe of richly embroidered silk and satin, with flower-pot shoes (which raised her little feet three inches off the ground) and her hair dressed in the monumental Manchu fashion – its blue-black tresses parted in zigzags and then piled up and over a huge gold bar balanced across her head, with a flower garden at each end, supporting loops, chains and tassels of pearls. The old man couldn't recall very much because he was only nine at the time, but he did remember noticing that the Emperor was 'rather ugly with thick lips' and the Empress 'beautiful and sad', and that they were both so still throughout the long ceremony that he wondered if they were actually alive.

And he could remember every word of the Imperial Rescript, which, like all other citizens of Manchukuo, he'd had to learn by heart. As night fell on the plains of Liao-ning beyond the grimy window of our Soft Sleeper on the North-East Express, the old man wrote down in his pad, in a firm and clear hand, some of the propagandist gobbledegook which had been so deeply etched on his memory fifty-five years ago.

The people of Japan respect their Emperor and love their superiors as they do Heaven and Earth; and every one of them is loyal, brave, public-spirited and sincerely devoted to his motherland. This is why they are able to enjoy domestic peace, resist foreign powers and take pity on their neighbours ... Let all our subjects in Manchukuo strive to observe this our Rescript for ever and ever. By the Command of the Emperor.

The English travel writer Peter Fleming, author of the classic *Brazilian Adventure* and brother of the creator of James Bond, had a meeting with the Emperor during a visit to Manchukuo the previous year – 1934. And in *One's Company – A Journey to China* he offers a strikingly more attractive picture of the Japanese puppet:

Mr Pu Yi is a tall young man of twenty-nine, much better-looking and more alert than you would suppose from his photographs ... He has very fine hands and a charming smile. He was wearing dark glasses, a well-cut frockcoat, a white waistcoat, and spats ... His Excellency understands English, and I suspect speaks it as well, but he prefers to give audience through an interpreter.

Peter Fleming's interview with the Emperor produced nothing more enlightening than bows and smiles and lots of '*Wang-t'ao*', meaning 'the kingly way of benevolent rule', the formula which provided the puppet with a neat answer for every question put to him, whatever the subject. (P'u-yi's Chinese premier, the puppet Cheng Hsiao-hsu had fed him the line after gleefully tipping off his Japanese masters that 'His Majesty is like a blank sheet of paper on which your army can paint whatever it likes.') So, whether the question was as harmless as 'Does your Excellency ever broadcast to his people as the King of England did recently?' or as potentially explosive as 'Has not the use of bombers on anti-bandit operations resulted in the destruction of much innocent life and property?', the answer was invariably the same: a smile, a bow and a *Wang-t'ao*. Nevertheless, the young Emperor exercised such charm that his even younger English interlocutor was happy to interpret the relentless prevarications as mere 'reticence'. 'Mr Pu Yi,' he decided, 'is surely the most romantic of the rulers of this world.'

*

RIGHT on schedule, at 6.17 a.m., the North-East Express pulled in to Ch'ang-ch'un railway station, and there, on the platform, waiting to welcome us, were the smiling faces of Professor Wang and his assistant and translator, whose family name was also Wang, which was rather confusing.

I asked Loud Report how they'd managed to recognize us among the hundreds and hundreds of other passengers from Peking who piled out of the train.

'Big nose, Misiter Socotolan.' (In the bathroom later I studied my nose, but couldn't believe it was so very different from a Chinese one – yet the Chinese think that all Europeans have huge noses, red hair, beards, and eyes as mysteriously and disturbingly polychrome as a cat's.)

Loud Report was disappointed that there was no reception committee: he'd hoped the faxes that flashed between Peking and Ch'ang-ch'un would ensure a full-scale official welcome with a line of work-unit hands to shake, a limousine with sunglass windows and a Red Flag on its bonnet, and a breakfast banquet waiting at the hotel; he'd promised me that the Northern Chinese were specially hospitable – now what I would think? I reminded him that he'd also promised that they were informal, and I was very relieved to discover they really were.

It wasn't till much later that I learned the importance of the welcome in the Chinese scheme of things – and its value as a yardstick of the visitor's credit. The honouring of a guest, particularly a foreign one, is an essential – and charming – part of Oriental hospitality, and the social code provides a range of welcomes according to the perceived status of the guest. A university professor or a doctor or a company director with an acknowledged position in a substantial organization and a sheaf of letters of introduction on grandly headed paper merits the whole works, with reception committees, guided tours of approved factories, speeches, presents and banquets; a self-employed genealogist with inadequate references is lucky indeed to find two Wangs waiting for him.

Loud Report had been hoping for a lavish reception for a variety of complicated reasons which I failed to understand till afterwards: he didn't want me to lose face, because if I did then he would, too; he thought that official hospitality would spare my pocket; he hoped for a little reflected glory himself; and, most complicated of all, he had a hunch – and he was right, and I wished I'd anticipated this myself – that, as an honoured guest, 'a scholar from BBC Corporation', my courting the professor for his learning, in the presence of his superiors, might add a little international sheen to the professor's local reputation, and that an understanding of the value he might place on this kudos could be a useful bargaining point.

All this might have happened if the documents we had so expensively transmitted from Peking had been sufficiently complete and impressive to entice the work-unit directorate to put their suits on. But our papers lacked one vital ingredient: an introduction from a legitimate work unit in Peking. And this oversight was to backfire on us later.

Professor Wang was a short, tubby, moon-faced man in a tight suit with the tie knotted rather short of the top button of his shirt; on his head was a cloth cap with a little peak. His smile was warm and open but his eyes bored through his spectacles with a beady look. The professor greeted me effusively, shaking my hand with both his and hanging on as he introduced his assistant and interpreter, Wang Hsüeh-liang, a bright-eyed, brown-faced half-Manchu postgraduate student, who wore a short-sleeved, blue shirt and chocolate trousers. Mr Interpreter Wang was as monosyllabic as the professor was prosy, but his apparently still waters certainly ran deep – and quite often, while translating his superior's words, his tongue poked a little mound in his cheek.

They had booked us into the city's best hotel, the Ch'ang-pai Shan Guest House, an eleven-storey concrete box on the edge of a large park and next door to a colossal brick building that had once served as Manchukuo's Supreme Court and was now an air force hospital. Most of Ch'ang-ch'un's prominent buildings – and the wide tree-lined avenues and the car factories (of which its industry is chiefly composed) – date from the same short period of Japanese occupation in the 1930s, though the city was first developed by the Russians when they pushed the Trans-Siberian Railway down into Manchuria at the turn of the century. Many of these big, ugly, Westernized administrative buildings have still got military watchtowers on top. Ch'ang-ch'un is not a pretty city.

In my large, comfortable, air-conditioned, south-facing bedroom on the eighth (mainly Japanese) floor of the Ch'ang-pai Shan Guest House – Loud Report having insisted on installing himself in a cheaper, shared room on the fourth (solely Chinese) floor – we got down to business, around a little coffee table vibrating with the combined power of four Japanese micro voice-recorders.

First, credentials – and the two principals remained demurely silent as the seconds extolled their respective virtues. Professor Wang was introduced by Mr Wang as Associate Professor of History and head of the P'u-yi study section at the Chi-lin Academy of Social Sciences, the author of several books on the last Emperor and an acknowledged authority on the demise of the Ch'ing dynasty: 'a very important man,' said Mr Wang, with an impressive nod of his head. He himself, he added, in a quieter voice, was a research associate at the Chi-lin Academy: his special field was Sino-American relations, and he was currently writing a book about United States policy in Manchuria in the years 1895–1911 – but he was also a member of Professor Wang's P'u-yi study section: 'I am becoming quite interested in last Emperor,' he said loyally, but without much conviction.

Loud Report then gave a résumé of my curriculum vitae, repeated my objectives and produced some further documents accrediting me variously, and truthfully, as genealogist, Radio 3 announcer and private press printer – adding, with rather less regard for the truth, 'Misiter Socotolan is important English scholar,' and, rashly, 'He know everything about last Emperor's life.' Professor Wang's smile twitched a little. Then he narrowed his eyes and fired a salvo of test questions, through Mr Wang.

'What day did P'u-yi accede?'

I wasn't going to be bowled for a duck: 'To which throne?'

Professor Wang laughed. 'Ch'ing.'

'The second of December 1908.'

'Why was the Great Ceremony of Enthronement considered so inauspicious?'

'Because the Emperor howled all the way through and his father, Prince Ch'un, comforting him, said, "It'll soon be finished."'

'How much red meat did the royal family eat in any one month in 1909, on average?'

'Over two tons.'

'And 388 chickens and ducks. Name one of the herbs which the Eunuchs of the Imperial Dispensary had to carry when the Emperor went for a stroll in the Forbidden City. In the summer.'

'Essence of Betony for Rectifying the Vapour.'

'See?' crowed Loud Report, in triumph.

'Good,' said Professor Wang. 'So far. Now we try a Manchukuo question. To what did P'u-yi kowtow three times in the palace air-raid shelter in Ch'ang-ch'un?'

'An egg.'

'Why?'

'Because he'd become a committed Buddhist and he was praying for the reincarnation of the soul of the chicken that had laid it.'

I passed and spent the best part of the next three days asking Professor Wang for answers to some of the eleven typewritten pages of questions I'd prepared at home in England. But first, and this took the longest, I had to correct and amplify the skeletal pedigree of the Aisin-Gioro family which I'd compiled from printed sources. Professor Wang's memory of names and dates never failed him, and he shared my fondness for colourful, if irrelevant, detail. What happened, I wanted to know, to Beitzu P'u-ju, grandson of Prince Kung? Ah, P'u-ju – well, he was a son of Beileh Tsai-ying, second son of the first Prince Kung and heir by adoption to Yi-ch'ia, first Prince Chung – the eighth of nine sons of the Emperor Glory of Right Principle. In 1901 Tsai-ying was cashiered by the Empress Dowager Beneficent Indulgence for complicity in the Boxer Rebellion and the title Prince Chung was bestowed on his cousin Beileh Tsai-t'ao, seventh son of the first Prince Ch'un. But when Tsai-ying died in 1909 the new Empress Dowager, Honorific Abundance, restored his title posthumously to snub the Regent, the second Prince Ch'un. As for P'u-ju himself, he was a painter so famous that he was known simply as the Northern P'u. He led a rather reclusive life in Peking's Fragrant Hills in the 1930s; in the 1940s he was a representative in the National Assembly; and after Liberation in 1949 he settled in Taiwan with his wife and son. He died in the 1960s.

This sort of family history, known perhaps only to Professor Wang – and of no possible use or interest to the rest of the world – was grist to my mill. For it I had given up a month's holiday and travelled halfway around the world. With it I could complete my genealogical chart. And from that I hoped to be able to calculate which of my list of seven possible contenders was the most likely claimant to the Dragon Throne.

But if Professor Wang's scholarship was music to my ears, it was the stuff of dreams for poor Loud Report, who should have been celebrating his birthday that first day in Ch'ang-ch'un; instead, in the new shirt I'd given him, he was sound asleep on the bed beside the professor's chair.

THE first known ancestor of the House of Aisin-Gioro and the real founder of Manchu rule in China was a sixteenth-century warrior called Nurhachu, chief of a tribe of marauding nomads renowned for their skills as horsemen, huntsmen and shepherds.

In a series of successful skirmishes at the end of the fifteenth century Nurhachu won control of the whole of the northern part of Manchuria. As the Ming Emperors who ruled the rest of China grew complacent and lazy, so Nurhachu grew bolder and more acquisitive, and in 1616, after seizing more land, he declared his territories the 'Ta Ch'ing Kuo', the Empire of Great Purity, and dubbed himself the Manchu Emperor. Three years later he won a great battle against the Ming army, which pushed the southern frontiers of his Manchu empire right down to the Shan-hai Pass on the borders of Hopei Province, only a few miles from Peking itself. But Nurhachu never managed to breach the Ming defences along the Great Wall, so the vast bulk of China remained beyond his reach. For the remaining seven years of his life, enthroned in the fastnesses of Manchuria, he rehearsed his role as Emperor of all China, but died before the cue came.

As a Manchu, with racial roots in central Asia, Nurhachu was really a Tartar − big and soldierly − not a Chinese at all; this important distinction explains much of the hostility which persists between Manchus and Chinese to this day. But he was a great admirer of the ancient Chinese civilization, the 'Celestial Empire, which had been an old country for forty centuries'. In his own capital of Shen-yang he built a replica of the Mings' power base, the imperial palace of Peking, and even called it by the same name, the Forbidden City, and modelled his court on theirs, complete with eunuchs and concubines − only he insisted that the eunuchs should never be Manchus and the concubines never Chinese: a house rule which remained unbroken till 1943, when Aisin-Gioro P'u-yi, then puppet Emperor of the Japanese state of Manchukuo, took as his third concubine a schoolgirl of Han nationality.

Nurhachu recruited Chinese troops for his army, borrowed Chinese governing techniques for his administration, imitated their system of settled agriculture and ironworking and even introduced elements of their language. But he resolutely clung to one immediately visible Manchu characteristic and bequeathed it to his successors as a sign of their superiority over the ethnic Chinese races: whereas the Chinese traditionally wore their hair knotted on top or piled in a coil hidden under a cap, the Manchus had always shaved their foreheads in a moon shape and let the rest of their hair grow into a long pigtail, often artificially lengthened with black thread. The pigtail remained the hallmark of the Manchus until 1921 when the fifteen-year-old ex-Emperor P'u-yi, newly introduced to spectacles by his tutor Johnston and restless for further Western influences, suddenly snipped his off – the eunuch-barber having refused to do it for him. In both the Manchu and the Chinese hairstyles, the idea was to protect, as a gesture of filial piety, that which had been inherited from father and mother and was therefore sacred. (In the same way eunuchs, after castration, or 'leaving the family' as it was delicately called, pickled their parts – known as *pao*, or treasure – and kept them safely, out of the way, on an upper shelf, so as not to offend their ancestors, who might then restore them to wholeness in another life.)

Nurhachu died in 1626, and for the next eighteen years the Manchus continued to make forays against the Great Wall – till at last, in 1644, they knocked their way through. Taking advantage of a Chinese mutiny, they routed the Ming army, scaled the Great Wall and marched down to Peking, where the Ming Emperor, deserted by his guards, was defended by nothing more terrifying than a few thousand armed eunuchs. The Manchu bandits were soon pouring into the Forbidden City and the Ming Emperor, filled with despair, climbed up Prospect Hill and hanged himself from an acacia tree, having first written a touching little note blaming himself for his country's problems and imploring the invaders to spare his people. In a typically Oriental response the Manchus punished the tree for conspiring in an imperial crime by wreathing its delicate branches with heavy metal chains.

It was another forty years before the Manchus decided to move to Peking and occupy the former Ming palaces in the Forbidden City. By then Nurhachu's grandson, Favourable Sway, the first Manchu Emperor to rule in China, had died and the throne had passed to his son, the energetic Lasting Prosperity, who first consolidated his predecessors' conquests in Northern China, Korea and Inner Mongolia and then took Taiwan, Outer Mongolia, Turkestan, Tibet, Burma, Vietnam and Nepal, leaving, in fact, little of the Far East free of the Dragon's claws.

For a hundred years the Manchu invaders brought peace and prosperity to the Chinese dominions. But by the middle of the nineteenth century, the dynasty began to run out of steam. Hidden behind the high walls of the Forbidden City, safe in the seclusion of its own secrecy, the court gave itself up to an orgy of intrigue and corruption under one of the great monsters of Chinese myth-history, the Empress Dowager Beneficent Indulgence, Secondary Consort of the Emperor Universal Plenty, a despot known variously as Old Buddha, Venerable Buddha and, to a handful of favoured eunuchs, Real Father. She probably poisoned her co-Regent the Empress Dowager Tz'ü-an (Primary Consort of Universal Plenty), certainly encouraged her own son, the Emperor United Rule, in his pursuit of such rococo sexual excesses that he died young, the victim of untreated syphilis which festered his lower trunk into a network of ulcerated holes through which his kidneys could be seen; possibly murdered his pregnant widow; and, in breach of all the rules of dynastic succession, Beneficent Indulgence placed on the throne her baby nephew, the late Emperor's cousin – a child constitutionally incapable of fathering children.

When, as an adult, this new Emperor, Brilliant Succession, showed a dangerous interest in the reform movement, the Venerable Buddha had him locked up in a windowless pavilion in the Imperial Park, west of the palace, where he died a decade later, emaciated and half mad. In 1900, at the time of the Boxer riots, the imprisoned Emperor's favourite concubine Pearl so angered the Empress Dowager by begging her to stay in Peking and not to flee that she was rolled up in a carpet and thrown down a well by two eunuchs, who sat on the lid till the concubine's cries had died away.

The Empress Dowager was merciless towards anyone who opposed her, or even upset her. When she caught a young eunuch staring at her facial tic, she had him thrashed to death. But when the eunuchs didn't look straight at her, she would poke at their faces with the pointed golden finger-stalls which protected the six-inch nails she grew on the third and fourth fingers of each hand. Her one object in life was the preservation of her power; anyone who stood in the way was flogged, dismembered or sliced up.

Despite Sterling Seagrave's reassessment of Beneficent Indulgence – in *Dragon Lady* – her forty-seven-year reign was as vicious and corrupt as any in the long history of imperial China – and the belief persists that she was indeed the hell-hag of popular legend. The contemporary

Western accounts which started the legend at the turn of the century may have sprung from the twisted pens of demented sinologists – one at least has been unmasked as a fraudster and sex fantasist of Gothic proportions – but the Dragon Lady's own great-nephew, the last Emperor, P'u-yi, was in no doubt about the resemblance of the legend to the real thing. In his autobiography, *From Emperor to Citizen*, he writes,

Tz'ü-hsi had a very highly developed lust for power, and was most unwilling to abandon any power that came into her hands. From her point of view the principles of moral conduct and the ancestral code existed to suit her needs, and she was certainly not prepared to let them inhibit her. Whether it was her own flesh and blood, her in-laws or palace officials, the same principle applied: those who obeyed her flourished and those who crossed her were doomed.

Beneficent Indulgence was not a modest despot. In nearly half a century of absolute rule she never issued a more memorably self-satisfied edict than one published in 1898, when reformist ideas were threatening her supremacy; it was written in the name of the powerless Emperor languishing in his palace cell and, like all imperial edicts, it was signed by Vermilion Pencil, the Gilbert and Sullivan euphemism for the Son of Heaven, whose name was too sacred to utter:

By the accumulated wisdom of six successive Sovereigns, our dynasty has succeeded in establishing a system of government, based on absolute justice and benevolence, which approaches very nearly to perfection ... Is it any wonder, then, that our soul is vexed when abominable treachery and the preaching of rebellion have been permitted to exist and to be spread broadcast; when high officials, lacking all proper principles, have dared to recommend traitors to the throne, in furtherance of their own evil designs? When we think of these things, our righteous indignation almost overwhelms us. Respect this.

Enervated by idleness and plenty, corrupted by luxury and vice, the Manchu dynasty was unable to resist the foreign powers gathering like vultures to gobble up the Empire. The beginning of the end came in the late 1890s, with the emergence of a powerful secret society originally called the Plum Blossom Fists, later reorganized as the Society of the Righteous and Harmonious Fists, and known to history as the Boxers. Originally they stood against the Manchu dynasty itself, but Beneficent Indulgence skilfully redirected their revolt against

Europeans; she even offered a price for the head of every 'foreign devil' killed. In June 1900 the Boxers were unleashed on the foreign legations in Peking. The Western powers retaliated with a massive relief expedition, an Allied army of some 20,000 men, which soon made mincemeat of the Boxers and then broke the Manchus' back with a crippling reparation demand – of five times the government's annual revenue – and the punishment of all those responsible.

It was a blow from which the Ch'ing Empire never really recovered – though Beneficent Indulgence did her best, on her return from the ancient dynastic capital of Hsi-an, south-west of Peking, whither she and the Emperor had fled, disguised as peasants, in a cart, the day after the foreign troops arrived in Peking. She executed the ringleaders, ordered the cancellation of all her anti-foreign edicts – in the interest of 'historical truth' – threw a party for the legation wives, charmed them with smiles and presents, and published a series of edicts reforming the educational, military and administrative systems.

But it was too late and it backfired on the dynasty, for the very changes designed to save the Manchus served only to highlight their inadequacies. Anti-Manchu groups sprang up everywhere, and in 1905 they united under the banner of the Revolutionary Alliance, led by Sun Yat-sen; the seeds of Communism were sown.

In 1908, just as Beneficent Indulgence felt her power slipping away, the imprisoned Emperor Brilliant Succession, though not yet forty, suddenly died. No one knows why: maybe he was poisoned by the reactionaries at court. Certainly Beneficent Indulgence, his aunt, was inordinately cheerful when the news was announced – for his death gave her the chance to appoint as his heir (he himself was childless) another infant, so that she could retain power at least till his majority.

Eight years earlier, apparently in response to calls from the Manchu diehards for the appointment of a successor to the still heirless Emperor United Rule, but actually in advance of a coup to depose the titular Emperor Brilliant Succession, Beneficent Indulgence had appointed an heir apparent. And in a further piece of political sleight-of-hand she had bestowed with it the innocent-sounding title of Ta-a-ko, or Great Elder Brother. The chosen heir was a fat, coarse-featured, hot-tempered boy called P'u-chün, a first cousin once removed of the Emperor Brilliant Succession, described variously as 'vicious, rude and overbearing' and 'a most notorious reprobate'. But as his father, Tsai-i, Prince Tuan, had been one of the ringleaders of the Boxer Rebellion,

Beneficent Indulgence had been forced, under foreign pressure, to rescind his appointment in 1901 – and to debar Prince Tuan's descendants from the throne for ever (that is until she changed her mind again).

It had been thought that she would then nominate Beitzu P'u-lun (son of Beileh Tsai-chih), eldest great-grandson of the sixth Manchu Emperor, Glory of Right Principle, to restore the throne to the senior branch of the Ta Ch'ing dynasty. But she argued that his claim was annulled by his father's having been adopted from a junior branch; besides, she didn't like his proposer, Prince Ch'ing.

In the event her choice fell on P'u-yi, the eldest son of the late Emperor's brother, Prince Ch'un. She had two good reasons for this decision: Prince Ch'un's mother was her own sister, and his wife was the daughter of her faithful friend, adviser and, perhaps, lover, Jung Lu, the most powerful official in the Empire. By nominating Jung Lu's grandson she would be fulfilling a promise she'd made years before – that the eldest son of his daughter's union with Prince Ch'un would be chosen heir, in recognition of Jung Lu's lifelong devotion and, in particular, his loyal service to the dynasty at the time of the Boxer troubles; at the same time, by appointing her sister's grandson, she would be honouring her own ancestress, Tz'ü-kao of the Yehonala clan, Nurhachu's Empress. And so Aisin-Gioro P'u-yi, aged two years and three-quarters, became the tenth and, as it turned out, the last Manchu Emperor.

But Beneficent Indulgence never lived to enjoy further power as his Regent: within twenty-four hours of the inexplicable death of her nephew, the Emperor Brilliant Succession, she had a sudden fainting fit at lunch and, in the words of her biographers, Bland and Backhouse, 'At 3 p.m., straightening her limbs, she expired with her face to the south, which is the correct position . . . for a dying sovereign.' Between lunch and death, the old woman was sufficiently clear-headed to edit her Valedictory Mandate and to dictate the final paragraph, which began: 'Looking back upon the memories of these last fifty years I perceive how calamities from within and aggression from without have come upon us in relentless succession, and that my life has never enjoyed a moment's respite from anxiety.' She then said goodbye to her favourite eunuchs and ladies-in-waiting.

And still she had strength for one final custom, this dreadful but indomitable woman who had ruled China for half a century. Would she care, her attendants asked, to pronounce her last words? *In articulo mortis* Her Majesty the Empress Dowager Tz'ü Hsi-Tuan-Yu-K'ang-I-Chao-Yü Chuang-Cheng-Shou-Kung-Ch'in-Hsien-Ch'ung-Hsi made the shortest and aptest pronouncement of her long life:

Never again allow any woman to hold the supreme power in the State: it is against the house law of our dynasty and should be strictly forbidden. Be careful not to permit eunuchs to meddle in Government matters: the Ming dynasty was brought to ruin by eunuchs, and its fate should be a warning to my people.

IT was a tradition in the great Ch'ing dynasty, as it always has been in constitutional monarchies in the West, that the throne should pass from father to son, but, unlike the European inheritance system which operates on the feudal principle of primogeniture, the Manchu succession didn't necessarily fall to the eldest living son: a son, ideally, but a son selected, in secret, by his reigning father.

Since the time of the very first Manchu Emperor to rule in China, Nurhachu's grandson Aisin-Gioro Fu-lin, who ascended the throne in 1644 and assumed the reign title of Favourable Sway, heredity had been the rule of succession. This not only preserved the purity of the blood royal, ensuring a direct line of male descent for nine generations from Nurhachu to the syphilitic Emperor United Rule, but it also conformed to the one absolute rule of imperial succession which had been in existence in previous Chinese dynasties for thousands of years: that the heir should be a younger male of the next generation.

The Manchu Emperors, like their Chinese predecessors, ruled under the aegis of the mandate of Heaven, so it was essential that they should placate their celestial mentor with a series of seasonal sacrifices at the ancestral temples and tombs. These sacred rites played a vital role in the complicated pattern of relationships which underpinned the imperial system. Their purposes, broadly speaking, were to reassure the imperial ancestors that their line was still going strong; to acknowledge, with a great show of humility and respect, the debt due to them for the responsibilities and privileges of kingship; and to perpetuate, on behalf of the people, the bond between Heaven and Earth. The rituals required the Emperor to prostrate himself in the triple kowtow, thrice repeated, before each of the ancestral tablets, while a bullock, a perfect specimen of two years old, was offered up as a sacrifice in a green porcelain furnace nearby. According to tradition these sacred ceremonies of ancestor-worship and oblation to Heaven could be performed only by a male Emperor of the generation immediately succeeding that of his predecessor; the temple rules were so strict that the very presence of anyone of the same generation as the late Emperor automatically invalidated the entire proceedings.

Such was the potency of ancestor-worship that an Emperor who failed to comply with its regulations risked alienating his ancestors, thereby jeopardizing both his temporal power and, much more seriously, his spiritual future.

For two-and-a-half centuries the House of Aisin-Gioro faithfully obeyed the injunctions of its imperial forebears and the throne passed properly from father to son. To ensure fair play the Emperor Harmonious Rectitude initiated the practice of naming his successor in two secret edicts in his own handwriting: he kept one hidden about his person at all times, while the other was sealed and placed in a box suspended above the throne in the Palace of Heavenly Purity. Neither edict could be revealed till his death. But the system wasn't foolproof – nothing in the Forbidden City ever was – and sometimes one or both of the Succession Edicts mysteriously disappeared.

With one Empress, up to two secondary consorts of the first rank, and as many as 108 oficial concubines of the second and third ranks, all of whom could bear a legal heir, the Manchu Emperors were unlikely to run short of eligible sons: Nurhachu fathered sixteen, and his great-grandson, the Emperor Lasting Prosperity, more than doubled this record, with a tally of thirty-five – plus twenty daughters.

Then came the decadent Emperor United Rule, his brain and body so riddled with sexual disease that the Aisin-Gioro seed lost its fruitfulness. Dying, at the age of only eighteen, without a son to succeed him, he ended the Manchus' record of an unbroken line of descent in tail male. (In fact, his widow A-lu-te was pregnant at the time of his death, but she and her unborn child died in mysterious circumstances a few days later; it was generally assumed that they'd been murdered by Beneficent Indulgence.)

In the event of a childless Emperor, the house rules allowed for the appointment of some other prince of the imperial clan – not necessarily the next in line – so long as he was of the succeeding generation. Various parties put forward candidates to claim the throne in succession to United Rule, but his canny mother, Beneficent Indulgence, had bold and controversial plans of her own. Loath to relinquish power to an adult Emperor, she looked around for a suitable royal minor for whom she could stand proxy as Regent. Her sister's son Tsai-t'ien fitted the bill in every respect but one: he was male, three years old, a prince and younger, certainly, than his predecessor, but he belonged to the same generation as the Emperor United Rule, who was in fact his first cousin. This should have disqualified him, for it left the imperial ancestors with no heir eligible to worship them. Assailed by a storm of protest, Beneficent Indulgence had resorted to an expedient without precedent in the history of the dynasty: she issued an edict adopting the child as son of his late uncle, the Emperor Universal Plenty, her husband. It was arrant jiggery-pokery, of course, but it provided the first nine Manchu Emperors – from Nurhachu to Universal Plenty – with a legitimate heir who could lawfully carry out the rituals of ancestor-worship, and so it silenced the majority of Beneficent Indulgence's critics. But it didn't satisfy everybody, for there was one big snag: so long as his cousin, the boy Tsai-t'ien, now reigning as the Emperor Brilliant Succession, remained on the throne, the last Emperor, United Rule, was himself marooned, heirless and un-worshipped, a zombie hovering in imperial limbo.

This unsatisfactory state of affairs so distressed the diehard conserva-tives at court that one of them, the Censor Wu K'o-tu, staged a dramatic protest suicide in a temple near the Emperor United Rule's mausoleum, having first petitioned the throne with an indictment of the degeneracy of the ruler of the Empire, couched in the most gentlemanly terms, as befitted an orthodox Chinese scholar. (A year earlier, the same Wu had distinguished himself for his fearlessness – and an elegant turn of phrase – when he presented a secret memorandum urging the throne to excuse foreign dignitaries from kowtowing to the Emperor 'in order that our magnanimity may be proved and our prestige exalted'. Censor Wu pointed out that, as 'barbarians' who thought of nothing but money, they couldn't begin to understand the ancient principles involved: '. . . one might as well bring together dogs and horses, goats and pigs, in a public hall and compel these creatures to perform the evolutions of the dance'. Beneficent Indulgence agreed and the kowtow was reserved for Chinese alone.)

The Censor's suicide had a profound effect on Beneficent Indulgence. Stung by so public a protest against the invalidity of the succession and her violation of dynastic traditions, she made a solemn pledge that the Emperor United Rule wouldn't be left permanently without a personal heir. And when the Emperor Brilliant Succession died in 1908 Beneficent Indulgence, whilst again upsetting the conservative elements by choosing P'u-yi to succeed him – for P'u-yi was a further step away from the main branch of the family – at last provided United Rule with a personal heir by appointing P'u-yi his son by adoption. It didn't matter that United Rule had been dead for thirty-four years, or that P'u-yi himself already had one consanguineous father, Prince Ch'un, and, by dynastic tradition, one other adopted father, his immediate predecessor, the Emperor Brilliant Succession, the great thing was that the rules had been obeyed at last.

What happened to the succession when P'u-yi died, childless, in 1967? By then the Empire itself had been extinct for fifty-five years: there was no Dragon Throne – the Emperor, according to Communist dogma, had been replaced by the people themselves, represented by the Party, led by Chairman Mao. The Ta Ch'ing dynasty may have been overthrown, but the Aisin-Gioro family lived on in surprising numbers. So who might have succeeded the Citizen Emperor in 1967? Not, certainly, his own flesh and blood, for in spite of the best efforts of five wives he never became a father. He did, however, have three brothers. The eldest, P'u-chieh, born in 1907, is now the head of the Aisin-Gioro clan, but would have been ineligible as heir to the throne by virtue of belonging to the wrong generation and the succession couldn't be passed through his blood, for his two marriages have brought only daughters; the third of P'u-yi's brothers, P'u-jen, son of Prince Ch'un by his second wife, was ineligible for the same reason, though he might have fathered a son; and the second, P'u-ch'i, died in 1918, aged three.

In the maze of Manchu genealogy it is inestimably helpful – and we have to thank the Emperor Lasting Prosperity, father of those thirty-five sons, for thinking of it – that all the male Aisin-Gioros of any one generation share the same first given name. The last Emperor's generation were all P'u something; their fathers were all Tsai, and their sons Yü; the present generation of males are all Hêng. It's a measure of the dynasty's confidence in its indestructibility that generic names were provided for five more generations of sons after the present, ending with Ki at the beginning of the twenty-second century.

The Manchu system of honours and titles was more complicated, but no less soundly based on common sense. With nine clearly defined exceptions, hereditary nobility, as we know it in Europe, didn't exist in Manchu China; and even in the cases of those nine exceptions, the possession of a title carried no special privileges beyond, for example, the wearing of a sable robe or the double-eyed peacock's feather, the right to sit in the Emperor's presence or to ride into the Forbidden City on horseback or in a sedan chair. Despite subsequent Communist propaganda to the contrary, birth was never valued above personal achievement; the determining of social rank was more a matter of bureaucracy than of aristocracy, so that a senior mandarin who had won high office through his own distinction was more generally esteemed than a prince.

The honours system might almost have been designed to maintain this healthy balance in favour of personal effort, for the twelve degrees of rank distributed among the princes of the imperial houses automatically diminished one grade in seniority with each succeeding generation. The sons of Emperors usually became princes of the first or second order on reaching manhood; their sons bore the title 'Beileh', or prince of the third order; a Beileh's son became a Beitzu, or prince of the fourth and most junior order; a Beitzu's male descendants shared various grades of the title Kung, or Duke, for four generations; and the most junior Kung passed on to his sons for another four generations four grades of a title similar to General; in the thirteenth generation, the male descendants of an Emperor returned to the common herd, with only a yellow girdle to remind the world of their illustrious blood.

The nine exceptions were the Holy Duke of Yen, the descendant of Confucius, whose title was genuinely hereditary, and eight princes of the blood, known as the Iron-capped Princes, who maintained their titles in perpetuity as a reward for the part their ancestors played in the Manchu conquest of China.

Candidates for the Pretendership

From the few printed sources available in England – most of them pre-dating the Communist Liberation of 1949 – I made a list of possible Pretenders before leaving for China:

1 Despite his obvious ineligibility on generation grounds, the last Emperor's elder surviving brother, **Beitzu P'u-chieh**, hereditary Prince Ch'un, was the name I put at the top of the list: he was, after all, head of the family – if,

indeed, he were still alive – and, while the finer points of dynastic etiquette were unlikely to hold much sway in the People's Republic of China, his seniority in itself might.

2 Next on my list came a putative nephew: **any son of Beitzu P'u-jen**, the last Emperor's half-brother.

After that I listed, in order of seniority, four of the great-grandsons of the Emperor Glory of Right Principle, who had been claimants on the last occasion on which the throne had fallen vacant – in 1908, following the death of the Emperor Brilliant Succession. It was highly unlikely that any of these four candidates were still alive – and, anyway, as same-generation cousins of P'u-yi they themselves wouldn't be eligible – but they might have eligible sons and grandsons.

3 **Beitzu P'u-lun**, son of Beileh Tsai-chih (formerly known as Tsai-chung), who was the senior candidate in 1874 and in 1908, by right of succession in the legitimate line through his grandfather, Prince Yi-wei, eldest son of the Emperor Glory of Right Principle. But his opponents argued that his claim was invalid, because his father was, in fact, the first cousin once removed of Prince Yi-wei, and only adopted as a son.

4 **Beitzu P'u-ch'eng**, son of Beileh Tsai-lien (one of the Boxer leaders), who was the elder son of Yi-tsung, Prince Tun, the fifth son of the Emperor Glory of Right Principle. Boxer-tainted descendants should be automatically disqualified, but the Chinese have a memory as short as it can be long.

5 **Beitzu P'u-chün**, son of Tsai-i, Prince Tuan (another leading Boxer), who was the second son of Yi-tsung, Prince Tun. In 1900 the Venerable Buddha appointed P'u-chün as heir apparent, with the title Ta-a-ko. But a year later, under pressure from the Allies, who wanted reparation for the deaths and damage of the Boxers' rampage, she demoted him and sent him, with his father, into exile in Ürümch'i, 2,000 miles away to the north-west. Strictly speaking this should have debarred him from candidacy, but see 4.

6 **Beitzu P'u-wei**, son of Beileh Tsai-ying (second son of Yi-hsin, first Prince Kung, sixth son of the Emperor Glory of Right Principle). P'u-wei's claim rested on his having been adopted in 1898 by his uncle Beileh Tsai-ts'eng, who would have succeeded the Emperor United Rule if Beneficent Indulgence hadn't borne a grudge against his father, Yi-hsin, the first Prince Kung.

7 But it seemed to me that a stronger candidate than any of these was an imperial clansman I knew only by his nickname, **Little Jui**. He makes frequent appearances in P'u-yi's autobiography as one of the three 'nephews' who were his constant companions in Manchukuo in the 1930s and early 1940s, in the Siberian POW camp in the late 1940s, and in Fu-shun in the 1950s. Of

all the nephews Little Jui was P'u-yi's favourite, as he records in the Chinese version of his autobiography, *From Emperor to Citizen*:

> He came from a fallen princely family, and I had summoned him to Ch'ang-ch'un when he was nineteen to study with the sons of other impoverished noble houses. I had regarded him as the most obedient and honest of the court students. He seemed less gifted than the others, but he served me better than his cleverer companions. He showed his loyalty to me throughout our five years in the Soviet Union . . . Just before my return to China I nominated him as my 'successor' in the event of my death, and his joy at this can be imagined . . .

This tantalizing reference to 'my "successor"' is never taken up again, nor is Little Jui ever unmasked. But the abridged version of the autobiography, edited by Paul Kramer, and published in the United States in 1967, under the title *The Last Manchu*, offers a few more clues:

> Little Jui was the descendant of Prince Tuan [*sic*] of the Ch'ing House. His family had declined in importance after his grandfather and uncle had become involved in the Boxer Rebellion . . . Among the young students of the Inner Court [in Ch'ang-ch'un] he was considered one of the most trustworthy and sincere. I realized that he did not have as high an IQ as the others, but he was not tricky and it had been better for me to have someone steady like him about. During our five years in the Soviet Union his loyalty had been complete and, thus, when I was about to return to China and feeling that my life would be in danger, I had discussed with my brothers-in-law and my brother the problem of 'selecting an heir to the throne', for I had decided to choose Little Jui. After he had learned of this decision, needless to say, his devotion was really beyond words.

Had this really happened? Were there any documents to prove it? Did P'u-yi have any further thoughts on the subject before his death in 1967? If Little Jui were still alive – and there was no statistical reason why not, for he would be barely seventy-five – did he still regard himself as P'u-yi's heir? But, most important of all, who was Little Jui and where was he now?

L OUD Report woke up as the Wangs left to join their families for lunch. 'Professor very nice man,' he said when they'd gone, 'but I think he waste his time with these Manchu.'
   'How do you know? You were sound asleep!'
   'Eyes closed, but ears listening to Interpreter Wang.'
   'And did he get anything wrong?'

'Nothing. Interpreter Wang very clever man.'

I rang down to the reception desk to order some sandwiches for lunch. 'Sorry, no room service.'

'No room service?' I was outraged. 'But this is a big, new hotel full of Japanese. There must be room service.'

'Sorry,' said the clerk, unmoved, 'no room service.'

'Then how are your guests supposed to feed themselves?'

'In the restaurant,' he replied, not unreasonably.

The restaurant seemed to be shut, though there wasn't a notice to say so, and it was still only half past one. Loud Report was as surprised as I was, so we walked in anyway – and five Chinese waitresses, sitting around a circular table in the middle of the otherwise empty restaurant, raised their faces from their rice bowls and turned to stare at us in amazement.

'Is it possible to have some lunch, please?' I asked, rather acidly. The girls – and they were only girls – continued staring for a moment, then one of them got the giggles and sprayed a mouthful of rice all over the table. Loud Report, sensing my irritation, walked over to their table and, with the friendly smile which all Orientals use as a disarming device, repeated my question in Chinese. They listened while he spoke, then pointed at the clock, shook their heads and returned to their eating. Loud Report didn't argue.

'Restaurant closed,' he told me, with his eyes averted in embarrassment.

'But,' I exploded, in the rude, loud voice that Occidentals use when they want to make themselves understood abroad, 'if the waitresses can eat, why can't the guests?'

'Chef gone home,' replied Loud Report, lamely.

At the reception desk the clerk coolly confirmed that, yes, the restaurant was closed.

'But it's only half past one.'

'Restaurant close at one.'

'When I asked you on the telephone just now for some sandwiches, you said there wasn't any room service so we'd have to eat in the restaurant.'

'Right,' he said, nodding seriously. 'No room service. Eat in restaurant.'

'But we can't,' I all but screamed at his expressionless face, 'because the restaurant is closed.'

22 P'u-chieh, brother of P'u-yi (then puppet Emperor of the Japanese state of Manchukuo), with his Japanese wife, Saga Hiro (a cousin of the Mikado), and their first child, Hui-sheng, whose disembodied head emerging from the pram pre-echoes the famous photograph of the aged Chairman Mao swimming in the Yangtze to prove he was still alive, outside their newly built bungalow in Ch'ang-ch'un in 1940.

23 P'u-chieh's bungalow in Ch'ang-ch'un is now a kindergarten.

24 The kitchen of the kindergarten, with the origina tiled floor.

25 The Emperor's brother's bath has been redundant since the fall of Manchukuo in 194

26 P'u-chieh in the uniform of a Japanese officer cadet with his Japanese bride, Saga Hiro, on their wedding day in Ch'ang-ch'un in 1938. The Mikado hoped that Saga Hiro would provide a Japanese heir for the Manchukuo throne.

27 Aisin-Gioro Hui-sheng, the elder of two daughters of P'u-chieh and Saga Hiro. She and her Japanese lover died together in a tragic suicide pact in a pine forest on Izu Island near Tokyo in 1957, when she was only eighteen.

28 A Japanese propaganda poster of P'u-yi as Emperor of the puppet state of Manchukuo (1934–45). The Chinese tunic, in imperial yellow, was a ploy to convince his people – and P'u-yi himself – that the administration was a step towards the restoration of the Ch'ing dynasty.

29 As a protest against the Japanese, Beauty in Flower continued to wear the court dress of the Manchus for her rare appearances in public as Empress of Manchukuo. As a refuge from a childless, loveless marriage, she took to opium and died, aged only forty, in 1946, eight years after this photograph was taken in the Imperial Palace in Ch'ang-ch'un.

30 Duke Yü-yan, favourite 'nephew' of the Emperor P'u-yi, during the Manchukuo period – and superintendent of the imperial testosterone injections – with his Manchu bride, Ma-chia Ching-lan, on their wedding day in Ch'ang-ch'un in 1943.

31 The Tatala concubine, Jade Years, P'u-yi's favourite Secondary Consort, in her bedroom in the Imperial Palace in Ch'ang-ch'un in 1938. She died four years later, aged only twenty-two – murdered, P'u-yi claimed, by the Japanese military. He gave her a huge state funeral and kept her fingernails and hair, which are now buried under the earthen floor of Yü-yan's Peking dwelling.

28

29

30

31

33

34

32 The Han concubine, Jade Lute, P'u-yi's third Secondary Consort. They married in 1943 when she was still a schoolgirl. She claimed later that he spent much of his time beating her.

33 Jade Lute divorced P'u-yi in 1956 when he was two-thirds of his way through the ten-year re-education programme at the War Criminals' Prison at Fu-shun.

34 In 1987 Jade Lute returned to the Imperial Palace in Ch'ang-ch'un to relive her memories of the Manchukuo period.

35

35 The 'new' Imperial Palace in Ch'ang-ch'un, which the Japanese built for P'u-yi. He was convinced it was full of bugging devices and refused to live there.

36 The author and Mr Interpreter Wang outside the 'old' Imperial Palace in Ch'ang-ch'un, known as the Salt Tax Palace because of its pre-Manchukuo incarnation. It is now open to the public and is as popular as a National Trust stately home.

36

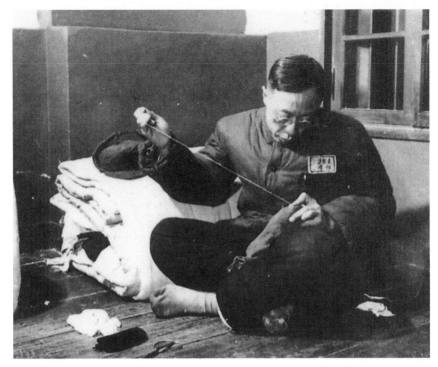

37 Self-help in the War Criminals' Prison in Fu-shun: when his 'nephew' Duke Yü-yan, a fellow inmate who 'reformed' before him, refused to be his 'valet' any more, P'u-yi was forced to darn his own socks.

38 Ex-Emperor P'u-yi receiving the news of his Special Pardon Order on December 8th, 1959: 'My motherland has made me a human being,' he said.

39 Duke Yü-ts'ung, son of Beitzu P'u-lun, wearing a coat of Japanese armour made in 1351. Yü-ts'ung was a *pan-tu*, or fellow student, of P'u-yi in Reginald Johnston's classes in the Forbidden City from 1919 to 1923.

40 Duke Yü-ts'ung (seated) with his elder son Hêng-ming outside their house in Pei-hai Park in Peking in about 1964. According to contemporary Communist sources Yü-ts'ung was 'a wastrel . . . who lived like a beggar'; like the rest of P'u-yi's court, he fell heavily from grace when Manchukuo collapsed in 1945.

41 The dilapidated gateway to Yü-yan's *hu-t'ung* dwelling in Peking, not far from the site of his ancestral home, the Palace of Prince Tun.

42 Loud Report sheltering from the storm on his way to the Pretender's lair.

'Yes.'

'This man is mad,' I said to Loud Report. Then, turning back to the clerk and trying hard to control my temper: 'Where is the manager?'

'Asleep.'

'Then wake the bugger up!'

I was suddenly overwhelmed with a sense of *déjà vu*. So was Loud Report.

'Misiter Socotolan,' he said softly, 'you remember angry Englishman at Peking Station?' I did, and with shame I remembered my sanctimonious response.

We left the hotel and went to look for a restaurant in the town, but the first two we found were just as firmly closed. So we returned to the hotel restaurant, ostentatiously sat ourselves at a table near the still dining waitresses and stared at them ferociously. I thought that if we sat it out for long enough they wouldn't have the gall to ignore us, but it was easier than that. Within a moment, one of the girls came over to our table and took our order as naturally as though they'd never refused us in the first place, nor ever told us the chef had gone home. Here was Chinese 'face' at work again: if they'd given in to us straight away, they'd have lost face; by making a scene we had gained face.

The girls weren't to blame for turning us away in the first place: they were taught to obey, as blindly as soldiers, rules drawn up for the convenience of the management – and, in return, they were paid the equivalent of £200 a year each. The hotel leaflet might boast that 'Serving guests is our first concern', but serving lunch after 1 p.m. was no concern of the comrade-waitresses, to whom such revisionary notions were incomprehensible.

It was Loud Report's birthday, and I thought I'd cheer him up. 'There's a very pretty girl doing the housekeeping on my floor,' I said. 'Very pretty indeed. In fact, I've never seen such a beautiful girl. She's short and slight and soft, with a fringe and a pointed chin, big round eyes and shiny lips. She's so light, her feet so small and her steps so short that she floats like an angel. And she's modest too: when I said "Good morning" to her, she lowered her eyes and blushed. I think you'd like her.'

'I know,' said Loud Report, his eyes misting over. 'Her name is Winter Stone.'

*

65

ONE way and another, we'd all had lunch and were now back in my hotel bedroom, gathered around the four little tape-recorders. I had some routine but important questions to soften up the professor before I sprang the big one.

Across the battery of microphones I smiled at Professor Wang, who smiled patiently at Mr Interpreter Wang, who in turn smiled glassily at me as he drew out the nub of each English question and passed it on in Chinese to the professor.

I had read that P'u-yi's brother P'u-chieh acted as a consultant to Bernardo Bertolucci during the making of the film *The Last Emperor* in 1986. He would then have been seventy-nine. Was he still alive?

Indeed he was, said Professor Wang: he was a member of the Standing Committee of the National People's Congress – the highest organ of state power; vice-president of the State Council's Nationalities Affairs Commission; adviser to several companies and, like so many other members of the Aisin-Gioro clan, a distinguished calligrapher and poet. On his release from the War Criminals' Prison at Fu-shun in 1960 he had gone to live in a house in Peking, which had been left to him by his late father, Prince Ch'un. His Japanese wife, Saga Hiro, had joined him there later and together they'd lived a life of happy domesticity until her death at the age of seventy-three in 1987. They had had two daughters: the elder, Hui-sheng, had died in 1957; the younger, Yün-sheng, had married a Japanese aristocrat who worked in the car industry, and together they'd raised a family of five children.

(P'u-chieh was married first to a Manchu aristocrat called T'ung Shih-hsia, a niece of the Pearl concubine who was murdered in the well; she stayed behind in Peking when P'u-chieh went north to join his brother in Ch'ang-ch'un; and in 1935 a secret emissary of the Japanese army persuaded her two brothers to give their permission to an annulment of the marriage in order to free P'u-chieh for a Japanese wife.)

What about P'u-yi's half-brother, P'u-jen, I asked Professor Wang – what had become of him?

He and his father Prince Ch'un had survived both the Japanese occupation of Manchuria and the ensuing civil war, and had subsequently opened a private school. When this was closed down by the Communists, they became primary school teachers in the state system. They lived in the Northern Palace just outside the Forbidden City until a few months before Prince Ch'un's death in 1951, when money troubles forced them to sell up to the People's Government. Part of the estate was later given to Sun Yat-sen's widow, Soong Ching-ling, who died in 1981, since when it had become a museum in her memory; the other buildings had been taken over by the Ministry of Health. P'u-jen had now retired, but still served the people as a committee member of the West City District Political Consultative Council in Peking. Like many other members of the Aisin-Gioro family, after Liberation, in order to avoid persecution, he had changed his name to Chin, a common Chinese name equivalent to the Manchu 'Aisin', meaning gold. He and his second wife, Chang Mao-ying, had two sons, the younger of whom, Chin Tzu-chung, now worked for his uncle P'u-chieh.

What, I wanted to know, had happened to the imperial family records, which had been maintained so assiduously by the court eunuchs since the start of the Manchu dynasty?

Professor Wang explained that all the records and seals and portraits, like everything else in the Forbidden City, had been 'dispersed' after the dissolution of the dynasty in 1924. But now, as part of a formal government policy, they were all being brought together again at centres in Peking, Ch'ang-ch'un, Shen-yang and T'ien-ching. In addition the last Emperor's widow, Li Shu-hsien – the nurse he married as plain Mr P'u in 1962 – owned a quantity of diaries, letters and other personal papers bequeathed to her by her late husband, and these she had lent to Professor Wang for his projected history of the family. He had already used them for a number of shorter works about P'u-yi – interest in the former imperial family has been growing in China since the fall of the Gang of Four – and he was at present editing the diaries, which run to 500,000 Chinese characters. 'Professor Wang is not the only writer on the subject,' explained Mr Interpreter Wang, in a reverential aside, 'but he is certainly the best informed and the most scholarly.' Professor Wang nodded enthusiastically as Mr Wang told me this, so I felt obliged to make a little speech acknowledging the privilege of sitting at the feet of so great a man. Professor Wang was delighted, and generously offered me access to 'all that I know'. We shook hands and would have embarked on a round of toasts if there'd been anything to drink; Loud Report, glad of the opportunity to escape, trotted off to find some beer.

Meanwhile I asked the professor about my other Pretender candidates – without revealing why I was interested in them.

P'u-lun had been, he said, 'somebody at court', and had 'sucked up to Yüan Shih-k'ai' (the first President of the Republic, established in 1912). He'd made an immense fortune and had lived the life of Riley on a great estate in Peking. P'u-lun had died before 1934, leaving three sons, including Yü-ts'ung, who had been closely associated with P'u-yi – first as his *pan-tu*, or companion student, in Johnston's classes in the Forbidden City, then as a member of the personal guard in Ch'ang-ch'un. On his father's death he had sold the family place at Kuan-wai for '50,000 silver coins'. But he had been a 'wastrel', had Yü-ts'ung, and had 'soon become poor'. After losing his fortune he had joined P'u-yi's court in Ch'ang-ch'un, and when Manchukuo collapsed in 1945 he had paid his way back home to Peking by singing ballads from the Pa-chiao Opera. On reaching Peking in 1947 he had moved in with his aunt's brother, 'selling waste, like a beggar'. After Liberation in 1949 the Party had 'taken pity on him and given him work', first as a calligrapher – the refuge of all Aisin-Gioros – then as a gardener in Pei-hai Park in Peking. His life had been very hard, but when P'u-yi was released from Fu-shun War Criminals' Prison in 1959 he gave what assistance he could. Yü-ts'ung died in 1965, leaving two sons, one of whom, Hêng-ming, was now vice-president of the Peking Forestry Department's three environmental commissions.

P'u-ch'eng, too, was no longer alive. He had married a high-born Manchu of the Fu-ch'a clan called Ching-kuei. They'd had two sons: Yü-t'ai, who died in Ch'ang-ch'un in the 1940s, and Yü-yan, who married twice and had three sons, all of whom were still alive.

P'u-chün, the Ta-a-ko who was exiled to Turkestan in 1901, had married a Mongolian aristocrat called Lo-shih, daughter of A-la-shang-ch'i Lo-wang. They hadn't got on very well, said the professor, because P'u-chün was 'a playboy, addicted to drinking, gambling and playing with whores'. Having ruined himself in Turkestan, he'd returned, penniless, to Peking, where he'd spent the remaining years of his life as the guest of his brother-in-law, T'a-wang, who was Minister of Mongolian and Tibetan Affairs in the government of Chung Hua Kuo Ming. P'u-chün had died in the T'a-wang Mansion in the early 1930s and had been buried in the backyard of Chia-hsin Temple. P'u-chün's eldest son, Yü-wei, was said to be mentally deficient.

P'u-wei had died in 1936, aged fifty-six, leaving ten sons, of whom the eldest now living, Yü-chan, was one of P'u-yi's favourites in the court at Ch'ang-ch'un. In a ceremony in the Imperial Palace in the summer of 1937, P'u-yi restored to the seventeen-year-old Yü-chan the title of Prince Kung (which had been given to his great-grandfather, Yi-hsin) along with the Kung estates in Peking and various family relics. Yü-chan had become a devout Zen Buddhist and had cut off all his hair, hence his nickname, the Bald Prince. In 1945, after the fall of the Japanese, he'd been arrested by the Russians – along with P'u-yi – and had been sent to a POW camp in Siberia, and thence to Fu-shun War Criminals' Prison in Manchuria. After seven years' 're-education' he had been pardoned and released. Since the fall of the Gang of Four he'd become a noted calligrapher, working for the Arts Academy of China in the Park of the Altar of the Sun in Peking. 'Foreigners, especially Japanese, buy his work,' said Professor Wang. 'He lives in a two-room flat in Peking, with his Han wife, Kao Chin-hua, and they have a good life.'

Loud Report had been gone a very long time and the Wangs were muttering darkly. I had to keep the professor talking. Changing the subject, I asked him if he knew where P'u-yi was buried. I knew he had died of cancer in a public ward of the Capital Hospital in Peking in 1967 and that his body had been cremated without ceremony, but I didn't know what had happened to his ashes. He was a former Emperor, after all, and the Chinese had been committed monarchists for 4,000 years: even though the Cultural Revolution was then in full swing, some sort of concession must have been made to the ancient procedures of imperial dispatch?

Professor Wang quickly corrected me: P'u-yi's ashes weren't those of an Emperor or even a former Emperor, but of a citizen of the People's Republic; as such, they had been interred, perfectly properly, in the masses' graveyard at Eight Treasure Mountain Cemetery in the northern suburbs of Peking. But twelve years later, at the end of the Cultural Revolution, the Communist Party Central Committee had decided to honour the former Emperor and pardoned war criminal who had so distinguished himself with seven years of selfless devotion to the people at the very end of his strange life. Unable, in the modern People's Republic, to arrange anything as counter-revolutionary as a funeral, Teng Hsiao-p'ing had called instead a memorial meeting, at which he had elevated Citizen P'u to the status of people's leader. And, to prove he meant business, Mr Teng had then bussed the Party faithful out to Eight Treasure Mountain and formally installed the last Emperor's 'bone-ash casket' among his Party peers in the Hall of Revolutionary Heroes.

Professor Wang was most anxious that I should understand the remarkable generosity the Communists had shown to P'u-yi ever since they came to power. As a former Emperor, he could have been sent into exile; as a war criminal – a Japanese collaborator – he could have been executed. Yet when the Russians handed him over to Chairman Mao in 1950, he wasn't even punished. Instead he was offered the privilege of re-education, or, in Party jargon, 'remoulding through labour and study'. By this means his thinking had changed; no pressure had been put on him, but, over the course of ten years in the war criminals' prison in Manchuria, he had gradually come to understand that emperors were bad and the people good, that the people ruled China now and that he was one of the people. As a citizen of the People's Republic, he was a free man at last. Had he not burst into tears on receiving his special pardon in 1959 and uttered the memorable words: 'My motherland has made me into a human being'? And when, the following year, he was given voter's rights for the first time, had he not said: 'As I put the ballot into the red box, I felt that I was the richest man on earth. Along with my 650 million compatriots, I was now the owner of our 9,600,000 square kilometres of territory'? Did his autobiography not end with the significant words: 'Only today, with the Communist Party and the policy of remoulding criminals, have I . . . become a real man'?

'The success of the last Emperor's reform,' said Professor Wang, 'proves that a man's thinking can change.'

I said I appreciated all this: the Communists had shown extra-ordinary sophistication in pardoning P'u-yi. I didn't say, because I didn't want to alienate the professor, that the whole operation had been motivated less by a civilized sense of generosity than by sheer political expediency. As Jung Chang explains in *Wild Swans*, 'Mao's stated policy was: "We kill small Chiang Kai-sheks. We don't kill big Chiang Kai-sheks!" Keeping people like P'u-yi alive, he reasoned, would be well received abroad.' The remoulding of P'u-yi represented one of Mao's master-strokes of propaganda: the Son of Heaven brought down to earth, the Lord of Ten Thousand Years humbled, re-educated and released into the world as a citizen voice-piece of Chinese Communism.

Anyway, we now had P'u-yi honoured at last. What about ancestral sacrifices? With no heir, and in the inhospitable climate of Communist China, who was to carry out these arcane and degenerate rites so that

P'u-yi's soul could rest in peace with the souls of his imperial ancestors who'd already 'mounted the Dragon chariot' and 'proceeded on the long journey'?

Professor Wang explained that the state maintained all the imperial tombs, 'though, of course, none of the Aisin-Gioro family have carried out the ancestral rituals since Liberation'. Nevertheless, P'u-chieh did still pay an annual visit to the North-East to worship at the family tombs in the city of Liao-yang, just south of the ancient seat of the Manchus at Shen-yang. And the last Emperor's widow, Li Shu-hsien, went out to Eight Treasure Mountain as often as she could, 'to pay her respects and to dust the bone-ash casket'.

And so, at last, I reached the burning question. Who was Little Jui?

Professor Wang looked blank. I wrote the name down for him and the Wangs went into cabinet.

'Ah!' said the professor, 'Hsiao Rui,' and it was my turn to look blank until Mr Interpreter Wang explained that 'Hsiao' was Chinese for 'Little' and 'Rui' was the Pinyin form of the character which the Wade–Giles system of romanization – still in use when P'u-yi wrote his book in the 1960s – renders as 'Jui'.

If only from relief at a mystery solved, we all laughed. But the greater mystery remained: who was Hsiao Rui?

The doorbell rang and in came Loud Report with six cans of beer. He looked both worried and excited. I dealt with the first first: 'Anything wrong, Loud Report?'

'Terribly sorry, Misiter Socotolan,' he gasped, for he'd been running, 'no bottles of beer in hotel, so I have to buy tins: Hong Kong beer, very expensive. Terribly sorry.'

'Don't worry – it really doesn't matter' – nothing mattered except Hsiao Rui's identity – 'thank you for finding any beer at all.' Loud Report's brow cleared, leaving just the wild gleam in his eye.

'Anything else, Loud Report?' I asked pointedly as I poured out the beer.

Politely begging the Wangs' pardon, Loud Report beckoned me to the door, where he whispered urgently in my ear: 'Winter Stone wants to make your bed.' For all the drama of his manner he might have been David Copperfield bearing the message to Clara Peggotty that 'Barkis is willin''.

'It's not really very convenient at the moment,' I said. 'We've reached a rather crucial point in our discussions.'

'But housekeeper will make trouble.'

'Can't she come back in an hour?'

'Misiter Socotolan, please, you speak to Winter Stone – she wait outside door.' And as he opened it there she was, resting her head against the frame like a tiny shy caryatid. In a trembling voice Loud Report introduced us.

'How d'you do?' I said, sticking out my Western hand.

Lowering her long-lashed lids, inclining her head and blushing delicately, Winter Stone acknowledged the clumsy greeting with no more than a faint curling of the fingertips of her right hand, which she held at an angle across her chest; she said nothing, but formed her lips into a small 'o' and exhaled slightly. The effect of this performance was intoxicating: Loud Report's heart beat so fiercely that his shirt rose and fell like a tent in a thunderstorm, and I lost my tongue.

At last Winter Stone broke the ice: peeping under her fringe, she smiled encouragingly and my voice came back. I said I was sorry she hadn't been able to clean my room, but I was having a meeting that was likely to last another hour: would she mind coming back then? Winter Stone accepted this with a tilt of her head and a *moue* of her lips and was about to float away down the corridor when Loud Report suddenly produced his camera.

'You'd better be quick,' I said, 'or the Wangs'll wonder what's going on.'

We went down to the end of the corridor and posed by the window. I felt infinitely clod-hopping beside this dainty Circe.

'Misiter Socotolan,' called Loud Report, peering into his Japanese camera, 'please to put arm around beautiful girl.' Gingerly I did, fearing that the weight of my arm might crush her. In response she yielded and I felt a wave of warmth where her softness pressed against my ribs. I tried to smile but could only bare my teeth. Loud Report flashed and, no excuse for further contact remaining, Winter Stone melted from me. Loud Report was less coy when his turn came to pose. But again the contact was broken the moment the flash went off, as though only the camera condoned a cuddle in Communist China. And so, in fact, things are – for public displays of affection between members of the opposite sex are classified as 'behaviour that corrupts public morals'; I often saw the charming sight of two boys holding hands or putting their arms around one another's necks, but I never saw anyone hugging or kissing – and a couple of months after I left

China, I read that official notices had been posted around Peking University banning all physical contact.

As Winter Stone wafted off to continue her work, carried away on the toes of her little sandalled feet with her hands stretched out horizontally at her thighs like vestigial fairy-wings, Loud Report gazed after her in a dazed trance. When, at last, she was out of sight, he turned to me with cloudy eyes: 'Misiter Socotolan, you like Winter Stone?'

'I think she's wonderful. But we must get back – the Wangs are waiting.' And I hastened down the corridor towards my bedroom.

'May I ask personal question?' said Loud Report, scurrying along beside me. I nodded my head. 'Do you have girlfriend?' I shook my head. 'Aren't you very lonely?' I smiled enigmatically – and wondered how many more of Loud Report's personal questions I'd be able to parry with nods and smiles and non-committal looks before I was forced to explain that, although I had neither wife nor girlfriend, I wasn't at all lonely or unhappy, because there were other sorts of partners.

The Wangs were deep in a discussion which our reappearance did nothing to disturb; the beer was finished. When they were ready I reminded them that we'd reached the question, the crucial question, about the identity of Little Jui, Hsiao Rui – top, though I didn't let on, of my list of Pretender contenders.

Gathering up his notebooks and switching the tape-recorders back on, Professor Wang provided in a few words one of the answers I'd come so far for: Hsiao Rui, he said, was the nickname of Duke Aisin-Gioro Yü-yan, already identified as the son of Contender Number 4, Beitzu P'u-ch'eng, son of the Boxer leader Beileh Tsai-lien, grandson of Yi-tsung (second Prince Tun, the fifth son of the Emperor Glory of Right Principle) and great-great-grandson of Mien-k'ai, first Prince Tun, who served as superintendant of the Imperial Bureau of Music before he fell foul of the palace for what Arthur W. Hummel in his work, *Eminent Chinese of the Ch'ing Period 1644–1912*, calls 'familiarity' with young eunuchs and actors and other 'inferior persons'. So the Little Jui of P'u-yi's autobiography – Duke Yü-yan, as we must now call him – had a double claim to the throne: on the one hand he was the chosen heir of the last Emperor himself, on the other he was a legitimate claimant in his own right, as a senior descendant of the Emperor Glory of Right Principle through the 1908 claimant Beitzu P'u-ch'eng.

Would I be showing too much interest in a dangerously political area, I wondered, if I were to press the professor harder on this point? I decided it was worth the risk.

'There's a curious paragraph in P'u-yi's autobiography,' I said in as disbelieving a tone as I could muster, 'in which Little Jui, I mean Yü-yan, is described as P'u-yi's chosen heir. How could this possibly be?'

'It's true,' said Professor Wang, whose interest suddenly intensified at this obscure reference. Leaning forward in his chair and stabbing the air with a finger for emphasis, he said that in prison in Siberia in the 1940s P'u-yi had issued an edict-in-exile formally adopting Duke Yü-yan, his favourite and most devoted 'nephew', as his son and heir. As a mark of special favour, he had excused Yü-yan from addressing him as 'Imperial Majesty', which had been court practice in Peking and Ch'ang-ch'un, or as 'Above', the quaint code they'd adopted in prison; instead Yü-yan was permitted to call his sovereign 'Great Uncle'.

After a period of re-education in Fu-shun Prison in the 1950s Yü-yan had publicly renounced his claim to the throne. But he and P'u-yi remained close friends till the last Emperor's death, and Yü-yan continued to address him as 'Great Uncle'; even now he called the last Emperor's widow, Li Shu-hsien, 'Great Aunt' – though she was a decade his junior.

'So Yü-yan is still alive?' I tried to sound casual, but my heart was thumping.

'Of course. He's a calligrapher, and he lives with his wife and youngest son in a ramshackle hut in Peking, in the Tartar City – not far from your Bamboo Garden.'

'Really?' I hoped I was sounding no more than politely interested; in fact, I was mesmerized. 'I suppose I'd better try to track him down,' I said, pretending to stifle a yawn.

'No problem,' said Professor Wang, 'I can give you a letter of introduction.' This was too good to be true, but what was the use of a letter of introduction to the wrong man? At the risk of losing all the ground I'd gained, I had to ask two more questions. I adopted the flannel tactic.

'Professor Wang, I know it's a foolish question, and you must forgive me if it seems impertinent too, but if circumstances were to change in China – as, indeed, they've already changed in Eastern Europe – and – I know it seems absurd – if the Party were to lose power, and if, by some monstrous quirk of fate, there were to be calls – as there have been in Romania, Bulgaria, Hungary, Yugoslavia – for a restoration of the monarchy, is it at all possible that Yü-yan might consider himself a candidate?'

The professor did at least laugh. 'It is not possible,' he said.

'But imagine it, if you can, in the abstract, as a hypothetical proposition: would Yü-yan be the undisputed heir, or might there be other claimants?'

'It could only be Yü-yan,' he replied confidently.

'Not P'u-chieh, or P'u-jen, or his son Chin Tzu-chung, or Hêng-ming, or the mad Yü-wei, or even the Bald Prince?'

'Only Yü-yan could claim the throne,' ruled the professor evenly, 'because only Yü-yan was chosen by the Emperor.'

'But you said he renounced his claim later?'

'He says he did,' he answered warily, 'but no one, and nothing, ever, can change the will of an Emperor.'

PUSHING his black bicycle across the park as he took us home for dinner, Professor Wang, in shirt-sleeves and cloth cap, gazed in the direction of Ch'ang-pai Shan's snowy peak and recounted the legend of the birth of the Manchus.

It was an impressive performance, the professor carefully enunciating each word in a voice that ranged dramatically from the bass of Boris Christoff to the soprano of Yma Sumac, the bicycle brakes providing occasional squeals of emphasis. But he might have been quoting statistics from Teng Hsiao-p'ing's Four Modernizations Programme for all I knew. And Loud Report, for once, was no help: yielding to a combination of factors – unfamiliarity with the fantasy of mythology, the professor's actorish telling of the tale, Manchu overkill, the memory of Winter Stone's warm softness, and birthday excitement, he simply wept with laughter, falling over the professor's back mudguard, bumping into a ginkgo tree, gasping, moaning and hooting like a wounded castrato. A little irritated, I pressed him for an explanation: it was very important, I said, portentously – how could I possibly understand the Manchu Empire if I didn't know the story of its birth. He tried to tell me, but he got no further than three lady spirits taking their tunics off before he collapsed into hysterics again. So I was grateful when, two days later, the professor, translated this time by Mr Interpreter Wang, repeated the whole story for the benefit of my tape-recorder. It went something like this:

'It was comfortable in King K'u-lun's Palace, but there wasn't much to do and the three princesses were rather bored. One day the King and Queen went to the Peach Festival leaving the girls alone at home.

'"What shall we do now they've gone?" asked the eldest, Princess En K'u-lun, who was tall and thin and hyperactive.

'"I don't know," sighed the middle one, Princess Chen K'u-lun, who never had any original ideas.

'"We could fly away," suggested Princess Fu K'u-lun. She was the youngest and the prettiest and the most enterprising of the three. "We've always wondered what happens beyond the clouds," she said. "Now is our chance to find out."

'The princesses put on their best silk *ch'i-paos*, the long dresses with high necks and slit skirts, and kicked off their little wooden platform shoes, because they always preferred flying in bare feet. Then with a series of quick, strong flutters of the wrist, they took off and disappeared into the clouds.

'After a day or so, they came to a mountain covered with dazzling snow, part of the long, high range which runs along Chi-lin's southeastern border from Yan-chi to T'ung-hua, dividing Manchuria from North Korea.

'"Isn't it absolutely beautiful?" exclaimed Princess En K'u-lun.

'"I want to go home," complained Princess Chen K'u-lun, whose wings were aching.

'"Let's call it Ch'ang-pai Shan," said Princess Fu K'u-lun, ignoring her.

'On the top of the newly named Mount Ever-white there was a volcanic crater with a lake so deep and still and clear that it seemed to reflect the very firmament itself; this they called T'ien-ch'ih, or Lake Heavenly.

'The princesses were hot and tired after flying for such a long time – and Princess Chen K'u-lun's constant grizzling was getting on her sisters' nerves – so they decided to stop for a swim. Before diving in they slipped out of their dresses, which they left in three separate piles on the shore.

'While the sisters were swimming, two large crows with red berries in their beaks flew over the lake. One of the birds, distracted by the sight of the three naked princesses splashing in the water below, momentarily lost its concentration and dropped a berry on to Princess Fu K'u-lun's *ch'i-pao*.

'When she had finished her swim and waded ashore, Princess Fu K'u-lun noticed a curiously sweet smell in the air. It was so enticing that she sniffed and sniffed until she traced the source to her dress, and there in a fold lay a small red berry, so plump and smooth that she couldn't resist licking it, and when she did it tasted so unbelievably good that she ate it in one. Almost immediately the young princess felt warm and heavy all over, so she lay down and went to sleep.

'"Wake up, sister," said Princess En K'u-lun, drying herself with some lotus leaves. "We ought to get back to the palace before they notice we've gone."

'"I don't think I want to go back," said Princess Fu K'u-lun, yawning. "It's so nice here. Besides," she added, "I don't feel like flying at the moment."

'"Well you can't possibly stay here, on top of the mountain, without any clothes on," said Princess Chen K'u-lun, her teeth chattering as the sun disappeared behind a cloud. "You'll catch your death of cold."

'"I don't care," said Princess Fu K'u-lun. "I'm staying."

'"Oh dear!" said Princess Chen K'u-lun, starting to cry.

'"Don't be silly," said Princess En K'u-lun to both of them. "We've got to go. All of us. Now." And she pulled Princess Fu K'u-lun to her feet, buttoned her into her *ch'i-pao* (which looked somehow tighter than before) and flapped her wrists for take-off. But, try as she might, she just couldn't get Princess Fu K'u-lun off the ground.

'"What on earth is the matter?" asked Princess En K'u-lun testily.

'Princess Fu K'u-lun hung her head and gently rubbed her stomach. "I'm terribly sorry," she said, "but I think I'm pregnant."

'"Oh that!" exclaimed Princess En K'u-lun, who, being the eldest, knew a bit about life. "Well, you'd better lie down for a few months." And she and Princess Chen K'u-lun went off to build a maternity nest in a tall and sturdy cypress tree not far from the lake's edge.

'When it was finished, they laid the pregnant princess in it, curled her into a ball and covered her with leaves. Then they kissed her.

'"Goodbye, sister," said Princess En K'u-lun. "You'll feel better when you've had the baby."

'"Then you must raise him," added Princess Chen K'u-lun. "It may take sixteen years. We won't wait."

'And with that they both flew away.

'In due course Princess Fu K'u-lun gave birth to a strapping baby boy who could talk and hunt and fish as soon as he was born, and the two of them lived together happily at the top of the cypress tree by the lake on Ch'ang-pai Shan.

'One day when he was sixteen the boy, who was now exceptionally strong and handsome, with thick black hair that hung down his back, asked his mother who his father was and the princess told him the story of the swim and the crow and the red berry.

'"Your family name," she said, "is Aisin-Gioro and your personal name is P'u-k'u-li Yung-sun. You are the Son of Heaven and the father of the Manchus. Your mandate is to put the country in order. The time has come for you to leave home. But first you must receive the sign." And so saying she cut off the hair at the front of his head and carefully plaited the rest into a tidy pigtail. "Now your people will recognize you. Go, and govern."

'Princess Fu K'u-lun took her son down to the bottom of the mountain where there was a river and, in the river, a boat. Aisin-Gioro P'u-k'u-li Yung-sun stepped in and waved bravely to his mother as the boat floated downstream. He was sad to be parting from her, but he knew he must.

'After waving him out of sight, Princess Fu K'u-lun climbed back up the mountain for a last look at the tree house where she'd raised the Son of Heaven. Then she flew home to the palace to rejoin her sisters.

'Meanwhile, Aisin-Gioro P'u-k'u-li Yung-sun sailed on down the river till he came to a place where three families were fighting. They'd been fighting for years. It was a leadership struggle. None of the three families was strong enough to win, but none was weak enough to lose, so the fight just went on and on – even though all that any of them really wanted was a peaceful life.

'When the warring families saw Aisin-Gioro P'u-k'u-li Yung-sun standing like a god in the prow of his boat, they stopped fighting and went down to the river to welcome him.

'"Hail!" they called.

'"Hail!" he replied. "I am the Son of Heaven. This" – he indicated his pigtail – "is my sign. I've come to govern you so that you can lead a peaceful life."

'The three families were overjoyed. They put down their weapons and prepared a banquet, and when it was over and everyone was feeling full and contented, the head of each family chose his most beautiful daughter and presented her to the Son of Heaven so that he should have three wives to look after him while he ruled.

'Peace soon settled on the land; the people prospered, as they were now able to devote all their energies to farming and hunting; and they were so grateful to their saviour that all the men in the land, then and for ever afterwards, wore their hair shaved at the front and plaited into a pigtail at the back as a sign that they were Manchus and proud of it.

'And when Aisin-Gioro P'u-k'u-li Yung-sun died, his son inherited the divine mandate, which in time he passed on to his son, and he to his, till the Aisin-Gioros ruled the whole of China. And everyone was happy under the Manchus.'

My tape-recorder listened more respectfully than either Loud Report or Mr Interpreter Wang, whose cross-infecting hysteria no pillow would stifle. I never did discover what tickled them so much: it may have been the professor's sing-song voice, exaggeratedly sounding the four different tones that distinguish Chinese from any other language, or it may have been my face, which I set in a state of what I hoped was polite receptivity.

CHINESE, even when spoken untheatrically, is to Western ears comical, mysterious and ugly. It seems to burst out of the mouth in a series of jagged bits. The ear can't detect the line of a sentence because the tones which in Europe shape and emphasize groups of words are used, in Chinese, to convey meaning to every single syllable. Standard Chinese has four different tones: the first starts high and stays there; the second starts low and rises; the third starts high, drops and rises again; and the fourth starts high and drops. And each computation of syllable and tone has to be learned in order, for example, to distinguish *mǎi*, sounded on the third tone and meaning 'to buy', from *mài*, sounded on the fourth tone and meaning precisely the opposite, 'to sell'.

Occasionally I would take a stab at a Chinese word, just to show willing, but however immaculately I thought I was reproducing it, by means of the BBC Pronunciation Unit's own modified phonetic version of the Pinyin romanization, I never failed to baffle my listener. The fact that I felt it necessary to manoeuvre my head and even my shoulders in the direction of the prescribed tones may have been as obfuscating as it was farcical. The result, anyway, was that my meaning never became clear till my listener had tasted the sounds in his own mouth, rolled them around on his tongue and finally cast them in recognizable tones.

Whenever I stopped someone in Peking and said, '*Ch'ing, Chiu Kulou tsai na-li?*' with a smile and an eyebrow raised hopefully, I imagined I was asking the way, please, to Drum Tower Street – home of the Bamboo Garden Hotel. Generally the '*Ch'ing*' – 'please' – and the '*tsai na-li*' – 'where is' – got through, but the crucial '*Chiu Ku-lou*', whether sounded high-level sustained, high rising, low dipping or high falling, remained, it seemed, as incomprehensible as the physical contortions that accompanied it, till at last, having attracted by now a crowd of gawpers, I was rescued by someone shouting triumphantly '*Chiu Kulou!*' which is what I thought I'd said in the first place.

Professor Wang lived in a grey and crumbling block of flats on a housing estate just south of Nanhu Park. It was dark when we reached it and there were no lights to guide us up the bare concrete stairs, past the bicycles leaning against the banisters, to the Wangs' flat on the fourth floor. Mrs Wang, a pretty woman in an apron, was waiting at the door of Flat 4510.

It was a small flat, clean and tidy, but poor and ill-maintained by Western standards: later I realized how superior it was – bigger and better furnished – to most Chinese homes. A tiny hall doubling as dining room stood at the centre, with a kitchen and bathroom to the right, a study-cum-sitting room to the left and one if not two bedrooms at the end. In it lived the professor and his wife and their two teenage boys, with a television, a telephone and lots of books and papers.

Professor Wang said it wasn't ideal, but it was cheap – about £2.50 a month – because it belonged to his work unit, the History Study Institute of the Chi-lin Social Sciences Academy. Soon, he hoped, they would give him a bigger flat, with more room for his sons and his books.

After I had exchanged my walking shoes for a pair of rubber house sandals Mrs Wang showed me into the study and sat me down, with a cup of green tea, on a black leatherette sofa beneath a bunch of plastic grapes, a Tower of London calendar, a scroll of calligraphy by P'u-chieh and a bare hook soon to receive the professor's cap.

When, later, Mr Interpreter Wang arrived from his flat in the same block, we had a ceremonial exchange of gifts: I gave the professor and Mr Interpreter Wang and their families some routine little presents which I'd brought out from England; the professor, more usefully, presented me with the English-language version of his paperback about P'u-yi's final seven years, *China's Last Emperor as an Ordinary Citizen*.

While waiting for Mrs Wang to prepare dinner Professor Wang showed me some of P'u-yi's letters and diaries which the last Emperor's widow, Li Shu-hsien, had lent him for his researches. Among them were: a page from his diary for February 1961, in which, in a hasty scrawl, he writes:

I was born into a feudal family and received a feudal education. That kind of education is poisonous, for it says that the Emperor is the Son of Heaven, the biggest landlord, the very state itself, that the territory of the whole country belongs to him and all the people are his slaves . . .

the certificate authenticating his membership of the Chinese People's Congress in 1964, the last official position he held before his death in 1967; an invitation from Premier Ch'ou En-lai to a banquet celebrating the sixteenth anniversary of the founding of the People's Republic in 1965 – the menu included roast chicken and boiled salt-water duck, with mooncake for pudding; and, most poignant of all, his very last note to his wife, Li Shu-hsien, scribbled from his hospital bed in Peking on October 10th, 1967:

Younger Sister, I feel very weak. When you come, pray bring me the *tzu-ho-ch'e* medicine [a powerful restorative made of powdered placenta – similar to a traditional eunuch remedy called Hung Pills made from the menstrual discharge of a beautiful teenage virgin]. I'll take it tonight. *Yao-chih*. ['Younger Sister' was the private nickname P'u-yi used for his wife; '*Yao-chih*', 'to glorify', was his private nickname.]

Eleven days later he died.

Professor Wang also showed me a cutting from the Chinese paper *Wen Hui Daily* in 1989, in which Li Shu-hsien disclosed that these documents were nearly destroyed by P'u-yi himself at the start of the Cultural Revolution. The couple were living quietly in a peaceful villa in a tree-lined lane in the Tartar City when one day in 1966 they received a threatening visit from a young Red Guard, who handed 'Comrade P'u-yi' a notice ordering him to surrender his prized

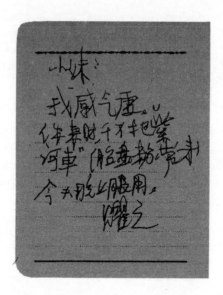

Fig. A: P'u-yi's last note to his wife, Li Shu-hsien, as he lay dying in hospital in Peking in 1967.

photograph of himself with Chairman Mao on the grounds that as a 'criminal of history' he had no business to pose with the people's leader. P'u-yi was 'thunderstruck and seemed to lose his mind', his widow writes. 'There is a Cultural Revolution now,' she quotes him as saying. 'It isn't necessary for me to keep all my books any longer.' The article continues:

After this he started to tear his books apart, and then, together, we brought cases of books to a peaceful little corner in the garden where he lit a fire. When the books were almost completely burned he asked me to bring out the boxes containing his calligraphy in order to destroy them as well . . . He also wanted to destroy his sketches, his poetry, his diaries, etc. Perhaps it seemed to him at the time that to burn all of this was his own revolution . . . I couldn't stand it any longer. Weren't the memories of our beautiful time together contained in those diaries? . . . Suddenly I had an idea. I said: 'Dear Pu, I seem to hear somebody knocking on the front door. Could you go and have a look . . .?' P'u-yi was rather nervous at this point and really believed that there was somebody at the door. Slowly he walked to the door and listened . . . then he suggested he should go out into the street to check. That was all the time I needed to take ten sketches and diaries out of the fire. I didn't mean to keep them as a record for posterity but only as a personal memory. P'u-yi came back from the street having found nobody and, feeling frustrated, he said that it must have been a ghost. I was very happy, and looking back I know I did the right thing . . . to keep all this information was no easy task. It is the legacy of China's last Emperor and proof of 2,000 years of her imperial tradition which was finally buried by history. Their historical value is immeasurable.

Over dinner I asked the professor if there was any indication in the diaries that P'u-yi had lapsed from the Party line after leaving Fu-shun in 1959: had he, for instance, shown any interest in becoming Emperor again?

'No,' said the professor, 'but subconsciously he couldn't help thinking like an emperor sometimes. For example, when he arrived at Fu-shun, the first thing he did was to visit the men's room, but he forgot to take any paper in with him because he was so used to other people . . . er . . . doing that for him.'

Edible fungus and tomatoes in sugar were among the delicious things Mrs Wang had prepared for the four of us, but to my surprise she didn't join us at the little round table in the hall. Instead she hovered in the entrance of her kitchen, occasionally filling our plates and always smiling. She resembled, I suddenly realized, her namesake, the last Emperor's beloved 'breeding mother', or wet-nurse, the selfless and devoted Mrs Wang who breast-fed him till, astonishingly, he was eight years old, when, without telling him, the High Consorts dismissed her from the Forbidden City. ('What little humanity I learned from her before the age of eight,' P'u-yi writes in his autobiography, 'I gradually lost afterwards.') We drank a toast to the health of Mrs Professor Wang, all of us taking care, as we touched glasses, to obey the charming Chinese code that requires each person to present his glass slightly below the level of that held by the most senior person present. Accordingly I clinked the professor's just below the rim, but he insisted on awarding me greater seniority and promptly hit back with a clink on my stem, which honour bade me reciprocate with a touch lower still.

Ill-mannered though it was at the dinner table, I was determined to ask my professor more questions; and he seemed just as keen to answer.

'Did P'u-yi feel he'd been a bad Emperor?' I asked.

'Yes. He writes a lot about that in the diaries.'

'Did he regret that he'd had no children?'

83

'Very much. He loved children.'

'Isn't it surprising, then, that he should have spent so much time flogging them?'

Professor Wang laughed gaily. 'The children he beat were only servants.'

B Y P'u-yi's own admission corporal punishment was his staff of life as puppet Emperor of Manchukuo – the Japanese state founded on the principle of *Wang-t'ao*, or 'the kingly way of benevolent rule'. Apart from eating and sleeping – both of which he indulged to excess in order to fill the long empty hours in his prison-palace – his daily life comprised 'floggings, curses, divinations, medicine and fear'.

The ritual of an imperial beating allowed some latitude in the matter of strokes, but the active element was usually a wooden paddle, a horse-whip or a bundle of bamboo rods and the passive element always the bare buttocks. The venue was the labyrinthine basement of the Imperial Palace, home of the boilers and the eight eunuchs who looked after the drugged Empress. It was known by the stagily sinister name of The Dungeons, as though it were a set in a Hammer horror film. But the menace was real. When the Emperor pointed towards the floor and commanded, 'Take him downstairs!' the effect in the little puppet court was as devastating as the Queen of Hearts' croquet match. The flogger was usually a senior courtier, perhaps one of the 'nephews' – including Duke Yü-yan – and sometimes the Emperor himself. The victim could be almost anyone at court, but was usually a member of the junior household staff, especially the corps of twelve page-boys, and sometimes even one of the 'nephews', but never the Empress, the imperial siblings or their spouses.

The twelve Chinese page-boys – the 'servants' Professor Wang had referred to – were recruited from a charity orphanage in Ch'ang-ch'un, their parents having been murdered by the Japanese. The aim of the institution, according to P'u-yi himself, was 'to teach them to be slaves, to wear them out through heavy labour', so they wouldn't have any energy left for escape or revenge. Employment at the palace must have seemed, at first, a dream come true; all too soon it proved a nightmare. The boys were given rags to wear and cheap maize to eat; in return they were expected to work up to sixteen hours a day, with sometimes a night-watch, too. Cold and tired, they would often fall asleep on the radiators and wake in the morning covered in burns. They were always being beaten and, if the weals were bad, they were thrown into solitary confinement till the wounds had healed. 'So wretched was their life,' P'u-yi confessed, 'that at the age of seventeen or eighteen they were as small as ten-year-olds.'

One of the pages – a boy called Sun Po-yuan – was beaten to death. After trying to escape he'd been caught and savagely flogged. He'd fled again, this time through the central-heating ducts under the palace floors, but he got disorientated in the criss-crossing tunnels and couldn't find a way out. After crawling in circles for two days he was so dehydrated that he had to give himself up. P'u-yi, in a fever of fury, prescribed the interminable flogging session which finally killed the boy. Fearful that Master Sun's ghost might take his own life in revenge, the Emperor spent the next few days on his knees, kowtowing to his ancestors and reciting scriptures in front of a Buddhist altar. He also ordered that the assistants who'd administered the fatal flogging should lash their palms with bamboo rods every day for six months as a penance.

As a condition of employment all the staff of the Imperial Palace had to take an oath of obedience to a long list of household rules, many of which had less connection with their work than with the Emperor's paranoia – for example, 'irresponsible conversations' and 'covering up for colleagues' were both punishable offences. At the bottom of the declaration, which they all had to sign in advance, was a clause to the effect that if the signatory disobeyed any of the rules, 'May Heaven strike me down with a thunderbolt'. The thunderbolt favoured by the Son of Heaven was 'severe flogging', and if the Emperor didn't think it was severe enough, then he had the flogger flogged, and doubly hard. In this way the entire household got drawn into the Emperor's sado-masochistic web of internal discipline.

P'u-yi's favourite servant, Li T'i-yü, known as Big Li, who served him from the collapse of the Ch'ing dynasty and the expulsion from the Forbidden City, right through the T'ien-ching interlude and the Manchukuo Empire, and then shared the fourteen years of prison – in Siberia, under the Soviets, and in Manchuria, under the Chinese Communists – grew to hate his master. 'This person P'u-yi,' he wrote in a confession to the governor of Fu-shun, 'was cruel, frightened of death and extremely suspicious. He was also very cunning and thoroughly hypocritical. His treatment of his servants was inhuman.'

85

P'u-yi acquired his taste for beating as a small boy in the Forbidden City, where floggings were part of the fabric of daily life: Beneficent Indulgence had dozens of eunuchs beaten daily and claimed they loved it. P'u-yi was brought up with the sight and sound of eunuchs publicly thrashing one another all over the Forbidden City, and it wasn't long before he joined in. By the age of seven he was already an old hand. 'Flogging eunuchs,' he wrote in his autobiography, 'was part of my daily routine.' He would fly into a rage if the eunuchs forgot to kowtow to him or failed in some other way to observe the minutiae of court etiquette, and quite often – though usually only in the case of a young eunuch or a page-boy – he would wield the paddle himself. Things got so bad at one point, before the arrival of his tutor, Johnston, who disapproved of flogging almost as much as he abhorred the eunuchs, that one of the Manchu tutors complained to the High Consorts, his mothers, that the boy Emperor had personally flogged seventeen teenage eunuchs in a single week.

Beheading was the officially prescribed punishment for a whole range of thieving offences, which the palace eunuchs – from Chamberlain to Keeper of the Cats, from Sergeant of the Imperial Concubines to Holder of the Privy Pot – had been practising since remote antiquity, but it was rarely invoked: a sore, sometimes raw bottom must have seemed a small price to pay for the retention of the head. Rather too often the floggings went well beyond the limits of the merely admonitory into the realm of full-blooded perversion.

When P'u-yi was about twelve, one of his mothers, the High Consort Lustrous, discovered him posing in front of a glass while kitted out in the uniform of an officer of the Republican Army, complete with plumed cap, sword, leather belt – and foreign socks. The jape had been organized by two young Eunuchs of the Presence on the orders of the boy Emperor himself, who had a passion for dressing up – a foible he was to indulge as an adult, when his favourite outfits ranged from Prince of Wales check suits with golfing cap and co-respondent shoes, to Mussolini breeches, Hitler jackboots and film-star dark glasses. Lustrous was so incensed at this breach of form, and its dangerous political implications, that she sentenced the two guilty eunuchs, mere boys, to 200 strokes of the heavy rod and, with no break for recovery, she then dispatched them, torn, bleeding and virtually insensible, to a period of hard labour in the palace cleaning department, where, as she well knew, they would be further abused by the older eunuchs and their multi-purpose besom handles.

As an infant P'u-yi was himself often roughly treated by the eunuchs. Once, soon after his ascension, he gobbled up six buns, one after the other, and got so ill that the Chief Eunuch turned him upside-down and banged his head on the brick floor, 'as if I were some sort of human pile driver'.

But this little act of thoughtless cruelty wasn't unavenged for long. The moment the boy realized he was the Son of Heaven he took full advantage of his new-found power. When he was about seven, he had what he later called 'a brainwave': 'I wanted to see whether those servile eunuchs were really obedient to the divine Son of Heaven. I picked on one and pointed at a piece of dirt on the floor. "Eat that for me," I ordered, and he knelt down and ate it.' Another time he half-killed an ancient eunuch by dousing him with a fire hose. And on a third occasion, excited by a performance of a Chinese Punch and Judy show, he would have 'rewarded' the eunuch-puppeteer with a piece of cake made of iron filings, if his wet-nurse, Mrs Wang, hadn't stopped him just in time. 'Master,' she said gently, 'he'll break his teeth.' 'I'm hoping so,' said the boy Emperor. 'I want to see him breaking his teeth, just this once.' 'All right, then,' conceded the merciful Mrs Wang, 'but why don't you put dried lentils in the cake instead?'

If P'u-yi learned the art of whipping in the Forbidden City, he certainly had the opportunity to practise in Ch'ang-ch'un, where his role as puppet Emperor in a palace guarded by Japanese soldiers and monitored by Japanese spies left him both idle and dangerously frustrated. With no official duties but the signing of documents prepared by his Japanese controller, what else could he do? He could, and did, study ants, collect precious stones, improve his calligraphy, play tennis, ride his bicycle around the palace compound – he wasn't allowed outside the gates – read English magazines, play with his dogs, consult the oracles and worship at his private Buddhist shrine; and, as he got more enmeshed in the Japanese trap, and further removed from his dream of restoration, he turned increasingly and obsessively to Shintoism, the Japanese religious system which recognizes the Mikado as the direct descendant of the Sun Goddess.

But flogging gave him the greatest pleasure, and it's difficult to understand why without reaching the conclusion that P'u-yi was at best mentally disturbed and at worst plain bad. And yet, he was easily taken in by a hard-luck story and gave thousands of dollars away to a variety of petitioners; he banned the killing of flies in the Imperial

Palace and he became a vegetarian on moral grounds. We know that he was chronically frustrated because of his inability to produce an heir, and presumably he felt just a twinge of guilt sometimes about his feeble submission to the Japanese. What more natural than to take it out on someone weaker still? But ritual floggings? To the point of death?

When P'u-yi arrived in Ch'ang-ch'un to take up his post as Chief Executive of Manchukuo, he was accompanied by only one wife, the Empress Beauty in Flower: his Secondary Consort, Elegant Ornament, had run off and divorced him in T'ien-ching the previous year. For all the companionship her husband gave her, Beauty in Flower might as well have bolted too, as P'u-yi himself admitted later. But she stayed for two reasons: on the one hand, as a Manchu of noble birth, she had a natural respect for the divinity of the throne; on the other her status brought certain tangible fringe benefits – notably spending money – which she found irresistible.

If Beauty in Flower had felt neglected before, her life was infinitely more lonely in Ch'ang-ch'un. In the Concessions at least there had been plenty of parties and shops, so she could play the part of Empress and spend the proceeds. In Ch'ang-ch'un there were neither and, unlike her weak and selfish husband, who was obsessed with the hopeless notion of restoration, she loathed the Japanese and made no attempt to hide her feelings: she very rarely appeared at state occasions, and when she did she always wore the old Manchu court dress, never the prescribed Japanese kimono.

It wasn't long before Beauty in Flower found solace in the 'ointment for limitless longevity', and no sooner had the Japanese got wind of her habit than they fed it – and fed it so generously that she was soon a helpless addict, smoking an incredible two ounces of opium a day, plus at least two packets of cheap cigarettes for good measure. P'u-yi, who could barely bring himself to speak to the Empress, sent to Peking for some unemployed eunuchs conversant with palace ways to come and look after her. Eight arrived, and one, who survived till recently, reported that her need for the drug was so overpowering that she had to smoke two pipes at once, with two eunuchs in attendance as stokers.

Blessed with good bones, Beauty in Flower, even at the height of her addiction, retained the outlines of her haunting beauty, but her figure shrivelled. Once every three months or so the Emperor would grit his teeth and pad along the corridor for a duty visit to his haggard wife and, according to the eunuch, he always left in a bad mood.

A S a teenager the Emperor had had no difficulty coupling with girls: hadn't his eunuchs supplied him with gaggles of young palace maids to sap his precocious night-time energy, so they could get some sleep? But ever since his wedding night, he'd been impotent. 'He wanted to,' Professor Wang explained, 'his sexual desire was normal, but he couldn't.' 'Why?' I was determined to get to the bottom of this. 'He was impotent.' Impressed by the interpreter's grasp of a specialist vocabulary and refusing to be silenced by a little warning glint behind the professor's spectacles, I haggled for a definition: 'Was the problem mechanical, chemical or psychological?' Both Wangs rose to the occasion: 'Erection.'

(P'u-yi had good reason to know that the fault was his, not Beauty in Flower's, for during the Ch'ang-ch'un years she had a baby by his chauffeur. For this act of treason the chauffeur could have been executed: instead he was dismissed with $500. The baby, a girl, was exterminated at birth before her mother's very eyes by a Japanese doctor with a hypodermic – a barbarity which played no small part in the Empress's subsequent lapse into madness.)

His impotence tormented the Emperor. He believed his entire future depended on his producing an heir in order to secure the Manchukuo throne, to continue the fight for the restoration of the Dragon Throne and to appease his disappointed ancestors. Convinced that the Japanese would put his brother P'u-chieh on the throne if he didn't soon solve the succession, he threw himself into an orgy of cures, from traditional Chinese medicines to injections of the male hormone testosterone. By his own account he devoted several hours a day to medication and the indulgence of his hypochondria. But nothing worked for the impotence; nor could he find a cure for his piles, which were so chronically bad that he sometimes couldn't walk.

When his brother, then an officer cadet at the Japanese equivalent of Sandhurst, announced his engagement to a Japanese girl, Saga Hiro, daughter of the Marquess Saga, a cousin of the Mikado himself – P'u-yi became desperate. By Manchukuo law P'u-chieh and any son born of his forthcoming union were to succeed to the puppet throne if, as seemed all too likely, P'u-yi died without issue. This was perfectly logical, but P'u-yi, pushed to paranoia, persuaded himself that the Japanese, impatient to impregnate the Manchukuo succession with the blood of the Sun Goddess, were plotting to murder him in favour of his more fertile – and more malleable – younger brother.

Invoking his imperial prerogative, P'u-yi did what his ancestors would have done – only a great deal more modestly: he took a concubine. Imperial China had always taken a realistic view of man's essentially polygamous nature. Marriage, according to an ancient saying, is like a teapot: it's meant to fill more than one cup.

Three weeks before his brother's wedding P'u-yi secreted into the palace compound a new Secondary Consort, a Manchu aristocrat of the Tatala clan, called Jade Years; she was sixteen. Ever suspicious of the Japanese, he kept her in seclusion in a hut near the bungalow reserved for P'u-chieh and Saga Hiro. (That bungalow still stands today, very little changed despite the upheavals of the past fifty years, except that it's now a nursery school with Donald Duck on the walls and the royal bath – such a glamorous novelty in Northern China then – lies abandoned, tapless and forlorn, outside the back door.)

Jade Years was another 'wife in name only', P'u-yi revealed in his Life. 'I kept her in the palace as I might have kept a bird in a gilded cage.' He may not have slept with her, but the Emperor seems to have been genuinely fond of his serious little child-wife, whose wrists and fingers he decorated with expensive watches, bracelets and rings. In 1940, when he went to Japan for a second meeting with the Emperor Hirohito, he mentioned that he was considering divorcing Beauty in Flower on health grounds, so that he could elevate Jade Years to Empress; the Mikado was not amused and vetoed the proposal as unworthy of a ruler whose mandate was in the gift of Heaven.

The marriage with Jade Years lasted no longer than five years. In 1942 she suddenly contracted typhoid and died the day after a Japanese doctor took over her case. P'u-yi was convinced that the Japanese had engineered her death and he publicly accused them of murder when he gave evidence at the International War Crimes Tribunal in Tokyo in 1946. For the next twenty years of his life until his pardon and fifth marriage, P'u-yi carried, next to his skin, a small purse containing the Tatala concubine's nails and hair.

No sooner had she died than the Emperor's minders suggested a Japanese replacement. This had been their intention all along, not only to keep closer tabs on their puppet, but also to cross-fertilize the succession. They offered him a selection of photographs to choose from – in much the same way as the High Consorts had set about providing him with his Empress in Peking twenty years before. All the girls were as young and virginal as his taste was known to favour, but P'u-yi rejected the lot: his new Secondary Consort had to be Manchu.

In 1943 he found himself a suitable twelve-year-old, but the relationship lasted only three days before she ran away. P'u-yi surrendered to the minders: all right, he said, any girl – so long as she's not Japanese. They produced Jade Lute, a fourteen-year-old commoner, not Japanese certainly, but by no means Manchu either: a tough little Chinese tomboy, handsome, pert and lithe, a waiter's daughter and, according to P'u-chieh's wife, who never missed an opportunity to denigrate the lower classes, she needed a good scrub – and a delousing – when she arrived at the palace.

P'u-yi said he married Jade Lute because 'being young, she could be educated in the way I liked'. The way the Emperor liked was decidedly peculiar. He wanted her to acknowledge him as a living god. He wanted to watch her having a bath. He wanted to give her little beatings from time to time. He wanted to sit beside her on the sofa in her drawing room during the day with the curtains drawn. 'Everyone thought they were having intercourse,' said Professor Wang, 'but they weren't – they were meditating and reciting Buddhist texts.'

Before he married Jade Lute P'u-yi took the precaution of getting her to sign a long list of rules and their respective punishments. 'When I had reason to complain of her behaviour,' he confided to the prison authorities in Fu-shun, a decade later, 'I would produce my list and tell her: "Read this." Then I would chastise her. Many's the beating I've given Jade Lute.' (And great was the revenge she took years later during the Cultural Revolution, when she bullied her former husband as he lay dying of cancer of the kidneys in Peking's Capital Hospital. 'In a fanatic state of mind,' writes Professor Wang in his book, *China's Last Emperor as an Ordinary Citizen*, 'she yelled, "I've come to settle accounts with P'u-yi, to denounce him! He oppressed me in the puppet court in the past and forced twenty-one rules on me."')

In August 1945 the Russians came, the Japanese surrendered and the Manchukuo Empire collapsed. P'u-yi and eight male relations and attendants, including his 'nephew' Duke Yü-yan, his doctor Huang Tzu-ch'i, and his major-domo Big Li, were arrested at Shen-yang Airport as they were waiting for a plane to carry them to safety in

Japan. They were bundled on to a Soviet aircraft and flown to a POW camp just the other side of the border, near Khabarovsk in Siberia.

'Can't I come too?' Jade Lute had sobbed, when the men left Ch'ang-ch'un Airport the day before.

'The plane is too small,' replied the Emperor. 'You'll have to go to Japan by train. In three days at the most you and the Empress will see me again.'

Jade Lute didn't see P'u-yi again till 1956 when she went to visit him in Fu-shun Prison, to tell him she wanted a divorce because she couldn't wait for his pardon. The prison governor, afraid that a divorce would 'slow down P'u-yi's re-education programme through sadness', allowed Prisoner P'u and his second Secondary Consort to share a cell for the night. Jade Lute admitted years later that they'd had 'a real husband-and-wife life' that night. Notwithstanding this stab of conjugal bliss, she went ahead with her divorce soon after that and married instead a television engineer by the name of Huang, with whom she still lives in the North-East today.

The Empress never saw her husband again. With other ladies of the court she spent the winter of 1945 as a prisoner of the Nationalists in Ch'ang-ch'un. Then she and Saga Hiro were flung into an open cart, with a sign identifying them as Traitors of the Imperial Puppet's Family, and sent 300 miles to the hill town of Yenchi, where they were imprisoned, separately, in concrete cells. Deprived of opium, Beauty in Flower went through all the terrible stages of withdrawal. The spectacle of the former Empress writhing in rags and screaming for drugs drew crowds to the prison, who queued up for a peep through her iron grille. But not everyone gawped. A Manchu peasant couple, moved as much by pity for the woman as by atavistic loyalty to the dynasty she once represented, persuaded the prison authorities to let them nurse the Empress at home on their farm in the Long White Mountains. There, in June 1946, Beauty in Flower died. But her ghost, it's said, still haunts the peaks of Ch'ang-pai Shan.

IF, as P'u-yi himself claimed, none of the women in his life were real wives, then whom did he sleep with? In the literal sense probably no one. His bed, still covered in imperial yellow silk, looks too small for two, at any rate on any permanent basis. Besides, there was a strict code of practice regarding the Emperor's bedroom assignations, for purely practical reasons connected with the succession.

In the Forbidden City, in the Empress Dowager's time, these matters were the province of the Eunuch of the Bedchamber, who would record the date every time the Emperor and his Empress made love, as proof in the event of conception. If the Empress was 'tired' – or the Emperor tired of her – the eunuch would wait till the Son of Heaven had finished his dinner, then crawl up to him on his knees, with a silver tray borne high above his head containing the names of all the concubines ripe for congress that night. The Emperor had only to choose the girl he wanted, turn her name-tag upside-down on the tray to mark it and retire to bed in the Hall of the Nurture of the Mind to get himself ready. The eunuch would then fetch the chosen concubine from the seraglio, strip her, wash her, wrap her in feathers and carry her on his back to the imperial bedchamber. Having deposited her on the Son of Heaven's bed, he would reverse out of the room and wait outside the door for a given time, at the expiry of which he would shout, 'Time up.' If there was no reply, he would repeat the words twice more before marching in and plucking the concubine from the Emperor's arms, having first asked His Majesty if he wanted her to bear his child. If the answer was 'No', and it usually was, the eunuch would take the necessary contraceptive measures, albeit rather late – but pre-coital precautions might have impeded the imperial pleasure; if 'Yes', he would note the date and other relevant details, again as proof in case of conception.

In Ch'ang-ch'un there was a small army of young men sleeping in and around the dispensary at the top of the stairs on the first floor of the palace, exactly halfway between the Emperor's apartments and the Empress's. It is inconceivable that any female could have slipped into P'u-yi's bedroom without the guards knowing: they were paid to stay awake all night, to protect the Emperor from assassins. And if the guards did know, it's equally inconceivable that none of them should have blabbed.

But it's not beyond the realms of possibility that the young guards themselves might have offered the Emperor some solace at night. To the suspicious mind there's a vaguely homosexual undercurrent in Reginald Johnston's book, Twilight in the Forbidden City – a suggestion that both the middle-aged bachelor author and his confused young charge might have shared, without ever discussing it – possibly without knowing it, even – an interest in the love that dare not speak its name.

Johnston had always deeply disapproved of the eunuchs' influence over the boy Emperor – 'those dangers to his moral and intellectual life that lurked in the dark corners of his own palace – the noisome miasma of the Forbidden City, the subtle poisons of a corrupt court'. For this reason he had tried, unsuccessfully, to persuade the Regents to allow him to remove P'u-yi to the healthier climate of the Summer Palace, where he could get that outdoor exercise which all good muscular Christians extolled for its purging of a boy's priapic urges. But he'd been more successful in his attempts to persuade the boy himself to send the eunuchs packing. So he wasn't best pleased when, after the evacuation of the Forbidden City in 1924, he heard that the imperial court in exile in T'ien-ching was still employing eunuchs. When he went to complain, however, he found something infinitely worse: a page-boy – not a eunuch (who wouldn't have known any better), but a fully equipped Manchu serving-child – who showed all the signs of being P'u-yi's lover: this isn't the terminology he himself used in his account of the visit, but the implication is there. There was nothing Johnston could do, because he wasn't tutor any more – the job had ended a year or two earlier, on the expulsion of the court from the Forbidden City, and he was now British Commissioner at Wei-hai-wei.

Perhaps it's just as well Johnston died in 1938, for he wouldn't have been at all happy about the rumours publicly circulating later that year – for all that they corroborated what he may have guessed already. They spoke of P'u-yi's increasing interest in boys and of a court of adolescents – half servants, half lovers – installed in the compound of his palace in Ch'ang-ch'un.

Nearly twenty years later, in 1957, P'u-chieh's wife, Saga Hiro, blew the gaff. In *Wandering Princess* (reprinted in Japan several times and later adapted as a film), she described her nomadic life after her husband's arrest by the Russians in 1945 and revealed – in a flashback to the Ch'ang-ch'un period – that P'u-yi had kept a male concubine since the T'ien-ching interlude at least – and possibly since his youth in the Forbidden City. She'd read about this sort of thing in history books, she noted, with a shudder of disrelish, 'but I never knew it existed in the living world'. Yet here was the Emperor, her brother-in-law, indulging in what she called 'perverted habits' with a page-boy. What hurt as much as the sexual irregularity was the male concubine's plebeian background. For the Wandering Princess was an old-fashioned patrician who strongly disapproved of social mongrelizing – so much so that when her own elder daughter, Hui-sheng, fell in love with a Japanese commoner, Saga Hiro made such trouble that the couple shot one another with a pair of duelling pistols in a tragic suicide pact in a pine forest on Izu Island, near Tokyo.

Saga Hiro names no names in her published diaries, but the implication is that the reigning male concubine throughout most of the Ch'ang-ch'un period was the servant Big Li, who had been brought up in the Forbidden City where his father had served Beneficent Indulgence. Big Li had been on P'u-yi's personal staff since the age of fourteen and was promoted to the rank of major-domo at Ch'ang-ch'un in the mid-1930s. Like Duke Yü-yan, Big Li had a hard life after the Russians threw him on the mercy of the Communist Chinese in 1950. At Fu-shun Prison he did manual labour in the cookhouse. On his release in the early years of the Cultural Revolution he was persecuted by the Red Guards without the benefit of the protecting hand extended by Premier Chou En-lai to the former Emperor himself. He now lives in a small apartment in Peking, surrounded by his family, including several grandchildren. According to P'u-yi's biographer, Edward Behr, who met him there, 'He is reluctant to talk about P'u-yi, but when he does the hostility is immediately apparent.' He was unable, Behr wrote, to forgive P'u-yi for his earlier 'wasted' life.

Approaching the subject quite unnecessarily delicately – for the Chinese distrust obtuseness quite as much as they dislike nonconformism – I asked Professor Wang about Big Li's 'past'.

'You mean,' he replied, with none of my coy reticence, 'the reports that he was the male concubine? I asked him about this when I interviewed him. "Did you have a homosexual relationship with the last Emperor?" I said. "No," he replied. "Never."' So much for that silly nonsense, said the professor's expression: he'd been tackled on a sticky topic, answered like a man and there was no more to be said. But I'm afraid there was.

'If,' I persisted, 'you'd had a chance to put the same question to the last Emperor himself, what do you think he'd have said?'

Professor Wang smiled. 'Why are you so interested in this homosexual theory? What evidence do you have?'

'None. That's why I'm asking you. You've read all his diaries and letters, spoken to all his family and friends. Do you think P'u-yi was homosexual?'

'Look,' said the professor, with an air of finality, 'it would have been quite impossible for the last Emperor to have boys in his bedroom because there were armed soldiers of the Palace Guard outside the door.' (The Palace Guard comprised 300 Manchu officer cadets subsidized by the Emperor himself. Their long-term purpose was to assist him in his restoration programme – that, at least, was the plan, but doubtless the Japanese had other ideas, for nothing in the Imperial Palace in Ch'ang-ch'un missed the eyes and ears of their spies; in the short term, they formed a protective barrier between the Emperor and the Imperial Guard, which came under the direct control of the Japanese Ministry of Defence.) Since these young men were themselves the very stuff of P'u-yi's fantasy – he even had a balcony built around the courtyard of the palace office so that he could watch them wrestling and he liked nothing better than to dress up in their uniform when no one was looking – this argument seemed naïve to the point of blindness. To my corrupt eye the pistol-holstered cadets outside the dispensary were less likely to have been the protectors of the last Emperor's honour than the paid invaders of it; they were his round-the-clock, always on hand, pleasure corps, hand-picked for their smooth good looks and hard figures, their compliance and discretion. But this was only a hunch, and Professor Wang was the expert, so I kept mum.

Communist China takes a puritanical line on homosexuality. Whilst there's no law specifically concerned with it, the unofficial view is that, at the very least, the love of a man for another contravenes the sacred principle of harmony. On these grounds a known homosexual can be forced into a sandwich board proclaiming his 'offence' and marched off to the local Party headquarters to make a public confession.

Imperial China, on the other hand, embraced homosexuality as warmly as the Ancient Greeks.

Two of P'u-yi's recent predecessors, his great-uncle the Emperor Universal Plenty and his first cousin once removed, the Emperor United Rule, were notorious bisexuals. They both haunted Peking's male brothels and they both died of sexually related diseases at an early age: Universal Plenty was thirty, United Rule only eighteen.

Universal Plenty's widow, Beneficent Indulgence, was so fascinated by the subject that she once paid a visit to a fashionable homosexual bath-house in Peking in company with her Chief Eunuch and a bizarre

English baronet, Chinese scholar and con-man called Edmund Backhouse (himself a sexual performer of so broad a church that he claimed not only to have seduced some of the court eunuchs but even to have slept, at her express command, with the ancient and painted Empress Dowager). 'It would amuse me to see all you dissolute young men diverting yourselves,' the absolute ruler of all China remarked to the eunuch. 'You must arrange for me to pay a visit in disguise.'

Excavating the imperial dressing-up boxes, the under-eunuchs produced the ideal camouflage for their royal mistress: a yellow riding jacket, a pair of men's trousers and a windproof cap to wrap around her head. But no disguise could hide Her Imperial Majesty Beneficent Indulgence. She was recognized the moment she set foot on the threshold of the hammam. 'Prostrations!' shouted a warning voice, and a hundred hot bodies leapt out of the baths, the steam rooms, the recovery cubicles, and flung themselves on the floor in terrified obeisance. Hugh Trevor-Roper, in his gripping exposure of Backhouse, *A Hidden Life*, reports that 'Her Majesty ordered the diversion to continue while she engaged in light *badinage* with those not immediately occupied.'

When the Empress Dowager had had her fill, she went back home to her palace, taking the reluctant Chief Eunuch with her. Backhouse stayed behind to finish his conversation with Prince Kung – a heavy-faced, lethargic man, according to the Italian diplomat Daniele Varè, with a mentality, 'of a somewhat ponderous calibre'. The prince, who was a regular *habitué* of this particular bath-house, asked Backhouse whether Queen Victoria would have come out *incognita* on such a jaunt. Backhouse thought not. 'Such spectacles,' he replied, pompously but accurately, and in perfect High Chinese, of course, 'such spectacles, though existing in London – and equally libidinous – are concealed from publicity by the cloak of hypocrisy.'

(Nearly a century later, the spectacles in London are even more libidinous and no longer concealed from publicity. A woman living near Hampstead Heath wrote to the *Ham and High* newspaper in 1992 to complain that people did not 'realize what a shock it can be (however broadminded you are) to come upon two men doing it "doggy fashion" in the middle of a public path, as I did the other day' – yet the cloak of hypocrisy still serves as a shield to protect Victoria's descendants.)

If homosexuality is as old as man, its charming Chinese name, *tuan-hsiu*, or cut sleeve, is almost exactly as old as Christianity. It was invented, by mistake, by the Han dynasty Emperor Ai-ti (6 BC–AD 1), who was having an affair with a young man called Tung Hsien. One morning, early, Ai-ti was woken with an urgent summons to an audience in the palace. Anxious not to disturb his lover, who was still sound asleep across the imperial sleeve, the thoughtful Emperor cut the sleeve off with a deft slash of his sword – and went off to work with one arm bare.

Suggestion is paramount in all Chinese nomenclature, less from coyness than from a sense of childlike playfulness. The very acts of sex themselves, known by such harsh and clinical names in the guilt-ridden West, are honoured in China by terms like 'the jade girl playing the flute' and 'playing with the flower in the back garden'. (But you've got to know your way around before entering this maze: 'Buddha leaping the wall', which might easily be defloration, is not a bedroom term at all but a *spécialité de la cuisine*, combining duck with seafood and pig's trotters.)

In the T'ang dynasty (AD 618–906) homosexuality reached epidemic proportions in Fukien Province, south of Peking. As in the ancient world it was common practice for an older man to take a younger male lover, whose family would welcome the older man as though he were a bridegroom. The prevalence of homosexuality in Fukien is said to have been connected with the province's historical reliance on the sea – and the tradition that women on boats brought bad luck.

By the early eighteenth century homosexuality was so widespread that, according to one contemporary writer, 'It is considered in bad taste not to keep elegant servants on one's household staff, and undesirable not to have singing boys around when inviting guests for dinner.'

The theatre was a ready source of supply of pretty catamites. In fact, in the nineteenth century it was generally assumed that boy actors were male courtesans, available to any official or scholar at a price. But their careers were short: by twenty they were considered to have lost their boyish selling power. Colin P. Mackerras, in his scholarly and fascinating study of the social aspects of the theatre in Manchu China, *The Rise of the Peking Opera 1770–1870*, says that the boys were often referred to as *hua*, or flower, which was then a common euphemism for prostitute. And the houses where they lived were frequently called *hsia-ch'u* which can also mean brothel. One nineteenth-century scholar, writing about these boy actors, speculated that they wouldn't have been so popular if female prostitutes hadn't been so wretchedly unattractive.

But relations between the boy actor and his patron weren't necessarily sexual. In the eighteenth century a respected Peking mandarin called Tsai-yüan was rumoured to be having a homosexual liaison with a popular boy actor called Ch'en Yin-kuan. But, in the most explicit terms, he denied it: 'Our necks and legs touch and we fondle one another. Although we are both aroused, we have no sexual connection.'

In the mid-nineteenth century, when the 'remote Barbarians' sent diplomats to Peking for the first time, they recoiled from this homoerotic ambience. In *John Chinaman*, published in 1901, but written in the 1880s, Edward Harper Parker, a retired British consul in the Far East, recalled his brushes with the Manchu court when he was a young man. All men's morals then, he maintains, were 'Turkish', and he'd felt 'a ghoulish sort of sensation' moving among them. One of the mandarins he had to deal with in Prince Kung's newly established Foreign Office was a Manchu called Ch'ung-lun – 'a curious man with a huge goitrous wen and naughty, twinkling eyes' who 'did me the honour to wet his finger and rub my cheek to see if I were painted'; another of the mandarins 'patted me and put his arm round my neck'. They were 'not very strong in virtue, any of them', Parker concluded.

In the Forbidden City, right up to the time of its final dissolution in 1924, a tradition of (necessarily passive) homosexuality was maintained by the eunuchs – most of whom came from Fukien. In their safely androgyne hands lay the sex education of all young males at court, including, when his turn came, the boy Emperor P'u-yi. Since the eunuchs used as teaching aids some explicit medieval carvings showing humans and animals locked together in scenes of riotous copulation, and since the child was encouraged to arousal by intimate caressing of these artefacts, it's not altogether surprising that he should have turned out odd. The amazing thing is that his ancestors, raised in the same hothouse of ignorance, corruption, prejudice, lust and disease, should ever have managed to produce him.

NEITHER the passage of fifty years nor even a Communist revolution has dispelled the pall of shame that hangs over the Imperial Palace in Ch'ang-ch'un like an invisible mushroom cloud. The place is now a museum, conscientiously restored by the People's Republic. And the authentic whiff of imperial decadence draws a ceaseless stream of visitors: Chinese in family parties with clunking Communist cameras and tour groups of Japanese pensioners immediately recognizable by their micro ciné-cameras, Benetton T-shirts and floppy sun hats.

The complex is surrounded by a high brick wall – punctuated, in Manchukuo days, by gun towers rising from every corner. Inside are three large buildings, lots of smaller ones resembling Nissen huts, with a tennis court and a swimming pool which even in P'u-yi's time never had any water in it. At the kernel is a sturdy grey brick building, like a stockbroker's villa in Surrey, designed by an architect suckled on temples. It was built at the beginning of the twentieth century as the head office of the salt revenue administration in Chi-lin Province and requisitioned by the Japanese military in 1931 as P'u-yi's private residence – simply because it was the most secure building in the city. P'u-yi never liked it – he thought it beneath his dignity to live anywhere so small and undistinguished, and referred to it, ironically, as the Salt Tax Palace – but, as a mere puppet, he was in no position to complain.

Immediately behind the residence, linked to it by a heavy gate and a courtyard, is a similar grey-brick building, where the Emperor went through the motions of administering his non-existent Empire. Here were his private office, banqueting hall, audience room, drill yard and the map room, where, like Churchill in his bunker below Whitehall, P'u-yi used to flag the course of the Japanese war machine through South-East Asia. But, unlike Churchill, P'u-yi dressed up for the job in jackboots and breeches. He wasn't alone in his adoration of Mussolini: Chan-tso-lin, the governor of Manchuria before the Japanese invasion, actually assumed the title of Generalissimo in 1927. Daniele Varè, who was Italian Ambassador to China at that time, notes in his reminiscences, *Laughing Diplomat*, that Mussolini was 'an unfailing subject of interest to Chinese generals, who would so willingly follow in his footsteps, if they could find some Fascists to follow them'.

Beside these two buildings is a large caramel-coloured purpose-built palace designed to replace them both, but it wasn't completed till 1945, by which time P'u-yi had lost all faith in his Japanese masters, and, suspecting, no doubt quite rightly, that it was alive with bugging devices, he refused to move in; his third Secondary Consort, the Han concubine Jade Lute, did, however, spend a few months alone in its cavernous state rooms before the end came. The building was destroyed in 1949 but rebuilt in 1953 as a geology college; it's now a library.

None of these three buildings has any architectural merit – in style they're no different from any of the other grandiose blocks with which the Japanese attempted to stamp their mark on Manchuria in the 1930s. But the internal layout of the residence throws an interesting light on the Emperor's domestic arrangements. It's divided into four distinct units providing self-contained accommodation for the Emperor, the Empress, the reigning Secondary Consort and the eunuchs and page-boys. There are no public rooms for getting together. Instead each set of apartments was designed to keep the royal family apart.

The Emperor's rooms, at the west end of the first floor, comprise a bedroom, study, Buddhist chapel, barber's chamber, dispensary and a king-size bathroom with a grand piano and a fish tank.

Down at the other end of the corridor the Empress had her bedroom, sitting room, bathroom and 'smoking room', where the sickly-sweet smell of opium lingers to this day, if only in the imagination. Pointing through the roped-off threshold, Professor Wang indicated the Edwardian *chaise longue* on which poor, neglected Beauty in Flower dreamed her lonely days away in a drugged haze.

None of the furnishings in the residence and office buildings is genuine: they're all clever copies of the originals, based on photographs and memories. What few relics have survived from the looting and destruction that followed in the wake of the Japanese surrender in 1945 are carefully preserved in glass display cases in a neighbouring building – and they're no more distinguished than the drab pieces in the Forbidden City or the Summer Palace or any of the other imperial residences of the Ch'ing dynasty; dark, heavy, fussy, West-influenced tat, like the contents of a maiden great-aunt's snuggery. But a white bearskin and some Japanese ceremonial swords caught Loud Report's eye – the only things that did in the whole of the Imperial Palace.

Our visit coincided with an exhibition, in one of the Nissen huts, of photographs and documents illustrating P'u-yi's life. I was amazed by the respectful, though never obsequious, awe with which the Chinese gazed at these icons. Hoping to capture their expressions on film, I produced my camera, ostensibly to photograph the ever-willing Professor Wang. But the moment it appeared the Chinese melted away, leaving the professor on his own. As the flash went off a girl guide ran forward, waving her arms and shaking her head in great agitation. 'No photography allowed,' she seemed to be saying. But 'I'm Professor Wang,' replied the professor, piqued that she'd failed to recognize him as the biographer of P'u-yi. 'Well, that's OK, then,' said the girl, retreating with a slightly doubtful look in her eye, as the professor, puffing his chest, posed for a second shot.

As we emerged from the exhibition, Professor Wang pointed across the compound to a long low building lying at right angles between the eastern ends of the residence and office buildings in the shadow of the new palace. 'That's where Yü-yan and the other "nephews" lived,' he said.

There were four other 'nephews' in P'u-yi's court when Duke Yü-yan and his older brother Duke Yü-t'ai were summoned to the North-East from Peking in 1936. The idea was that they should form a cadre of loyalists for P'u-yi's eventual restoration to the Dragon Throne. With this end in view they were to be dispatched to the military academy in Tokyo for officer training. But when P'u-yi cottoned on to the fact that he was simply supplying the Japanese army at his own expense, he changed his tactics and turned his aristocratic Manchu 'nephews' into housemaids instead. They were to form an elite corps, a sort of Chinese janissary, with special duties including floor-sweeping, valeting and bed-making: the Personal Guard, they were grandly called. And it wasn't so very peculiar, after all, for no Manchu Emperor had ever been served by anything but boys, through the entire history of the dynasty. P'u-yi persuaded them that it was a perfectly reasonable deal in exchange for their free board and lodging and education in classical Chinese, calligraphy, modern languages and world history.

The young Dukes Yü-yan, then eighteen years old, and Yü-t'ai were overjoyed to be invited to join their Emperor's court in whatever capacity: as well as providing them with an occupation, all found, it offered them an opportunity to display their loyalty to the toppled throne of the Ch'ings.

But sheer economics must have clinched the argument, for the two boys, left fatherless four years earlier, had been living a hand-to-mouth existence in the faded grandeur of their family palace in Peking, looted and stripped in successive onslaughts by the Allies, the Chinese warlords and the Nationalists.

The founder of their branch of the family was Yi-tsung (fifth son of the Emperor Glory of Right Principle), who inherited the Princedom of Tun from his musical uncle Mien-k'ai, the black sheep with the penchant for boys – a bent he took to such extremes that in 1838 he was found to be harbouring as prisoners in his palace no fewer than ninety under-age actors and eunuchs. Along with the title and the palace Yi-tsung seems to have inherited a certain irregularity as well. One of the few things known about him is that for inefficiency and disprobity he couldn't be bettered. On his appointment as Commander-in-Chief of the Manchu Field Forces, according to Beneficent Indulgence's English biographers, Bland and Backhouse, the army 'became more and more notorious for its tatterdemalion uselessness and the corruption of its commanders'.

Yi-tsung, Prince Tun, was born in direct line of succession to the throne and when, in 1874, his nephew the Emperor United Rule died, Prince Tun not unreasonably imagined that his eldest son, Beileh Tsai-lien, would be chosen to succeed. But the Beileh was passed over in favour of another of Prince Tun's nephews – on the grounds that Yi-tsung's adoption by the first Prince Tun had removed him from the direct line of succession and invalidated his sons' claims. For this slight Prince Tun never forgave Beneficent Indulgence, and he bequeathed this grudge to his sons, who became leaders of the Boxer movement, the original object of which, as we have seen, was the overthrow of the dynasty itself. It was only later, under Beneficent Indulgence's skilful manipulation, that the Boxers switched their hatred to the 'foreign devils'. The family fortunes went into rapid decline with the defeat of the Boxers in 1900, when Beneficent Indulgence, responding to the Allies' demands, locked Tsai-lien in a darkened room and, using a technique adopted later in the century by Chinese leaders of a redder hue, forced him to 'consider the error of his ways'.

The bad blood of the Tuns was inherited by Tsai-lien's volatile elder grandson, Duke Yü-t'ai, who blotted his copybook at the court of P'u-yi in Manchukuo in the 1930s. After a series of fights with his noble cousins, culminating in a bloody scuffle with the Emperor's favourite Beitzu P'u-cho (eighth son of Tsai-ing), Duke Yü-t'ai was thrown out. But P'u-yi was nothing if not soft when it came to family, and he arranged for the young man to live with his uncle Beitzu P'u-hsiu in P'u-yi's old house in T'ien-ching. So Yü-t'ai was well clear of Ch'ang-ch'un when the axe fell in 1945. Two years later, he moved back to Ch'ang-ch'un with his liberated Chinese wife – a Japanese-educated girl – and his uncle P'u-hsiu; they went to live with his wife's father, who had been Minister of Culture in the closing years of the Manchu dynasty. Yü-t'ai's aggressiveness, if not hereditary, was probably clinical, because he soon manifested symptoms of the manic depression from which he died in the late 1940s. His widow survived him and later remarried.

Yü-yan, his younger brother, was cast in a different mould. From the moment he arrived in Ch'ang-ch'un as a teenager he showed such exceptional devotion to the Emperor that he soon became a firm favourite, to whom special, very personal duties were entrusted.

'Like what?' I asked Professor Wang.

'Injecting the Emperor with male hormones,' he replied. 'For sexual energy.'

'But Yü-yan didn't have any medical training, did he?'

'Doctor Huang Tzu-ch'i gave the injections and Yü-yan washed the needles.'

'What was so special about that?'

'Only the people the Emperor trusted could do such personal things, because he was frightened of being murdered. And the relationship between P'u-yi and Yü-yan was very close indeed.'

Professor Wang, knowing my interest in Yü-yan, was anxious that I should understand just how he, of all the 'nephews' in the Personal Guard, had come to be chosen as the last Emperor's son and heir, and, as we wandered around the compound of the Imperial Palace, he cited various other examples of the special trust which the Emperor placed in Yü-yan.

In 1942 Yü-yan's eldest sister thought it was time that her shy little brother, then aged twenty-four – though he looked a good deal younger – met some girls. So she introduced him to a friend of hers, a girl who had been educated at a Japanese school in Ch'ang-ch'un and had a brother who taught at another predominantly Japanese school in the Manchukuo capital. But the men of the Personal Guard were expressly forbidden from consorting with the Japanese, even at one remove, and the Emperor was severely displeased. Ever since his own brother P'u-chieh had married the Japanese Saga Hiro – a political union which he'd been unable to prevent – P'u-yi had been paranoid about the Japanese. Believing that Saga Hiro was a spy, he excluded P'u-chieh from his secret counsels; he refused to eat with Saga Hiro at the same table; and he wouldn't take a mouthful of food from her kitchens until P'u-chieh had tasted it first, in case it was poisoned. The Emperor made it plain that Yü-yan – for all that he was the imperial favourite – would be sent to Coventry, just like P'u-chieh, if he saw any more of his 'tainted' friend. Dutifully Yü-yan told his sister that he didn't want to get married just at the moment, thank you.

The following year, 1943, the Emperor rewarded Yü-yan with a proper Manchu wife, an aristocrat of the Ma-chia clan called Ching-lan – a literary girl who wrote and recited poetry. She bore the Pretender two sons, Hêng-chen and Hêng-k'ai, and died in T'ien-ching in 1948, three years after the Japanese surrender; she was only twenty-eight.

When the Tatala concubine, Jade Years, was struck down with typhoid in 1942 it was Yü-yan to whom the Emperor turned for help. Unable to bring himself to watch her dying, P'u-yi sent Yü-yan instead. By Professor Wang's reckoning this was a signal honour, effectively recognizing Yü-yan as the Emperor's son – for, in the days of the Ch'ing dynasty, no other male would have been allowed to watch the soul of an imperial wife ascending to Heaven. Such signs of favour didn't pass unnoticed in the superstitious atmosphere of Manchu court life.

After Jade Years' death Yü-yan was appointed chief mourner, and, alone of the household, he was permitted to wear the Manchus' traditional mourning white. The funeral was quite the most impressive state ceremony ever staged in Manchukuo.

The concubine's body was dressed in robes of state, embroidered with the imperial dragon, and laid in a catafalque so huge that seventy-two bearers were needed to carry it from the Imperial Palace to the Emperor's private Buddhist temple in the city outside, the streets having been swept and strewn with yellow sand in advance. On top of the great catafalque the Emperor placed a bowl of wine, not a drop of which spilled on the slow progress to the temple.

Such was the Emperor's devotion to the memory of his favourite wife that when he was a prisoner of the Russians in Siberia in the late 1940s he smuggled a message back to Ch'ang-ch'un that the body was to be cremated in secret and the ashes sent to Peking for safe-keeping by Yü-yan's uncle, Beitzu P'u-hsiu. And such was his devotion to his chosen son and heir that he subsequently entrusted the ashes to Yü-yan himself; and to this day the mortal remains of the Tatala concubine lie in a casket beneath the earthen floor of Yü-yan's hut in Peking – as I hoped to discover for myself.

ON the night after our visit to the Imperial Palace I invited the two Wangs to dinner at my hotel. It was an ample – and mercifully unadventurous – menu, masterminded by the egregious Loud Report. Plenty of beer; plenty of toasts – the professor's glass vying with mine for the lowest position of maximum respectfulness required by the rules of Chinese etiquette; and plenty of formalized speechifying of no great substance or truthfulness, but, again, complying with the necessarily florid traditions of hospitality.

Loud Report and I thought it had gone rather well, and, watching the Wangs ride away on their bicycles afterwards, we congratulated ourselves. But my head was spinning with excitement at the prospect of meeting the Pretender back in Peking and perhaps this had desensitized my social feelers. And Loud Report was on another planet. He'd seen Winter Stone earlier in the evening.

'I like you,' he'd said, tentatively but with feeling.

'I like you,' she'd whispered back.

'May I kiss you?' he'd asked and, receiving no reply but a maidenly lowering of the eyelids, he'd pressed his lips to her cheek.

'Ahhh, Misiter Socotolan,' sighed Loud Report, clutching at his chest, in the hot Manchurian night, 'my heart is like a running mouse.'

Each absorbed in his own thoughts, we'd misread the signs.

THE Ch'ang-pai Shan Guest House stopped serving breakfast at nine, on the dot. So Loud Report and I used to meet in the breakfast restaurant at a quarter to. On what I hoped was our last day in Ch'ang-ch'un I was just trying to spread some margarine on my bread with a chopstick when Loud Report appeared, his face drained of colour, his forehead creased with worry.

'Big problems, Misiter Socotolan. I don't know what we can do. I never know anything like this in my life.'

Loud Report crumpled over the stained table cloth. Whatever the trouble, he needed some coffee. I joined the queue of toothpaste-fresh Japanese who were gazing in polite disbelief at the array of breakfast offerings scattered in untidy heaps on a soiled cloth over a trestle table. After four days I was an old hand and well used to tepid soup with a crust of congealed fat, greasy beansprouts, piles of tinned scrambled egg on a tray, cold white toast, jam-smeared marge and marge-smeared jam, the gallon jug of instant coffee and the tall thick glasses provided to drink it from. Their gorges rising, the Japanese tourists turned away to complain, politely and ineffectually, to the *apparatchik* collecting the breakfast tokens at the door. They wouldn't get anything better anywhere else, and after nine they wouldn't be able to return here either. I assembled some bits for Loud Report, together with the restorative glass of coffee. And then he told me the story.

At a quarter to six that morning he'd been woken by his room-mate returning to their shared bedroom with a girl.

'Don't worry about us,' the room-mate had said. 'You just go back to sleep.'

But Loud Report couldn't sleep, because the room-mate and his companion had sat on the end of the unslept-in bed and noisily worked their way through a picnic breakfast. 'Sleep, sleep,' said the girl, when she turned and saw him watching her. Loud Report rolled over, tucked his head under the pillow and thought of Winter Stone.

Later he was woken again by a bang on the door. He sat up. The room-mate and his guest had disappeared.

'Who is it?' he called crossly.

'Wang!'

Wang? He looked at his watch: it was five past seven. Wondering what on earth the professor wanted at that time of the morning, he'd pulled on some clothes and answered the door, where he'd found both Wangs, professor and interpreter. They hadn't been able to sleep, they said, because they felt that Misiter Socotolan had treated them so unfairly. For three days they'd told him all about P'u-yi, and all they'd got in return were some worthless presents and a wholly inadequate dinner. Unless they received a certain specified figure, in American dollars, in a sealed envelope at the airport on Misiter Socotolan's departure, the professor was sorry but he wouldn't be able to help with Duke Yü-yan and the other Manchu imperials in Peking.

Loud Report had been outraged by this unexpected and unfair demand, but nothing he said had any effect on the Wangs: they wanted money and that was that.

'Misiter Socotolan: very big problem – terribly sorry.' He shook his head, over and over again, bewildered, hurt and a little afraid.

'Look, there must be some mistake,' I said, trying to be sensible and positive. 'Let's telephone the professor and clear it all up.'

'Hawgh!' He nearly dropped his glass of coffee. 'No, no, please,

Misiter Socotolan, not to telephone professor. Professor say me not tell you about this – ah – meeting.'

I was outraged; in fact, I felt sick, as you do when friendly relations suddenly, inexplicably, turn sour. At no point had the professor ever mentioned a fee for his services – either in advance, during our initial contacts on the telephone from Peking, or at any time during our meetings in Ch'ang-ch'un. To demand money retrospectively was tantamount to extortion. I simply couldn't believe it, for the professor had volunteered a great deal more information than I had asked for, and indeed it was at his insistence that we'd lingered in Manchuria longer than I'd intended. As for Mr Interpreter Wang, he was the professor's responsibility – I'd never asked for a second interpreter: although he'd been a great asset, I could have managed with a combination of Loud Report and the tape-recorder.

My understanding was that the whole thing had been arranged through the professor's work unit, that it was an official contact, with the Wangs' time funded by the History Department of the Chi-lin Academy of Social Sciences. The notion of fees never entered my head, and if it had, I'd have dismissed it as being contrary to the spirit of international scholarly exchange; who ever heard of a professor accepting money for sharing information with a student of his subject? I assumed the professor understood that in return for his help I intended to write him up in a way that was sure to publicize and gloss his stature as one of China's leading authorities on the decline of the Manchus in general and the life of the last Manchu in particular.

Assuming anything in China is unwise. To Professor Wang the issue was probably no less black and white than it seemed to me. A Westerner with no academic bona fides but a money belt packed with dollars, wanted information which only he possessed. In accordance with the rules of Chinese hospitality he had invited the Westerner to his home city and offered to tell him all he knew. But the same rules imposed an obligation on the Westerner to offer some sort of 'consideration'. When the Westerner, having filled five micro-tapes, two notebooks and three rolls of film over the course of three days of intensive questioning, still showed no sign of raising the question of 'considerations', what else could the professor do but ask point-blank and hope that, in the time-honoured way, the parties might meet and talk and negotiate a compromise which would save face all round?

At breakfast that morning I didn't see it like that; nor did Loud

Report. To both of us the Wangs' demand was a threat; and as Loud Report pointed out indignantly, the sum demanded was about as much as Winter Stone earned in a whole year. My first response was to do what Reginald Johnston had done when he was 'squeezed' by the eunuchs for a massive tip on his appointment as P'u-yi's tutor: offer to pay in full, but demand an official receipt. On second thoughts I saw the role of Mr Interpreter Wang in a different light: unlike the professor he stood to gain nothing from my book, and if he really hadn't been lent by his work unit, then I really should pay for his services, even though I hadn't asked for them. So I decided on the following course of action: to ignore Professor Wang's claim; to pay Mr Interpreter Wang; and to send the cash, with a covering letter, to the director of their work unit, the principal of the History Study Institute of the Chi-lin Academy. Professor Wang had imperiously demanded a response by lunchtime. We decided to keep him waiting.

Loud Report deserved a holiday and I wanted to find the Empress Beauty in Flower's burial place. Instead of going straight back to Peking I suggested that once we'd sorted out the Wangs we might spend a couple of days exploring Ch'ang-pai Mountain.

'Aaah!' exclaimed Loud Report, his gloom evaporating in an instant. 'My father once go there. In the lake on the top' – his eyes widened and rolled in wonder – 'the water is blue, not green, but *blue*!' This was the lake where those fairy princesses were swimming when the crow dropped the berry that sowed the seed of the Manchus; I longed to see it, too.

It didn't look very far away on the map, but we discovered that the train journey took ten hours. So what the hell, I thought, we'll fly. But it wasn't that easy. At the booking office of the Civil Aviation Administration of China, having queued for an hour, we were told that as Loud Report came from a work unit in another city, he wasn't permitted to fly anywhere without a letter of introduction from a work unit in Ch'ang-ch'un. The Wangs being the only local people we knew, we were unwilling to pursue this. So we resorted to the railways – only to discover at the station that there weren't any train tickets available for three days.

More depressed than ever, we slunk back to the hotel and, unable to put it off any longer, telephoned the professor. Poor Loud Report! This difficult call, which lasted nearly an hour and a half, must have been one of the most unpleasant and challenging tasks he'd ever undertaken. As an only child, the son of doting parents, both of them professors, he'd probably never had to play such an adult role before. He was out of his depth but he was determined to stay afloat. He started politely but firmly, with a statement of my decision and a résumé of the reasons why. Across the hotel bedroom I could hear the professor's furious reaction. For eighty-odd minutes Loud Report, his eyes sometimes popping out of his head, the veins throbbing angrily on his neck, struggled to control his temper; each time it rose he seemed to hear the dangerous shrillness of his own voice and quickly brought himself under check again. It was a brave fight, but he lost.

With sweat pouring down his blanched face, tears of frustration and fear welling up in his eyes, he said, in a hoarse, choked voice, 'I'm terribly sorry, Misiter Socotolan, but you will have to pay. Professor Wang say if you not pay he send men from work unit to search your room and keep us in Ch'ang-ch'un. I never know anything like this before. Very bad business. Terribly sorry.' Loud Report was shaking. I sat him down and made some green tea. Shaking his head in baffled disbelief, he riffled through the dictionary looking for the word he wanted to express his feelings about the professor. At last he found it: stabbing 'ethics' with his index finger, he said, through clenched teeth, 'Professor Wang has not this.'

When Loud Report had first broken the news of the professor's demand, at breakfast, the ugly thought had crossed my mind, shamefully but persistently, that possibly he himself, my trusted and invaluable Boy Friday, might be a conspirator in the plot. If Professor Wang wasn't the teddy bear he seemed, perhaps Loud Report wasn't the *ingénu* he seemed? Anything was possible in this *Through the Looking Glass* world, where Western yardsticks kept measuring up all wrong. After all, I'd consulted Loud Report on the very question of 'considerations' the day we arrived in Ch'ang-ch'un and he'd dismissed payment out of hand: my presents, he reckoned, were more than enough – everything else would be covered by the work unit. Now I knew for sure, as I'd known instinctively the moment I met him, that Loud Report might be naïve but he was no turncoat. He'd been genuinely shocked and disgusted by the professor's demand; now he was frightened by his threats. If only for Loud Report's sake, I had no choice but to pay up, and in full; but still I would insist on a receipt.

In a quarter of an hour, as promised, Loud Report telephoned the professor with my decision. Instantly the professor, who had expected, at the very least, some haggling, was purring – and yes, of course, he would give a receipt. We refused his invitation to dinner, but agreed to go around to his flat to deliver his ransom. 'Misiter Socotolan,' warned Loud Report, 'please to be nice to professor. Problem not finish yet. I talk, you smile.'

It was raining, so we took a taxi. The professor was waiting in the doorway of his block as we arrived. Clapping us both on the back, he gave us a warm welcome and escorted us up the unlit concrete stairs, past the bicycles. Having removed our shoes, we went into the study, where, with the prescribed smile, I handed over two envelopes – one addressed to Professor Wang, the other addressed to Mr Interpreter Wang. (At Loud Report's insistence, I'd written the amount that each contained close to the respective name, in the subtle hope that the proximity of Mammon to Academe might provoke a little *frisson* of shame; it didn't.) With barely concealed impatience, the professor pulled off his spectacles, tore open his envelope and removed the dollar bills. First he counted them, then he rubbed them, and finally he held them up to the light to check them. Satisfied, he put his spectacles back on, and, beaming, bowed to me with his hands held together at chest level in the praying position – the traditional Chinese gesture of thanks. I smiled weakly, and Mrs Wang handed me a banana.

Then came the negotiations, and now that Loud Report knew the rules of the game he wasn't going to be outdone by Professor Wang. Misiter Socotolan, he said, wanted a document, which acknowledged receipt of the money, permitted full and free use of all material given and guaranteed no further demands. OK, said the professor, who was no one's fool – and loved haggling – but Misiter Socotolan's book must acknowledge, in full, and on each page on which it appears, each piece of the professor's material; and when the book is published, 'I want five copies.' Trying hard to remember to smile, I said I couldn't, and wouldn't if I could, give any such undertaking, but I would, of course, acknowledge his assistance in general terms and I would send him two copies of the book, if it were ever published – though I wasn't at all convinced that the professor would thank me when he saw how frankly I'd reported our encounters.

While the professor and Loud Report drew up the contract, as cautiously as a pair of country solicitors – the professor writing in Chinese on graph paper to Loud Report's confident dictation – I gave an English lesson to the two teenage Masters Wang, just home from

声 明

TONY SCOTLAND（英国）先生和王庆祥先生议定：1991年6月8日至9日在长春长白山宾馆，由王先生回答了TONY SCOTLAND先生提出的关于中国末代皇族历史变迁的一系列问题，TONY SCOTLAND已向王庆祥先生支付谘询费美金叁佰元整、向王学良先生支付口译费美金壹佰元整，总共肆佰美元。今后TONY SCOTLAND先生利用这部份谘询资料从事撰述，不须再向资料提供者支付报酬、但应说明资料来源。如该书能在英国出版，应向王庆祥先生酌情提供样书。王庆祥先生表示愿意协助出版该书的中文译本。特此声明。

声明（收款）人：王庆祥

声明（付款）人：

证人：朴锋锋

1991年6月10日于长春

Fig. B: 'Contract' under which the author paid Professor Wang for information about P'u-yi, dated June 6th, 1991, and signed by Professor Wang, the author and Loud Report.

school, and their mother plied me with further bananas and green tea. At last the contract was ready. Loud Report paraphrased it for me, the professor anxiously watching my face for signs of a negative reaction. But all was well. With beaming smiles we signed, shook hands and made polite speeches. The professor, still wearing his cloth cap, presented me with a bamboo fan in a box with a glass lid and his younger son gave me a bronze medal. 'Please,' said the boy in English, 'will you be my friend, Uncle?'

Now that the professor had got what he wanted – and Loud Report told me later that he'd been under great pressure from his work-unit director, who wanted a cut of the ransom – he reverted to his jolly, generous self and, over the next hour, he painstakingly wrote letters of introduction to Duke Yü-yan, the calligrapher Yü-chan and the 'Empress' Li Shu-hsien, and gave me addresses of various other members of the Aisin-Gioro family in Peking, including P'u-chieh; he also filled out the work-unit authorization that we needed for Loud Report to travel. As he wrote in a laborious hand, hunched over his desk, his wife hovered oddly in the doorway with a notebook and pencil, like a shy cub reporter. I asked Loud Report what she was doing. He reported that she had taken a fancy to my shirt (Marks and Spencer, blue cotton, long-sleeved, casual) and would I mind, please, if she sketched it? Obligingly, I untucked the tails and pirouetted to display St Michael's tailoring to best effect.

Our business done at last, we had a final banana and then posed for a family photo call.

Loud Report and I wanted some fresh air, so we decided to walk back to the hotel; Professor Wang, full of hostly consideration, insisted on escorting us part of the way. The park was unsafe for foreigners at night, he said, and the unlit road around it wasn't much better, so we walked right down the middle of the road, lest 'enemies' should be lurking in the dark behind the trees at the verge.

When the professor left us, Loud Report and I burst out laughing in sheer relief that it was all over. It had cost me money which I had set aside for travelling to other Manchu sites in China, and it had dealt a blow to my belief in the universality of friendship. But, when all was said and done, it was no pig in a poke I'd got in return: factual information, detailed and colourful, which I couldn't easily have gathered from any other source, and introductions to members of the imperial family, including my Pretender – and these were as precious as gold-dust. (And later, on my return home, I was to receive even more help from Professor Wang, more photographs, more documentary material, more genealogical details.) Moreover, I had learned yet another lesson about Chinese inscrutability. The professor's demand – its manner, extent and unexpectedness – still rankled, I still felt I had been tricked, and Loud Report still felt he'd been bettered by the professor and he smarted from the consequent loss of face. Through sheer inexperience we had all of us made mistakes, but we'd all, in different ways, gained from it.

This charitable philosophy wasn't uppermost in my mind when, returning from breakfast the next morning, I found the Wangs in the lobby outside my room. Something's gone wrong, I thought – they want more money. So I greeted them rather frostily and made them wait while I did my teeth. What could they possibly want now?

'The professor,' said Mr Interpreter Wang, 'wants to give you something.' And Professor Wang stepped forward with a copy of *A Pictorial Biography of Aisin-Gioro P'u-yi*, a weighty – and expensive – volume of photographs which he himself had compiled with the assistance of the last Emperor's widow, Li Shu-hsien. In the flyleaf he'd written an inscription: 'Dear Mr Tony Scotland; I hope this present will make a little contribution to your book and your study of P'u-yi family.' And that wasn't all: with it came a large envelope full of photographs and documents, including a comprehensive genealogy of the Aisin-Gioro clan, showing all the male issue of the nine sons of the Emperor Glory of Right Principle. Furthermore, the professor offered to put himself at my disposal for as long as it took to brief me about the surviving members of the Aisin-Gioro clan, especially the ones I was going to meet. These were valuable gifts indeed: I was overwhelmed and not a little ashamed that, for the second time, I'd misjudged the professor's intentions. Nevertheless, I couldn't quite banish from my mind the mean suspicion, which his unshaven, red-eyed face seemed to confirm, that, pricked by a bad conscience, he felt obliged to offer a more generous Roland for my multi-dollar Oliver: having secured, perhaps to his surprise, the full sum he'd demanded, the professor felt duty-bound to give value for money. Whatever his motives his generosity healed all misunderstandings and I thanked him rather extravagantly.

IT was night-time, tropically hot and pouring with rain. Sheltering under a mimosa tree on the pavement outside the hotel gates, Loud

Report and I, freshly bathed, were waiting for Winter Stone. It was her twentieth birthday, our last night in Ch'ang-ch'un and Loud Report was taking us all out to dinner. Winter Stone was late.

We tucked her presents into our shirts to keep them dry: Loud Report had bought some Italian biscuits in the foreign exchange store and I'd got some perfume and a BBC pen. Loud Report kept consulting his watch: 'She said she come after work, but work finish ten minutes ago,' he said anxiously.

'She's probably getting herself ready,' I replied, though secretly I suspected she'd funked it and gone straight home. When Loud Report first suggested this threesome dinner I had begged him to count me out; I felt sure that she'd have preferred a quiet evening alone with him. 'No, Misiter Socotolan,' he'd insisted, 'you must come. Winter Stone like you, she want you come, and I am nervous without you. You can speak English with her, but you must talk slowly and smile, so she is not frightened.'

The workers of Ch'ang-ch'un, returning home on their bicycles, splashed our trousers as they ploughed through the puddles in the pock-marked road. The delicate leaves of the mimosa tree offered little protection from the driving rain and soon our crisp clean shirts – white cotton for Loud Report, blue silk for me – were sticking to us (and Winter Stone's birthday presents) like cling-film.

'She not come,' said Loud Report, his brow furrowed with worry.

'Nonsense!' I replied. 'She's probably waiting for the rain to stop.'

At last there she was, clocking out at the guardhouse by the main gates: a little empress in a yellow blouse, black pants and black sandals with a buckle missing on the right one. Under a rainbow-coloured parasol, a birthday present from her sister, she tiptoed along the pavement watching out for puddles which were hard to spot in the dark.

We all shook hands. Loud Report was so nervous he couldn't speak; Winter Stone was so shy that she couldn't either. To break the ice I made some remark about her long hours at the hotel.

Winter Stone looked worried. 'Why-er?' she asked, in slow, careful English and speaking in a tiny-girl voice which we had to bend to hear, 'is-er my face-er red-er?' She raised a little white hand to her porcelain cheek in a gesture so delicate and feminine that Loud Report clutched his heart and started to pant, and I felt a sudden and unaccustomed surge of manly protectiveness.

'Your face is beautiful,' I blustered, 'like alabaster. Why do you think it's red?'

'You said-er I looked-er hot-er.'

'I said you worked hard.' Nineteen years a Radio 3 announcer and still I couldn't make myself understood. I laughed.

'You laugh at me-er.' Winter Stone raised her silken lashes and looked up at me reproachfully. I felt big and clumsy and longed to reassure her.

'I was laughing at me, not you,' I said, resisting the urge to touch her. She was as perfect and as perishable as a butterfly, this ethereal child-woman, and my protective instincts were aroused as powerfully as Loud Report's heartbeat.

Under cover of Winter Stone's parasol we splashed through the puddles to a restaurant which Loud Report and I had discovered earlier: a newly opened private-enterprise establishment run by three dancers from the Ch'ang-ch'un opera house. Judging by their expensive Western clothes and jewellery, the proprietors had no reason to regret their initiative; judging by their fare, they deserved their prosperity.

Seating us in a quiet corner, Loud Report made a speech: 'Please,' he said, 'you are my guests. I want you to enjoy, but I have not much money, so we have not many dishes. Terribly sorry.' Nevertheless, he ordered more than we could manage. It was a delicious dinner: chicken, pork and fish with lots of vegetables, including marinated mushrooms, sea cucumbers, aubergines, fried beancurd and pickled celery cabbage in a variety of sauces, sweet, sour, hot and salty. Winter Stone and Loud Report drank beer and I tried *maotai*, a Chinese firewater, distilled from sorghum grain – an experiment I didn't repeat.

One of China's more attractive eating conventions is a concern for one's neighbour's plate. Loud Report, usually punctilious about such matters, was too excited to pay much attention to anything but Winter Stone. She, on the other hand, played her part to perfection, a combination of mother, wife and little sister. Calling for a clean pair of chopsticks, she collected morsels from each of the serving dishes as deftly as a honey bee in a lavender bed and delivered her garnerings to our bowls with a grace that enhanced each mouthful.

As she worked she kept up a commentary in English, but so slowly and deliberately and quietly that we had to stop eating to catch her words. She told us about her family and her work. She had one brother, who was still at school and was good at drawing. She herself had gone to university to study English, but she'd got impatient with the slow progress she made and, believing that she would learn more quickly if she had to speak the language daily as part of a job, she chucked university and went to work at the Ch'ang-pai Shan Guest House. She liked the job and the people she worked with, and the manager was kind, but she still hadn't mastered English because she was too shy to talk to the guests. What she really wanted to do was to travel, specially to England. I told her I thought she'd be quite surprised by English life: the girls, for example, were much bolder than girls in China, and there was much less difference between the sexes; it wasn't uncommon nowadays, I said, for the husband to stay at home and look after the children, while the wife went out to work.

Winter Stone pulled a face. 'I don't-er like-er,' she said emphatically.

'You'd rather be a housewife?'

'Not-er. I want-er to be a worker, to be-er independent-er. But I don't-er want to be a man-er; I like-er to be woman.'

I said there weren't many girls like her in England; if she came to England, all the boys would fall in love with her, because she was so soft.

Winter Stone shook her head. 'Inside-er I am-er hard.' She smiled and a steely look in her eye, at odds with the girlish rest of her, confirmed that the Manchurian Siren wasn't cast in gossamer after all.

'I am pleased to see you can smile,' I said, teasingly.

'I am-er happy,' she said, 'happy-er to be here wizz-er you-er.' She peeped round a lock of well-cut silky black hair and smiled again, her pink lips, full and moist, sucking on the ends of her chopsticks.

'You often seem rather sad,' I said.

'I am-er rather sad-er.'

'Why?'

'For reasons.'

Loud Report had told me that Winter Stone was having trouble with one of the porters in the hotel, who was madly in love with her; although he was the best-looking boy in the hotel, she felt nothing for him and had told him so, but he wouldn't believe her. One night, just to show the porter what the score was, she'd walked out of the hotel on Loud Report's arm. The Apollo porter had given Loud Report a hostile glare, which, in Loud Report's words, had frozen his left side as effectively as Winter Stone's proximity burned his right.

When Loud Report left the table to pay the bill, I asked Winter Stone about the handsome porter: was he the cause of her sadness?

'The porter?' She looked surprised. 'Sometimes-er I like-er him' – she sucked thoughtfully on her chopsticks again – 'sometimes not. I don't-er know.'

Taking advantage of Loud Report's absence, I juggled with the opposing objectives of putting in a good word for Loud Report himself, whilst hinting that he wasn't entirely uncommitted: ever since realizing the extent of Winter Stone's effect on Loud Report, I'd felt concerned about Morning Mist, left behind in Peking.

'Loud Report is a nice boy,' I said, 'a good boy. He likes you very much, but there is a problem.'

'I know-er,' said Winter Stone, 'but not-er problem. We are only friends-er.'

It had stopped raining by the time we emerged from the restaurant. Back at the hotel gates I said goodbye, so they could be together.

'I will-er remember this night-er for all my life-er,' said Winter Stone.

FREE at last to leave Ch'ang-ch'un, we couldn't persuade the airlines office or the railway station to sell us tickets to Peking for another two days, because of unusually heavy bookings. I spent the time transcribing my notes and tape-recordings, and correcting and expanding my imperial genealogy, while Loud Report mooned about in a lovesick haze, stalking the corridors in search of Winter Stone and her trolley of sheets and cleaning things, or lying on my bed listening to a tape of a mournful guitar piece called 'Spanish Sorrow', which he played incessantly on his crackly Chinese cassette-player.

Loud Report couldn't forgive himself for mismanaging his farewell to Winter Stone on the night of the birthday dinner. When I'd left them, he'd called a taxi to take her home. After a while she'd said, 'It's not far now, let's walk.' Because it was dark and late and unfamiliar territory, he'd asked the driver to wait for twenty minutes. But Winter Stone's home had turned out to be miles away, and he'd had to leave her and run back to the taxi. Now he was mortified because he realized that she'd intended him to pay off the taxi when they left it and walk the long distance to her home, so they could talk. 'Winter Stone, Winter Stone,' moaned Loud Report, beating his head on the pillows. 'Morning Mist is my girlfriend, but I love Winter Stone. Oh! Loud Report is a bad boy. Winter Stone, Winter Stone!'

It was during one of these periods of noisy self-mortification that the Wangs reappeared, in their best suits, with the director and vice-director of their work unit. Quickly replacing 'Spanish Sorrow' with some more appropriate court music of the early Ch'ings, Loud Report rustled up some beer and cigarettes while Professor Wang made the introductions. And for the next hour we exchanged litanies of compliments that grew more wonderfully preposterous as the beer bottles emptied.

'The History Study Institute of the Chi-lin Academy of Social Sciences bows in deference to the honourable English scholar,' said Professor Li Chih-t'ing, the director.

'It is our privilege to extend the hand of academic friendship across the Seven Seas,' added Professor Wang.

I studied Mr Interpreter Wang's face to see if I was supposed to laugh or not. Deciding not, I heaped Ossa upon Pelion: 'On behalf of Her Britannic Majesty and the Chancellors of the two ancient seats of learning, who harbour in their breasts the desire to kindle the spark of communion with the scholar class of Manchuria, felicitations!'

The professors looked pleased. 'We all aspire to objective truth,' said the vice-director, Professor Sun Yü-liang. I had assumed that these compliments must be leading somewhere, but when the visitors rose to go it became apparent that our meaningless little obsequies had been an end in themselves, a necessary part of the Chinese sense of hostliness. The formalities had been done, each side had flattered the other, we'd all kept smiling and face had been maintained.

HAVING at last secured some plane tickets back to Peking, there remained only the painful wrench from Winter Stone. Early on our last morning I found her on duty at the reception desk and laundry depository on the fifth floor.

'Remember to keep smiling,' I said, rather too breezily, as she squeezed my hand with the tips of her fingers.

'I will-er try to be happylike-er,' she said, looking miserable. 'But-er you are going now-er and you will forget-er me . . .'

Loud Report played 'Spanish Sorrow' one last time. 'Stop!' she said, pushing the tape away. 'Too sad-er.' And a tear rolled down her cheek.

'You are like a soft bird,' said Loud Report, taking her in his arms. 'I will never forget you.'

Downstairs in the hotel lobby he collapsed on our luggage. 'Misiter Socotolan,' he said in a choked voice, 'I cannot leave her. I must stay.'

'What about Morning Mist?' I asked, brutally forcing him to face reality. He rolled his eyes and clawed at his heart, panting like a hot dog. 'I am a bad boy. What can I do?'

'You're not a bad boy. But you must pull yourself together, because here's Professor Wang.'

With the professor was yet another official of the work unit, Dr Chen Long-shan, an authority on the economic history of Korea. Determined to honour the English scholar right to the last, Professor Wang had kindly laid on a work-unit taxi to the airport. All the way there we paid one another elaborate formal compliments, while Loud Report sat in silent misery. But, within sight of the terminal, Loud Report, perhaps excited by the prospect of the flight, suddenly emerged from his private gloom – and all but provoked a revocation of the Wang–Scotland Accord: 'Ha ha ha!' he burst out. 'Misiter Socotolan say this morning he think last Emperor look like a monkey.'

'BOYS' BALLS!' said the T-shirt. Below the slogan was a drawing of a girl staring with undisguised interest at the bulging flies of a boy in jeans. Then came the punchline, 'Try our hormone supplement and she'll soon see the difference.' The young Chinese whose chest carried this enlarging message was ambling down Wang-Fu-Jing, the Oxford Street of Peking, with a ring in his ear.

The Chinese capital's newly acquired veneer of Western trendiness seemed even more extraordinary after a week of drab austerity in provincial Ch'ang-ch'un.

'Do you think he knows what it means?' I asked Loud Report.

He looked puzzled. 'What means?'

'Boys' balls.'

'Ah!' he exclaimed with a happy smile, 'nice English words. Very popular shirt. All my friends have.'

Ripping a page from my notebook, I sketched the crude outlines of the male privities, as Loud Report watched with interest turning to embarrassment. Then, defacing the most familiar graffito in the history of man, I crossed out the intromittent organ and jabbed at what was left. 'Boys' balls,' I explained.

Loud Report's jaw fell. 'Aaargh!' he cried, in shocked amazement, 'I can't tell my friends, I can't.'

English names and slogans were all the rage among the Peking young, and so little did their meaning matter that even when the printer misspelled beyond the point of comprehension, the English letters in themselves served as a valuable status symbol. But not all T-shirt slogans were worn in innocence. At a time when the Chinese Communist Party was celebrating its seventieth anniversary, cynical slogans were particularly popular: 'I'm depressed – leave me alone', 'Bored' and 'There's no way out – let's get drunk'. The indispensable *China Daily* reported that the rise of these negative messages was upsetting the Party, and it recommended more improving slogans emphasizing the positive teachings of Maoist socialism: 'Study hard', for example, and 'I ascended to the summit of Tai Shan sacred mountain', 'A single spark can start a prairie fire' and 'Sweep away all vermin'. But these ideological mottoes were old hat to the new young of Peking. For all that the Party still ruled, its influence was slipping. After T'ien-an-men Square nothing could be the same again.

'Are you a member of the Party?' I asked Loud Report as our bus hurtled down Chang-An Boulevard towards T'ien-an-men Square, *en route* to the Bamboo Garden Hotel.

'No, I'm not interested. My father is.'

'Don't you think you ought to join?' I asked, provocatively. 'After all there are a thousand million people in China and only fifty million in the Party, yet the Party runs the country. Isn't it your duty?'

Poor Loud Report squirmed. 'I told you before I love my country, I have faith in my country.' He laughed nervously and tried to change the subject: 'Misiter Socotolan, look – Western car, Benz!' Above the black limousine parked at the main entrance to the Forbidden City was the huge colour poster of Chairman Mao. I wasn't to be diverted.

'Why's Chairman Mao still there, when he's been gone fifteen years?'

Loud Report gawped. 'Mao gone?'

'Well, he's dead, so he's gone in that sense. And it's generally acknowledged that he made some serious mistakes, at least in his last years, so he's gone in that sense, too.'

Loud Report didn't like this; nobly he defended the Republic's great saviour, the God of Red Sun. 'Mao was the father of my country, he built my country, he make China important in the East. Chinese will always remember him, his contributions, his "ethics"? – the example he give. Mao is never gone.'

'And the errors?' I persisted.

'If he make errors, they are lesson for us.'

As the bus ploughed through the sea of bicycles in the lunchtime rush hour, we hung on to the overhead rails on the cool side, away from the sun. Dripping and thirsty, I continued to badger Loud Report with political questions which I knew he couldn't answer.

'If Communism makes everyone equal,' I barked unreasonably, 'how come you're so much better off than those two there?' And I nodded towards a pair of grubby country boys with unkempt hair, black nails and holey trousers rolled up to the knee; they sat with bulging sacks between their legs and a dazed look on their faces.

Quietly, humbly, Loud Report admitted that he was lucky: because he lived in the city, he'd had a better education and a better life generally than was possible in the country, where the great mass of people lived.

'Is that fair?'

'Not.'

'Will you change it when you're Prime Minister?'

'No one can change it. It is part of life. Sad part.'

I wondered what they were doing in Peking, all these bewildered-looking country people with their sacks – were they looking for work? Loud Report thought not, for the system doesn't allow the people to live and work in separate places, and if they were absent without leave from their country work units, the police would forcibly return them. The peasants thronging the city streets, he said, were either 'profiteers' – small farmers who'd come up to town to sell their produce – or tourists, or both.

(Domestic tourism has increased staggeringly in China over the past ten years: of the 302 million tourists who tramped round the great sights in 1990, 300 million were reckoned to be mainland Chinese, now freer and sufficiently prosperous to see something of their huge country for the first time in their lives. This visible manifestation of the dramatic improvement in living conditions which resulted from Deng's economic reforms in the early 1980s poses problems for the National Tourism Administration: the increased numbers of tourists are threaten-

ing the fabric of the great monuments and scaring off the more profit-
able foreign tourists. The Administration is taking steps to solve these
problems by raising entrance charges and by opening more sights.)

The peasants on the bus looked so poor and deprived it was difficult
to believe that they were either 'profiteers' or tourists. Don't be misled
by appearances, said the suddenly worldly Loud Report: Chinese
peasants had plenty of money nowadays; the problem was that they
didn't know how to spend it, so they wasted it on trifles instead of
improving themselves.

We left the bus at the Drum Tower and, in my hurry to get back to
the Bamboo Garden Hotel and on with the search for the Pretender, I
broke into a trot.

'Excuse me, Misiter Socotolan,' panted Loud Report, 'you mind I
ask question?' I braced myself for another assault on my love life, but
Loud Report had more mundane matters on his mind. 'Please,' he
began, in his highest, most plaintive mode, 'we walk more slowly?'

BACK in the Bamboo Garden I took stock. I had letters of introduction to the Pretender, Duke Yü-yan, to the 'Empress', Li Shu-
hsien, the last Emperor's widow, and to Yü-chan. And I also had the
address and telephone number of the head of the Aisin-Gioro family,
P'u-chieh, the last Emperor's younger brother. Whom should I approach
first, and how? My instinct told me to go all out for the Pretender
himself: with only a fortnight left in China it was essential that I
should devote all my efforts to the capture of the prey. But caution
warned me to go slowly: if I rushed at the Pretender, I might frighten
him off; far better, perhaps, to stalk him, corner him and pounce. So I
decided first of all to contact P'u-chieh; from him I might find out
more about the lie of the land.

Loud Report, for once, wasn't much help in these deliberations.
Torpid with lovesickness, he lay in an armchair, his arms lolling over
the sides, his feet up on my bed, quietly crooning the name of Winter
Stone. He did promise to rope in his father as interpreter and cal-
ligrapher once I'd drafted my letters. For the rest I was on my own.
But I couldn't concentrate.

'You're awfully depressing like this, Loud Report,' I snapped. He
reached for my Panama hat and covered his face. Thus muffled and
disembodied, his mournful Winter Stones were even more irritating.

'Dear Duke Yü-yan,' I began writing on a piece of Bamboo Garden paper. Then I thought better of it, scored it out and started again. 'Dear Mr Aisin-Gioro . . .' But that didn't look right either. I wondered what *Debrett's Correct Form* would recommend for a toppled prince of the blood remoulded as citizen – 'My once Lord Duke', 'Your ex-Grace'?

'Winter Stone . . . Winter Stone . . .'

'Dear Sir' had the advantage of simplicity, but still looked a little formal.

'Winter Stone . . .'

'Oh, do shut up, Loud Report. Winter Stone's miles away in Ch'ang-ch'un. It's all over now. You must come down to earth. We're back in Peking, and Morning Mist is expecting you to supper tonight.'

'Aaargh!' he cried. 'What can I do?'

'Take my hat off and telephone the Emperor's brother.'

It worked: given a task, Loud Report always jumped to. He found himself a pencil and some paper, switched on his tape-recorder and dialled the number I'd been given by the BBC correspondent in Peking, James Miles.

Meanwhile, I solved my etiquette problem with the simple 'Dear Yü-yan . . .', and tossed off a short note, introducing myself as a genealogist, seeking permission to ask him some questions about his family and suggesting that he leave with Red Universe a telephone number where I could call him back to make an appointment.

Loud Report had got through to P'u-chieh's phone number and was carrying on an animated conversation in Chinese, his eyes open wide, a smile on his lips. The signs looked good. When, at last, he put the phone down he mopped his brow and grinned.

'Mr P'u-chieh very big man, I think,' he said, impressed. 'I speak to his nephew, Chin Tzu-chung: soft voice, nice man – Mr P'u's secretary. He say Mr P'u-chieh give interviews, but only for forty minutes. We must talk to his work unit at Office of National People's Congress in T'ien-an-men Square. But very sorry no more interviews this month.' Loud Report drew a deep breath, respectful yet puzzled. 'P'u-chieh – very – big – man. But why? Because he is last Emperor's brother? I don't understand.' I hadn't the heart to suggest that a brainwashed imperialist happy to trot out the Party line for visitors was worth his weight in *yuan* to a beleaguered Communist dictatorship.

I wasn't so anxious to talk to P'u-chieh that I was prepared to pursue him through official channels. So then I turned my attention to Yü-chan, whose home address Professor Wang had given me in Ch'ang-ch'un; and before I left London the retiring British Ambassador in Peking, Sir Alan Donald, had given me his business card and work number in the Park of the Altar of the Sun. Loud Report telephoned and discovered that Yü-chan and his wife were away in Manchuria till the end of the month.

Having drawn two blanks, it was more important than ever that I played my last two cards right. Loud Report checked my letter to the Pretender and approved it, so I wrote a similar letter to the 'Empress', adding a request for permission to pay my respects to the ashes of her late husband at Eight Treasure Mountain. I decided to post hers, but to deliver his in person: after all he lived just round the corner. But first they both had to be translated. Loud Report was going to take them home to his father after his reunion with Morning Mist. Stimulated by his telephone calls, he dipped his whole head in the basin and felt ready for anything. I put him in a taxi, gave him a present he couldn't refuse, because he wouldn't find it till he'd left, and advised him to keep mum about Winter Stone.

IN Manchu Peking the princes lived in palaces with marble lions guarding the gates, the gentry lived in pavilions with lotus ponds and belvederes, and everyone else lived in single-storey courtyard dwellings, or *szu-ho-yuan*, hidden behind high walls in narrow lanes called *hu-t'ung*. The extent and decoration of the interior depended on each occupant's means, but the plan and architectural features – copied from the model of the Chinese temple – were always the same. At the entrance were heavy wooden gates painted scarlet under a sloping roof ornamentally tiled at the corners and along the ridge, with a wooden threshold standing a foot proud off the ground (to keep the street dust out) and, flanking the gates, squat stone carvings symbolizing the power of life and death. The gates opened on to a narrow hall forming a screen between the lane and the outer courtyard; this had a double purpose – to give some privacy and to keep evil spirits at bay (for it was believed that ghosts could only fly in straight lines, so that if a phantom accidentally floated through your entrance gates, it would immediately bump up against your courtyard screen and, being unable to turn either left or right, would simply reverse out again or evaporate). From the entrance hall, steps led down to a courtyard shaded by a large tree, usually a ginkgo, with a bronze censer nearby for ceremonial occasions; and, off this three-sided courtyard, in a scrupulously correct south-to-north polarity, were three or more residential halls with walls painted red and green, curved roofs of unglazed grey tiles and windows of rice paper stretched over wooden lattices. Richer people had more courtyards and more halls, often with elaborate bays and columns, and roof tiles in bright colours – though never yellow, which was the strict prerogative of the Emperor.

From the twelfth century till the middle of the twentieth this was the shape of Peking, the framework that supported the traditions of a great civilization: in the words of the Italian journalist Tiziano Terzani, writing about his travels in China in *Behind the Forbidden Door*, 'the rarefied atmosphere in which a scholar and his friends could view the blossoming of the chrysanthemum and spend a night writing poems to the moon'.

To the Communists this last refuge of individualism posed an irksome threat, and in 1966 the Gang of Four sent the Red Guards to break it up. The owners were arrested by people's judges, beaten, sometimes killed; the houses were stripped, looted and burned clean. All that remained when it was over were the bare buildings. Into these the masses surged, and 'the new régime entered the heart of Peking'.

Some of the former owners managed to claw back a room in their old dwellings. Yü-yan was one of them.

Yü-yan's *hu-t'ung* was in the vicinity of the Drum Tower – not far from the site of the palace where he was born – but no one could find it on the street map. At last we consulted the Head Post Office where a manly postgirl with rubber stalls on the tips of all her fingers flicked through the Bible-thin pages of an official directory and found it by the postcode.

Primed with chicken, duck and cucumber in a seafood sauce and a fruity white wine called Great Wall, Loud Report and I set off in search of the Pretender. We agreed that Loud Report should go in first to deliver my letters of introduction and to ask for a meeting, while I waited outside.

Just after we'd left the main road below the Drum Tower and disappeared into the maze of *hu-t'ung* which proliferate there, a storm broke and the rain came down in a solid sheet. We sheltered in a covered alley and watched the floodwaters raging down the lane with tins and corncobs bobbing about like flotsam.

Loud Report shook his head meaningfully. 'It's a sign, Misiter Socotolan. I tell you Manchu no good.' A sudden flash of lightning suggested the gods agreed. But it was soon over and we picked our way on stepping stones down the flooded lane to an old low-arched white-stone bridge spanning a piece of green water edged with willows. This was the ornamental lake, called Shih-ch'a, on the shores of which once stood the palaces of most of the near relatives of the Manchu Emperors, including the Tun Wang Fu (Prince Tun's Palace, Yü-yan's birthplace), the Pei Fu (the Northern Mansion, Prince Ch'un's Palace, where P'u-yi was born) and the Kung Wang Fu (Prince Kung's Palace, Yü-chan's ancestral home). For a moment the sun came out and the dazzling stone of the bridge, the gleaming still-wet tiles of the *hu-t'ung* dwellings, the faded red of their entrance gates, the glimmering turquoise of the lake offered a flash of old Peking; even Loud Report was impressed.

Loud Report asked in a shop for directions. 'Ah, you must want Yü-yan,' said the wizened old shopkeeper, with a quizzical look at me, 'first right out of the shop, then halfway down the *hu-t'ung*, on the left-hand side.' My heart was thumping.

Number 12. The Pretender's lair at last. A shabby entrance gate with its roof ridge broken but the tiles still intact, plaster peeling off the old brick walls; a carved stone tablet at either side of a well-worn wooden threshold; the courtyard number in Chinese characters and Arabic numerals above pale red double doors; one door ajar, and through it a glimpse of a black bike leaning against a wall.

Loud Report took a deep breath, mopped his face with his scented handkerchief, tucked his shirt in and smoothed his hair down. Then, gathering up the camera, tape-recorders and presents, he climbed over the threshold, turned back with a smile and a Victory sign and disappeared behind the spirit screen.

I carried my rucksack to the other side of the road and settled down on the threshold of the entrance gate opposite, so that I could watch any comings and goings unnoticed. I recalled Reginald Johnston's encounter with the impoverished Ming Pretender, Shining Merit, the Marquess of Extended Grace, who'd called at the Forbidden City in a borrowed hat and coat in 1924 and begged Johnston not to return the call because he lived in a hovel. 'He would have "lost face",' wrote the sensitive tutor, 'if he had had to receive me in such lowly surroundings.' Professor Wang had warned me not to call on Yü-yan unannounced, for he was 'self-conscious' about his rough home. I hoped he wouldn't be angry with Loud Report. But what would happen if he wasn't there and suddenly came back and found Loud Report snooping? Exactly what sort of place did he live in? Who else lived in the same courtyard? What did he look like, the Pretender? Did he think of himself as the heir of the Manchus, the legitimate successor to the oldest throne in the world?

Ten minutes passed. I tried to imagine where Loud Report was now and I got the strong feeling that he and the Pretender were having a cup of tea in a room some way to the left of the entrance gate. There was a lattice window there and, as the storm gathered again and the sky darkened, I thought I detected the glimmer of candlelight. I didn't like to cross the road for a closer look because there were two men in vests squatting in an entrance gate further up the *hu-t'ung*, having a smoke and carrying on a furtive conversation in undertones with occasional suspicious glances in my direction, and I was afraid they might report me to the Street Committee. Every now and then I caught their eye and smiled reassuringly; unconvinced, they grunted.

A bicycle came along with a boy and a girl wrapped in a tent-size mac of transparent plastic, through which I could see that the girl was sitting side-saddle on the back mudguard holding on to the boy's waist with one hand and, with the other, grasping a bowl of rice. There was a puddle in the lane just in front of where I was sitting and I assumed they would see it and avoid it, but they didn't and my white trousers, fresh for the Pretender, were spattered with muddy rainwater. I got up and leaned against the wall: the stone was still hot from the day's sunshine and steam soon rose from my legs.

In the distance someone was playing a *pipa*, the Chinese lute. Further down the lane, to my right, a well-dressed girl stood patiently under an umbrella, with the pessimistic air of a Londoner waiting for a bus. A clatter of hooves, and two skinny ponies trotted past with a wagonload of timber.

I'd been there about an hour: it was getting dark and I could no longer pick out the 12 on the Pretender's door. My imagination had started to invent various calamitous scenarios, when suddenly Loud Report emerged from the entrance gate and crossed the road. I ran to meet him.

'How did you get on?'

'Shhh!' hissed Loud Report, 'we must leave this place. Quick. Don't look behind you! They must not see you.'

43 On May Day 1962, two-and-a-half years after his pardon and release from the War Criminals' Prison, P'u-yi married, as his fifth wife, a 37-year-old nurse called Li Shu-hsien. He was then employed as a historical researcher for the Government and a seedsman at the Peking Botanical Gardens. This photograph was taken in March 1964 on a visit to Li Shu-hsien's birthplace in Hang-chou, a port not far from Shanghai.

44 Li Shu-hsien and P'u-yi setting off to work, soon after their marriage. 'Now he had an ordinary home,' wrote P'u-yi's ghost-writer Li Wen-ta, 'but to him it was extraordinary. He had had several wives in the past but never had a family life like others.'

45 Li Shu-hsien and P'u-yi (centre) on their wedding day, in the club of the National Committee of the Chinese People's Political Consultative Conference. Flanking the couple are P'u-yi's brother P'u-chieh and his wife Saga Hiro, and other members of the Aisin-Gioro clan, including: Prince Tsai-t'ao, P'u-yi's uncle (centre, between the bride and groom); Jun Ch'i, P'u-yi's double brother-in-law (behind P'u-yi's left shoulder), brother of the late Empress Beauty in Flower and husband of P'u-yi's third sister Yün-ying; and P'u-jen, P'u-yi's half-brother (third from the right).

46 Saga Hiro and P'u-chieh (left) with Li Shu-hsien and P'u-yi, at home in Peking in 1964. 'Trees may wither, stones may rot, but my mind will never change,' Li Shu-hsien had vowed to the former Emperor on their marriage two years earlier; 'Mountains may have tops, rivers may have sources, but the flower of our love will never fall,' P'u-yi had vowed in return.

47 The widow Li Shu-hsien at home in Peking. 'I'm only a woman, so no one helps me, and even though it's not so bad in China for a single woman, it's not so good either.'

48 The entrance to the block of flats in the Peking suburb of Ch'ao-yan, where Li Shu-hsien lives in retirement.

49

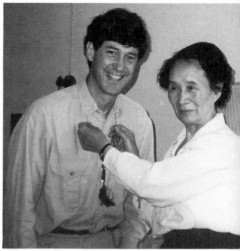

50

49, 50 and 51 At Aunt
Li's for dinner: the
widow of the last
Emperor presents Loud
Report with a white
shirt, the author with a
good-luck talisman –
and prunes – and Red
Universe with a purple
blouse.

51

52 Li Shu-hsien and her memories: photographs of her late husband, P'u-yi, on their wedding day, and of a happy meeting with Premier Chou En-lai shortly before P'u-yi's death in 1967. (A much-prized photograph of the former Emperor and Chairman Mao, taken at an informal dinner in 1961, was confiscated by Red Guards during the Cultural Revolution.)

53 and 54 The table was heaped with dishes: a dozen varieties of edible fungus, cold fish cutlets, hot sea cucumbers, sweet-and-sour carp – all prepared by Aunt Li, who hovered over us, assiduously replenishing our plates like an Oriental *Hausfrau* with an enigmatic smile, half solicitous, half wilful.

55

57

56

58

55 Eight Treasure Mountain Cemetery, Peking: the final resting place of the last Emperor of China. Despite its fairy-tale name, it is as flat as a pancake, and no more romantic than Golders Green.

56 The last Emperor's widow, Li Shu-hsien, wearing imperial yellow for her pilgrimage, beside the open cabinet containing P'u-yi's funerary casket in the Hall of Revolutionary Heroes.

57 The last Emperor's cedarwood funerary casket, bearing a photograph of Citizen P'u-yi as a 'revolutionary hero'. Beside the casket, a basket of plastic flowers and a glass vase containing the author's pilfered tribute.

58 'Hmmm!' said Loud Report, catching a whiff of the Emperor as he relieved me of the casket. 'He smell nice, like hôtel men's room.'

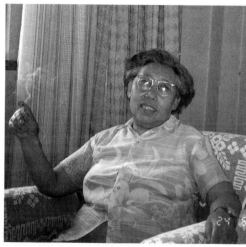

9

60

59 and *60* Journey's end: Yü-yan and his wife, Chang Yün-fang, at the author's climactic bedroom conference in the Ch'ien-men Hotel, Peking. 'And do you regard yourself, now that P'u-yi is dead, as the rightful ruler of all China?'

61 Yü-yan, with Loud Report breathing down his neck, reading the author's pedigree of the Manchu House of Aisin-Gioro.

61

62 Aisin-Gioro Yü-yan, great-great-grandson of the Emperor Glory of Right Principle, adopted son and heir of P'u-yi and Pretender to the Dragon Throne, signing his calligraphy for the author.

There was a roll of distant thunder and the clouds burst again as we ran down the dark *hu-t'ung* towards the lake and the shelter of a weeping willow.

'What happened?' I asked at last.

Loud Report was too puffed to answer. He put down the bag of cameras, tape-recorders and undelivered presents and wiped his face. Then, baring his teeth in a grimace as comically menacing as a Monkey King mask, he said, in a voice no less dramatic for being so out of breath:

'Tung-tung – (puff) – very – (puff puff) – dangerous.' And he rolled his big dark eyes ominously as he watched me wrestling with this incomprehensible piece of information.

'Who on earth is Tung-tung?' I asked.

'Tung-tung is Yü-yan's third son – my age, I think. He work in a bank and is very proud. He call himself *Chia-pin* like a royal prince – ha! stupid boy.'

'Look, I think you'd better have an Altoid and start at the beginning.' Ever since Ch'ang-ch'un I'd found that nothing subdued Loud Report's excitement more effectively than one of the Original Celebrated Curiously Strong Peppermints. I fumbled for the tin in my pocket and placed one on his tongue like a priest giving Communion.

Gradually the story came out.

Yü-yan and his second wife – a Chinese (not Manchu) lady called Chang Yün-fang – and their son Hêng-chün, known as Tung-tung, had all been at home when Loud Report called. Yü-yan was a frail old man, thin and small, and his wife was stout and short, with spectacles; they were both chain-smokers. Tung-tung, a sullen young man of twenty-five, had studied accountancy at the No. 112 Financial Occupation Training Senior Middle School for three years and was now working as an accountant at the Shih-szu (West 4) Bank in Peking.

The three of them lived together in a single room measuring, at a guess, eleven feet by seven-and-a-half. (The Government had offered them a new, larger home in a block of flats, I was assured later, but Yü-yan preferred to stay in the Tartar City *hu-t'ung* close to his studio in Prince Kung's Palace.) The parents' tiny double bed ran along one of the end walls, with a television set on a table at the foot. Beside the TV, beneath the only window in the room, was a desk with a chair next to it. Tung-tung's narrow bed stood against the long wall opposite the door, with its head separated from his parents' bed by a small canvas screen. Along the wall to the right of the door was a long cupboard and between that and the door was a wash-basin on legs and a standard electric fan. Loud Report didn't want to seem disrespectful, but actually he said, with a fastidious twitch of his nose, the crowded little room was rather dirty.

Had there been anything on the walls? I wondered.

'The walls?' repeated Loud Report, his eyes widening in disbelief. 'You want me to tell you about Yü-yan's walls? Why you ask these questions, Misiter Socotolan? Why you English interested in my country? I think this not natural.' Chastened but not silenced, I muttered something pompous about the value of international contacts. Then I gave him another Altoid and pressed him again on the subject of Yü-yan's walls. He said they were hung with examples of Yü-yan's calligraphy. He remembered one in particular – a philosophical text of just four characters – *Ho Lo Chih Yu* – which didn't make much sense in English.

'Try,' I urged.

'Ah, so difficult. It mean, I think, "This place poor but is my . . . my . . . Garden of Eden".' The Oriental equivalent of Sancho Panza's 'For whom God loves, his house smells savoury to him'. Or 'Home, sweet home'.

'Tell me about Yü-yan,' I asked. 'Did you like him?'

'Yü-yan very nice man,' he replied with conviction, 'like English gentleman. Yes, I like. And his wife.' Suddenly his voice changed. 'But I don't like Tung-tung. He watch me all the time. *Chia-pin*! Hah!'

'And what did Yü-yan say when you showed him Professor Wang's letter of introduction?'

'I think he not pleased with Professor Wang. He say he is just a writer. But he want to meet you.'

'That's wonderful! When?'

'Perhaps tomorrow. They will talk and then telephone Red Universe. But there is problem, Misiter Socotolan.'

'Problem? It all sounds perfectly straightforward to me – you couldn't have done better – I'm thrilled.'

'Tung-tung is dangerous boy. Not like his father. Tung-tung is not trusting. I am sorry, Misiter Socotolan, but I invite him come, too.'

'That's all right – I'd like to meet him.'

Loud Report came closer. 'Please, Misiter Socotolan,' he said, his voice soft with concern, 'please be careful with your questions.'

The storm was now directly overhead. There was a flash of white lightning and through the leaves I could see an empty rowing boat tossing about on the lake. A roar of thunder shook the ground, the wind whipped up and the trailing willow branches lashed about our legs. Excited, I pulled Loud Report to the water's edge for a ringside view.

'Why is Chinese lightning so white?' I asked.

'You are crazy!' he shouted, laughing. 'All the time questions. I think you are a spee.'

'Spee?'

'English spee. Like James Bong.'

'Who?'

Exasperated by my stupidity, Loud Report threw back his wet head and bellowed into the storm: 'Double-oh-seven.'

BREAKFAST at the Studio-of-the-tending-of-the-pines hadn't improved, despite my complaints. It was still coffee essence in a glass, milk in another – and never delivered till the coffee was cold – and a plate containing jam, scrambled powdered egg and two thick slices of undertoasted white bread. On the morning of the fifth day of the fifth month of the Chinese lunar calendar the menu changed. Just as I was paying for my breakfast, a girl emerged from the kitchen carrying a small hot plate which she pushed towards me with a smile. On it was a steaming pyramid-shaped object wrapped in reeds.

This, I soon learned, was *tsung-tzu*, a dumpling made of polished glutinous rice and crushed jujube berries, which supplements the breakfast of most families in China on the day of the Dragon Boat Festival. No one quite knows its origin. One theory is that when the ancient poet Ch'u Yuan drowned himself in a river in Hunan Province in the fourth century BC, dumplings were thrown in to distract the fish from eating his corpse, which was then recovered intact by a dragon-shaped boat. Another school of thought believes the festival started much earlier, when the Chinese regarded themselves as descendants of the dragon and worshipped the god Totem; on the god's feast day the people used to stuff dumplings into hollowed-out bamboos which they then bound in protective leaves and threw into the water to feed Totem for another year.

The Dragon Boat Festival is still primarily a peasant festival, a holiday from the busy farming routines of spring. And it's observed with special fervour in Hunan Province. In the early morning the people gather vine leaves, reeds and herbs, which are believed to have extra special medicinal properties at this time, and sweet flag and mugwort, which they festoon about their doors and windows to repel scorpions, vipers and toads. For lunch they have roast duck and salted eggs with the boiled leaves of Love-Lies-Bleeding and garlic cloves. Then comes an important ritual in which the adults prepare a potion of wine, red arsenic and tincture of cinnabar, with which the children draw circles on their foreheads to increase their courage and ward off evil spirits. And in the afternoon the young men leap into the river and race one another in long narrow boats decorated with dragon's heads and tails.

HOT and tired after a day at the Forbidden City – peering into the cluttered gloom of a hundred palace halls and longing for a Chinese Mark Girouard to answer practical questions about lighting, kitchens, bathrooms and sewerage – I decided to return to the Bamboo Garden by pedicab rickshaw. At the rank, in the failing light of early evening, I chose a young rider with beefy legs and bare feet. I knew from experience that it would be a waste of time attempting to enunciate my destination in Chinese, so I presented the hotel card and pointed to Drum Tower Street on my map. The other pedicab riders gathered around and joined in the fixing of the fare.

'*Yuan* 30' (about £3.00), my rider scribbled on a piece of paper, and general mutterings seemed to suggest that this was the going rate. Although it was double the taxi fare, my Protestant conscience wondered if I'd have been prepared to pedal someone halfway round Peking for anything less. Then I remembered what Loud Report had said about pedicab drivers – that they were lazy, greedy and deceitful to a man – so, for his sake, I haggled:

'Fifteen.'

'Fifteen?' he scoffed, 'twenty!'

And, without further ado, I agreed, knowing that all this bargaining was of purely academic interest, as I had every intention of giving him, at the finish, the full thirty he'd asked for.

I climbed aboard and settled into the padded seat below the fringed canopy, with my hands dangling out of the sides. I was determined to get the most from this new experience. The rider, sensing my greenness, made as much fuss about the strain of pedalling us off as if I'd been the Queen of Tonga.

At last we were away, bumping down quite the wrong street, but I presumed the rider knew a short-cut and, anyway, the slight breeze caused by our progress through the turgid windless air was such a relief that I couldn't have cared less.

It was a curiously exciting sensation being propelled along an unknown street in a hot foreign city by the physical exertion of a muscly stranger, and I projected a surge of gratitude towards his rippling back.

After perhaps a quarter of an hour he pulled up in the middle of a manic intersection. It was the rush hour: with bicycles, buses and taxis bearing down on us from every direction he coolly turned on his saddle, leaned towards me, with his hand on my knee for balance and, leering at my lap, he said, 'Big one?' Convinced that I'd misheard him, but unwilling to check at such a perilous moment, I offered the affirmative answer his tone seemed to expect: 'Yes,' I replied, to humour him, 'big one,' quite matter-of-factly, as though it meant 'Left here' or 'Warm evening'. He burst out laughing and, without waiting for the oncoming traffic to stop, he pedalled straight through it towards a dark side-street.

Several minutes later, still chuckling, he turned again and said, unmistakably, 'Fuck want?' A few feet away a woman in a tight dress was pretending to look in a shop window. 'Fuck want?' the rider repeated. I shook my head politely, 'No fuck, thank you – just Bamboo Garden.' He slapped my knee and laughed out loud.

The night was black. Nearly an hour had passed since we began our journey outside the Forbidden City. In a wide, unlit street in a part of Peking I didn't recognize the rider stopped under a tree, dismounted, removed his Mao jacket, folded it carefully and tucked it beside me on the seat. It was wet. He mopped his brow with his arm and looked at me for sympathy. But he wasn't too tired to haggle again.

'Fifty *yuan*!' he demanded.

'Twenty!' I replied, my voice faltering in the pitch dark of this lonely street. 'And make it snappy. I want to get home.' I hoped I sounded more confident than I felt.

Suddenly he bent down and took off one of his shoes. Then, raising it above his head, he made as if to hit me. I ducked, but the blow never came. Nervously – for the man wasn't quite all there and needed careful handling – I laughed. He then put his shoe back on, leapt aboard the bike again and pedalled off with renewed energy.

I didn't wait for him to find the Bamboo Garden. The moment I caught sight of the Drum Tower I jumped off near a traffic policeman, paid the twenty *yuan* I'd agreed – and no more – and walked home without looking back.

'Twenty *yuan*?' exclaimed Loud Report the next morning. 'You must be crazy. Those people are . . . are . . . they are cannibals.'

'Cannibals?' I repeated. 'Really?' Perhaps I'd had a luckier escape than I realized.

Puffing and wheezing with frustration, Loud Report flicked through his pocket dictionary. 'Sorry,' he said. 'Parachutes.'

MESSAGES at last from the Pretender and the last Empress – but in neither case the immediate entrée I'd hoped for.

Li Shu-hsien – or Aunt Li, as she seemed to be known in China – would be pleased to meet me, Red Universe reported on the telephone, but her 'agent' insisted on spending at least three hours with me first, to examine my credentials and to approve my questions; furthermore, a visit to Eight Treasure Mountain to see P'u-yi's last resting place was 'highly unlikely'.

Yü-yan was also prepared to meet me, but his 'agent' a Mr Kao – wanted me to submit my questions, in advance, to Mr Chang, principal of the Peking Institute of Calligraphy.

I was astonished that either of my imperial relics – one a poor relation, the other not an Aisin-Gioro at all but a good Communist housewife – should need an agent, and rather resentful that my legitimate approach through Professor Wang should require any further investigation. But it would have been foolish – and possibly damaging for Loud Report and Red Universe – to refuse to meet their requests, so, reluctantly, I agreed.

Back at the Bamboo Garden, the telephone rang. It was the Head of Chancery at the British Embassy, Mr Jim Hoare, with a telephone number for P'u-chieh. I thanked him, but explained that I'd got it from another source and had already made contact.

'How did you get on?' he asked.

'All right,' I said, 'but everything seems to be so difficult – it all takes so long.'

Mr Hoare laughed. 'Par for the course in China,' he said, 'but don't worry: just when you think it's hopeless and you'll never achieve anything, suddenly, all the obstacles evaporate, and everything falls into place for no apparent reason. It's very odd, but that's the way it is here.'

ONE of the distinctive sounds of Chinese speech is the burred 'urr', produced by a contorted throat technique involving gargling with the swallowed tongue. To Western ears it has something absurd about it, like a Cornish Yogi Bear mimicking the mating croak of a natterjack toad. At the box office of the Peking Concert Hall I had to perform this lingual feat in front of a crowd of music students. All I wanted was a ticket for the *erh-hu* recital that night – the *erh-hu* is the two-stringed fiddle which wails so mournfully in the pit of the Peking Opera – but I couldn't get my tongue round it. Every time I reached '*erh-hu*' I jutted my head forward, opened my mouth wide and produced such a strangulated gurgle that the ticket clerk thought I was going to be sick and slammed her little window. Eventually a kind student, realizing that I was neither retching nor dying but simply English, persuaded the ticket clerk to reopen her window and sell me the ticket I wanted.

Loud Report pulled his lemon face when I told him I'd been to an *erh-hu* concert. 'I – don't – like – *erh-hu*,' he said, '*erh-hu* so miserable.' In fact, it does have a rather sad voice, but it's a warm and mellow mournfulness like the cello. And at the bottom of its wide range, when its little rosewood body is resonating with all the richness of its larger Western cousin, then, I suddenly realized, it does actually sound like the unpronounceable first character of its own name.

An interruption prevented my pursuing this line of thought: halfway through Maestro Wang Liang-sheng's performance of *Listening to the Sough of the Pines*, a thin girl with spectacles strode purposefully down my row, put out her hand and said in English, 'Hallo. I would like to be your friend. I am reporter with New China News. May I sit?' Without waiting for an answer she took the seat and, in a loud voice, quizzed me for the rest of the concert – the music be damned – on my views about nationalism and the future of the EEC, the American 'invasion' of Iraq, 'petting' and the Prince of Wales.

If I couldn't hear very much of the *erh-hu* recital, I couldn't see very much at the Peking Opera, because it was full of television cameras. I wished it had been the other way round, for, while the *erh-hu* needs to be heard and not necessarily seen, the Peking Opera might be more palatable seen and not heard: the music is so unremittingly loud and shrill and disconnected. Visually the Peking Opera has something of the appeal of old-fashioned English pantomime, with exotic costumes – though no scenery at all – painted faces, mime, acrobatics and dance. For the uninitiated, comprehension is a problem, because of the complicated conventions of stylized symbolism: when an actor lifts his leg, for example, he's indicating, on a stage with no doors, that he's climbing over the threshold on his way out; an actress, for whom such a gesture would be inelegant, not to say impossible in a heavy gown, conveys the same message by drawing the shape of a doorway in the air.

Numbed by the screaming music and obstructed by dollying cameras, I remember little about my introduction to Peking Opera except that Loud Report, a never-failing source of surprise, took a peculiar shine to the conductor's head. 'Ah!' he sighed wistfully, 'he is like a scholar – like Mr John Major.'

The National Ballet of China provided a more memorable evening: a full-length work called *The Wild Geese are Flying South*. If the title promised romance (which the score – half Tchaikovsky, half Hollywood musical – duly delivered), the small print gave the game away: 'created to celebrate the seventieth anniversary of the founding of the Communist Party'. It was propaganda, of course, but artfully disguised as a tale of love and loyalty in the Sino-Japanese War in the 1930s.

It was winter in the mountains of eastern Manchuria – which explained why the geese were flying south. The hero, a Communist guerrilla, had been wounded by the Japanese and was looking for his unit. A pretty young peasant woman, whose husband was away at the war, took him home and nursed him back to health. As winter turned to spring, the soldier recovered. But duty called – he had to rejoin his unit. Cue for bravura solo for the hero in yellow silk jacket, tights, Mao cap and red scarf with revolver. Then, while the woman and her small daughter were out, he ran off into the woods, leaving his precious gold watch as a gesture of thanks.

In the second act the soldier was a prisoner in a Japanese POW camp, run by a mad and vicious Hitler lookalike: no holds barred in the depiction of Japanese brutality. The soldier stirred up a mutiny, the guards were overpowered and the Chinese prisoners escaped to a risky freedom in the Japanese-infested mountains. The soldier hero then discovered that his best friend was the husband of the woman who nursed him. They returned home to reassure her that they were both safe, and bravely she and her daughter waved them off to continue the struggle for the people.

It was curious that it should have taken a ballet sixty years after the event to bring home to me the reality of the Japanese occupation of Northern China. Throughout the performance I kept thinking that all this had actually taken place while P'u-yi was sitting on his throne in Ch'ang-ch'un – with Yü-yan washing up the testosterone syringes, Beauty in Flower puffing on her opium pipes and Big Li supervising the floggings. How much, I wondered, did P'u-yi know about the atrocities being carried out in his name? At the Japanese War Crimes Tribunal, in Tokyo in 1946, he claimed that the Japanese had forced him to go to Manchukuo against his will and he denied any knowledge of Japanese atrocities. But he was still a prisoner of the Russians when he gave that evidence, and fearful of the consequences of his return to Communist China. In 1961, just after his release from a decade of 're-education' in Fu-shun, he told a different story when he spoke to a Japanese delegation visiting Peking:

Through study in the Fu-shun War Criminals' Prison, I learned that numerous Chinese children died at the tip of Japanese bayonets. I have come to understand the past and myself through my humanitarian reform and come to know what is life and how to be a man. I feel pained by memories of the past. During those criminal days I worked in league with Japanese imperialists and betrayed my country by providing Chinese territory as bases for the enemy and press-ganging Chinese to work for the enemy. Thousands and thousands of families were broken up. I feel pain for those compatriots who died for the country.

The ballet left me in no doubt that anti-Japanese feeling still runs high in China today.

IF Loud Report hadn't yet quite recovered from his poodlefaking with Winter Stone in Manchuria, a week after our return to the capital he had at least made his peace with Morning Mist. They'd celebrated their reunion with a supper party in her parents' flat at which Morning Mist had shown me her stamp album and Sunshine, her younger sister, had performed an English reading, while Red Universe and her younger sister, First Light, compared notes about their Western bosses and Loud Report, the cook, had yelped, hollered and cooed in the kitchen. (At the table, between the shark's fin and the peppered pineapple, he'd revealed a striking new talent as an ear-waggler, holding the left still while moving the right, nodding the tops of both, and even revolving the two in opposite directions simultaneously. 'This is nothing,' he said modestly when applauded, 'one of my classmates can chew own nose.')

Now, though, there was a new threat to their relationship. Loud Report, discontented with the financial restrictions of perpetual studenthood and ashamed of trailing along in Morning Mist's wake had applied for a job as a receptionist at a grand hotel. In his scheme of things it was a humble post, but it was a foot in a promising door. The problem was that Morning Mist had grave misgivings: she was afraid it would expose him to corrupt Western influences – and pretty girls; she discounted his rejoinder that she, in her job, was no less invulnerable to the very same corrupt Western influences – and pretty boys.

And now the tussle had taken a dramatic new turn with the news that Morning Mist had just been offered a job as a secretary in the business centre of the very same hotel. It was a job so enticing that she couldn't possibly turn it down, but Loud Report was convinced that it dashed his own prospects.

'Surely it would be nice working together in the same hotel?' I said, unaware of the social subtleties involved. Loud Report looked at me pityingly:

'Misiter Socotolan, you don't understand. A man cannot work as receptionist in hotel where girlfriend is secretary.' His lip curled on the mean 'receptionist' and his eyes widened on the glorious 'secretary', so that I began to see, at last, the face he would lose playing Cinderella to Morning Mist's Prince Charming.

There was nothing for it, I advised – since I'd been asked – Morning Mist must take the job, and Loud Report would have to concentrate on completing his postgraduate studies, at the end of which he would be qualified for a better post in what would by then be a richer marketplace.

'But then, Misiter Socotolan,' wailed Loud Report, 'I will be old man.' In the meantime, for heaven's sake, he said, despairingly, how could he possibly compete with all those rich businessmen whispering their dictation into Morning Mist's ear?

It was to thrash all this out that I took Loud Report to Ma-k'ai for lunch. But we never got around to the subject of jobs and relationships.

The restaurant was even busier than usual, so we had to share a circular table at the back with an elderly Chinese couple, inconspicuously distinguished like the survivors of an *ancien régime*. 'Ni hao,' I said. 'May we join you?'

'Be my guest,' the old man replied with a friendly smile and a wave to the vacant seats. 'We don't often see tourists here.' He gave me an intense look for a moment. 'Where are you from?' His English had an American flavour and the ease of his conversation seemed at odds with the formality of his bearing. I tried to place him and guessed, correctly, that he was a professor; but I could never have put my finger on his subject, which was waste disposal.

He'd learned his English, he explained, at university – Ch'ing-hua, the Cambridge of China – and perfected it as an interpreter with the US Army, when the Americans joined the Nationalist Chinese in their struggle against the Japanese in 1941. It was clear that he disliked the Americans almost as much as the Japanese, from whom he'd fled as a boy in T'ien-ching in the 1930s. But he said he had had a special fondness for the English ever since meeting a young lieutenant in Manchuria during the war: 'His name was Robert – I can't remember the rest. He was older than me and very kind. We didn't keep in touch, but I have never forgotten him.' He paused, and his eyes swept me with a soft sad look. 'He looked like you.'

The professor and his wife, a professor of horticulture with the air of an ambassadress, were among the millions of Chinese artists and intellectuals persecuted by Mao's Red Guards during the Cultural Revolution. They lost their jobs, their home was ransacked and they were separated and sent to the country to 'learn through labour' for nearly ten years. I longed to ask lots of questions, but the professor was in charge of his own story; he told only as much as he wanted to tell.

While he talked, his wife was advising Loud Report about the menu. They often dined there, she said; as it was Hunan cuisine and Hunan was her native province, might she recommend the braised eel and hot red peppers in oil, with noodles and spicy bean curd? Loud

Report licked his lips as the horticulture professor called the waitress and repeated the mouth-watering words all over again – in the hectoring tone the Chinese always use with restaurant staff.

When our dishes had been delivered, I sensed disquiet on the table nearby: a respectable-looking woman suddenly leapt to her feet, pointing at our lunch and shouting at the waitress. Though they registered the disturbance, neither the rest of the protesting woman's party nor anyone else in the restaurant, least of all the waitress, paid any further attention. More curious than embarrassed, I asked Loud Report what the trouble was. He looked across and listened for a moment: 'Ah,' he said, 'the lady think our eel bigger than her eel.' After a while she sat down and finished her lunch. Like everyone else in China she'd only made a fuss to win face; her wrong hadn't been put right but she'd made a commotion, registered her dissatisfaction, and that's what counted.

When the professors had finished their lunch, they invited us to help ourselves from the remains of their serving dishes, and, when we declined, for we had more than enough ourselves – the Chinese don't stint in these matters – the professors called for a plastic bag, into which they scraped the left-overs.

'For the dog?' I whispered to Loud Report.

'Haw! No!' he replied, shocked at the notion that anyone might waste good food on a dog. 'For professors' supper.'

Then they sat politely sipping green tea till we'd finished.

'May I ask what you are doing here in Peking?' asked the waste-disposal professor.

'I'm on holiday,' I said.

'Looking for Manchu,' added Loud Report with a sneer.

The professors looked puzzled.

'I don't like Manchu,' explained Loud Report.

The professor of horticulture laughed. 'No? My husband's family is Manchu.'

'Manchu lazy,' persisted Loud Report, to my embarrassment. 'Sorry.'

Now the waste-disposal professor laughed. 'It's true,' he said.

'See, Misiter Socotolan?' cried Loud Report, vindicated at last. 'What I tell you?'

'Which Manchus are you looking for?' asked the waste-disposal professor.

'Aisin-Gioros, actually – surviving members of the former imperial family. But they all seem to be guarded by agents, and I'm not getting very far.'

'No? Well, here's one without any guards,' he said, with a mischievous smile. 'I am an Aisin-Gioro through my mother. My grandfather was Prince Yü-lang.'

I couldn't believe my luck! Prince Yü-lang was a well-known member of the imperial clan, and a Grand Councillor in 1910. His daughter was the second wife of Duke Jung, father of the Empress Beauty in Flower. But that wasn't his only link to the throne: he was also a direct descendant of the Emperor Enduring Glory through his grandfather, Tsai-ch'üan, fifth Prince Ting. I turned to the waste-disposal professor:

'So you are a cousin by marriage of P'u-yi – and perhaps even a pretender to the Dragon Throne?' I laughed to show that I was only joking. But the damage had been done. Imperceptibly the professor froze. Calling for the bill, he rose from the table, bowed slightly, wished me, in a loud voice for all to hear, 'Happy holidays,' and led his wife out of the restaurant.

I could have kicked myself for frightening off such a key witness, and I hadn't even got his name, so I wouldn't be able to find him again. I could only console myself with the knowledge that whoever he thought was listening wouldn't have learned very much more from my question than from the professor's own admission which prompted it. I wondered how much Loud Report had noticed and was relieved to see that he still had his nose in the rice bowl.

I may have lost the waste-disposal professor-prince, but another door was about to open. Back at the Bamboo Garden I was just looking up Prince Yü-lang in my reference notes when the telephone rang. It was Red Universe. Would I please go straight to the Ch'ien-men Hotel in the old Chinese quarter south of the Forbidden City: Duke Yü-yan was waiting for me.

THE Ch'ien-men Hotel is a large grey block with 410 rooms and three stars. The management describes the building as 'Chinese and Western classical in style'; in fact, it's a cross between multi-storey car park and Stalinist tower block. But it does have one attraction: it's the permanent home of the Li-yüan Peking Opera Theatre. Relishing the prospect of sharing the premises with the modern practitioners of an art-form so closely associated with the Manchu Emperors, I had originally planned to install myself at the Ch'ien-men for the whole of my stay in Peking, and I'd even given its address to friends at home.

In the event, and not for the first time, I changed my mind. But I had called in from time to time in search of letters, so I knew the place well by now – and I didn't like it. The atmosphere in the gloomy lobby was furtive bordering on sinister, the staff were cold and patronizing and the spivvy Chinese 'businessmen' who frequented the place whispered deals in dark corners or shouted showily into their new portable telephones; they may have been nothing more suspect than taxi-drivers (who enjoy five-star status in free-enterprise Peking), but they bore the stamp of black-marketeers. It wasn't just me – Loud Report picked up the same vibrations. 'Even in Manchu Empire,' he said, 'this was bad part of city.'

And now, as we went up in the lift to our rendezvous on an upper floor, clutching, for the second time, the bag of presents and cameras and tape-recorders, Loud Report shuddered: 'I don't like this place,' he said. In the glass on the lift wall I noticed a pimple on the end of my nose. The omens weren't good for an imperial audience.

To my surprise the audience chamber was a bedroom no different from any three-star overnighter anywhere in the world except for the lace antimacassars on the backs and arms of the chairs and the skirts covering the shame of their legs, and the lidded cups of green tea on the table. Why we should be meeting there I didn't understand – but this was China, where everything's upside-down and back-to-front.

An overweight little man of about forty, in an open-necked short-sleeved shirt, his lips pursed, his eyes calculating, met us at the door and introduced himself as Yü-yan's work-unit director, Mr Chang, principal of the Calligraphy Institute. And there at the dressing table, in an organized clutter of paper, brushes, seals and ink, his concentration focused on the thin fingers of his right hand as he deftly painted the characters of a calligraphic text, sat the Pretender to the Dragon Throne, Aisin-Gioro Yü-yan, *de jure* Emperor of China. When he'd finished his brushwork, he got up and shook hands, smiling more than politely. Small, frail, dapper, gentle, he was everything Loud Report had described, but his fine bones and small even features, his smooth skin, strong teeth and thick black hair belied his seventy-three years. He looked, in his crisp white open-necked shirt and grey flannels, like an off-duty prep-school master still confident of his effect on the undermatron.

But there were others in the room, lots of them: the Pretender's wife, Chang Yün-fang, shorter even than he and heavier, with grey hair, a cigarette in her hand and a disconnected, far-away look in her eye; Yü-yan's 'agent', Mr Kao, tall, unsympathetic, shifty-looking; a pretty young woman with a baby, who seemed to be Principal Chang's wife and child; a doe-eyed young artist from the Calligraphy Institute, who specialized in painting cats; a scruffy press photographer with his eye locked to a large old-fashioned camera; and a sour woman interpreter with a metal headband, who said she didn't know why she'd been asked along, because her language was French not English.

I wasn't sure whether they were all there for my meeting with the Pretender – and if so, why – or whether I'd caught the tail-end of someone else's session. As far as I could gather, the Pretender seemed to be holding court in his capacity as calligrapher; the object of the exercise was to sell his work; and the agent and the principal were the salesmen-negotiators. But I couldn't be sure and, as usual in China, no one offered an explanation. Bewildered though I was, antagonistic though I felt towards elements of this motley collection, I was determined to follow Loud Report's advice: sit still, shut up and keep smiling.

He, for his part, was to follow the plan we had worked out in the light of our misunderstandings in Ch'ang-ch'un: present credentials, explain the mission, establish the fee (if any), then haggle. I wanted a private meeting with Yü-yan, to talk to him about his life and views and family, and to photograph him. If necessary, I was prepared to make a modest payment, but only on condition that every *fen* of it went to Yü-yan himself.

Sitting on one of two single beds, with Loud Report on my left and the woman and child on the pillow to my right, the cat artist on the neighbouring bed (chain-smoking below a sign requesting No Smoking in Bed), Principal Chang, the Yü-yans and the agent on chairs beneath the window, the little room cloudy with cigarette smoke, its walls ringing with the gunfire of Chinese speech, I tried to smile, I tried really hard. But as the voices rose and the smoke thickened and the dollar signs multiplied in the agent's eyes, I could only fidget and seethe: what were these people talking about, why had their tones become so sharp, what was the Pretender thinking as he sat there so silent and dignified? Wasn't it rather unseemly discussing terms in front of him? Provoked beyond the limits of my short fuse, I exploded:

'Would you mind telling me just what the hell's going on here?' I shouted at poor Loud Report, who was doing no less than his very best on my behalf. He looked hurt, then irritated.

'Please, Misiter Socotolan,' he said through clenched teeth, 'smile and leave to me.'

'But what do they want? Why do they sound so cross. When's it going to finish?'

Loud Report put out a calming hand. 'It's all right. They say if you want talk with Mr Yü-yan, they know nothing about you, so you must pay $800. I tell them . . .'

I leapt off the bed. '*Eight – hundred – dollars?* Are you crazy? I haven't got $800. And if I had, I wouldn't pay it. I don't need to speak to Yü-yan that badly. What are we doing sitting in this horrid smoky little bedroom talking to these dreadful people? I've had enough.' I was all set to march out, but something in Loud Report's manner stopped me.

'If you go,' he said gravely, 'very very bad business, all is finished, never you speak to Mr Yü-yan, and maybe trouble for Loud Report. Please now, Misiter Socotolan, English boss, my friend, sit. Wait five minutes – and smile.'

Obediently, gratefully, I sat down, but I couldn't twist my angry face into a smile, so I stared at the floor.

The discussion continued and seemed less heated than before. After a few moments the Pretender got up and went to the bathroom. To my surprise Principal Chang followed him. Five minutes later they both emerged and the meeting seemed suddenly to reach a conclusion. Turning to me with a victorious wink, Loud Report announced that it was all over:

'Principal Chang is happy for you meet Mr Yü-yan and pay no money. But he want to see your questions first. No meeting until then. OK, Misiter Socotolan?'

'OK if you say so,' I thought, 'but I don't understand how they can have swung from $800 to nothing at all, and I don't really understand what we're all doing in this hotel bedroom anyway.'

'OK,' I said, with a tight-lipped smile. If it was all over, why wasn't anyone getting up and going? Perhaps they were waiting for me. Coldly I shook hands with Principal Chang and the agent; warmly with the Pretender and his wife, wondering if I should ever see them again.

In the lift going down I clapped an arm around Loud Report's shoulders and congratulated him on his diplomacy and wisdom and patience. It all seemed to have worked out satisfactorily, but I didn't know why, and I was deeply suspicious of the motives of Agent Kao and Principal Chang. Were they acting on behalf of the Public Security, or their own pockets? If the latter, why had they caved in so inexplicably in the matter of fees? What right had they to scrutinize questions which I wanted to put to Yü-yan? What would they be looking for: political taboos, or potential profits? And what had the Pretender and the Principal talked about in the bathroom? I was out of my depth.

'You are in China,' said Loud Report philosophically.

'Hmm,' I scowled.

Loud Report's forehead creased with concern. 'Misiter Socotolan,' he said, in a choked voice, 'my heart feel so heavy when I see your face so long. Please to smile.' He was irresistible, Loud Report, and I didn't deserve him.

It was wet outside and the roads were awash: cyclists hidden under plastic sheets splashed past, pedestrians ran for cover. The ordinariness of the scene cast a dreamlike blur over the meeting. An Imperial Audience in a hotel bedroom – it was absurd! I laughed aloud and turned to Loud Report to share the joke. Suddenly the button-eyed, stocky figure of Principal Chang caught us up. My mood had changed. If he could swing from $800 to nothing at all, the least I could do was to be polite. I grasped his hand and apologized for being angry, but explained that I hadn't understood what was going on; indeed, I still didn't. The principal looked pleased, if surprised. Dipping into his plastic briefcase, he fished out a wadge of photocopied pedigrees. These, he said, were just part of the famous Jade Register, the definitive imperial genealogy commissioned by P'u-yi in Manchukuo in 1937. The original belonged to Yü-yan. When next we met for the vetting of my questions, he would like to present me, he said, with a copy of the complete document; I wouldn't be disappointed – it was, quite literally, a hundred times more detailed than Professor Wang's reduced version. And there was other material he wanted me to have – but it would all have to wait till our next meeting. Having whetted my appetite, he withdrew the precious pages and slipped them back into his briefcase with a foxy look. The game wasn't over yet – and I was further than ever from understanding the rules.

'IT'S me!' cried the familiar voice on the telephone, with a squeal of laughter. 'Isn't this too exciting?'

'Annie? I don't believe it.'

Fey and attractive, the daughter of a Scottish baronet, Annie used to be my neighbour in Hampshire: a Titania trapped in the big house. Since then she'd broken free and taken up New Age healing. Now she was a wandering enchantress who could be relied on to surface in the most unlikely places.

'Where are you?' I asked.

'Just down the road.'

'In China?'

'Peking!'

'Whatever are you doing here?'

'"Overtoning" in Buddhist temples.'

I wasn't really surprised. Annie had 'regressed' in Texas for a doctorate in Inner Light Consciousness, 'networked' in Bulgaria with Orthodox monks, 'rapped' with the Russians on world peace; and, as an alternative practitioner, it was rumoured that she rubbed some pretty exalted feet.

Annie and an equally glamorous English friend, who makes silk flowers for some pretty exalted drawing rooms – and studies acupuncture in her spare time – were taking part in a pilgrimage to Tibet with a group of music and movement therapists, most of them women, from a summer school in Boulder, Colorado. All were committed in some way or other to pushing back the frontiers of conscious experience; Annie's particular bulldozer was a mystery called 'metamorphic technique'.

They'd come to Peking to chant mantras at dawn with a group of Buddhist monks on the great, circular, open-air altar in the Temple of Heaven. Here, on New Year's Day in the imperial past, the Emperor, as High Priest, used to offer up a live bullock as a sacrifice to bring blessings on his people over the next twelve months; it was a rite of such significance that the Chinese believed their very future depended on it.

The credentials of the Boulder chantresses were indisputably gilt-edged, but I did rather question – if only to myself – the authenticity of the Peking 'monks', who had only recently been readmitted to their temples – and were sometimes suspected of being reincarnated Public Security agents.

Peking's temples have served the state well since the collapse of the Empire: one of the capital's biggest Taoist shrines was for years a spy school; the temple near the Ch'i Chia compound was once the nerve-centre of the Public Security's phone-tapping operations; the Five Pagodas Temple behind the zoo was used to breed police dogs; and the Temple of Heaven complex itself, now a public park full of photo booths and ice-cream stalls, was in the 1930s a public execution ground.

The mecca of the Boulder party's pilgrimage was to be the great Buddhist stronghold near Lhasa, the Potala Palace, once the religious and political centre of Tibet, now the still-waiting seat of the exiled Dalai Lama. There, in a few days' time, they planned to join the persecuted monks in a programme of prayer and contemplation, culminating in a spiritual 'linking by chant' with the monks of the Tibetan monastery in Colorado. Annie demonstrated this deep chant down the telephone and tickled my ear with her bottom E; clearly the copula was more than symbolic.

If the Temple of Heaven, where Annie had been chanting, is the most photographed building in Peking, the city's most visible landmark must be the White Dagoba. It stands on a hill on Resplendent Jade Island in the south-east corner of Pei-hai Lake, rising up from the trees like a bollard with a rocket on top: striking, but not pretty. The Manchu Emperor Favourable Sway built it in the mid-seventeenth century to mark the first visit to Peking by a Dalai Lama. Immediately below the Dagoba, on the north side of the island overlooking the lake, is the Tower of Blue Reflection. And inside that is one of the best restaurants in China; it's called Fang Shan and it specializes in dishes from the court of the Manchus. With its Buddhist and imperial associations, Fang Shan was the ideal place for dinner for the three of us.

Booking wasn't easy, even with the clout of Annie's smart hotel. Fang Shan is the favourite haunt of Party leaders and foreign business-men. A week's notice is *de rigueur*: we gave three hours' and, to make matters worse, we planned to arrive at the time that most Peking restaurants close. The hotel receptionist laughed at the impossibility of our pulling it off, but Annie isn't easily beaten – and wasn't this time.

We took a taxi to Pei-hai Park and went in through the main gate. It was getting dark and the visitors were going home; only the courting couples stayed on, silhouetted in still and silent seemliness against the setting sun. We passed the Buddhist Hall of Receiving Light, high up on a fortified enclosure to our left; then through a decorative arch over the low stone Bridge of Eternal Peace, under another arch and on to Resplendent Jade; there we followed a winding path around the eastern edge of the island to the Tower of Blue Reflection, across a courtyard strewn with palms in porcelain censers, past a pair of marble lions and up a flight of steps into a pavilion as heavily rich and cheerless as a High Victorian church. This was the famous Fang Shan, its painted ceiling hung with decorated paper lanterns and silken swishes and supported by shiny blood-red columns, its walls panelled and papered. If the tables hadn't been covered with white cloths, we'd have fallen over them, for the place is so cavernous that the light cast by the lanterns never quite reaches the floor.

It was empty, or emptying, when we arrived, and the staff weren't pleased to see us.

'What you want?' snapped a tired waitress, decked out like a palace concubine, 'fifty, one hundred, two hundred and fifty, five hundred or one thousand?'

'One thousand what?' I snapped back.

'*Yuan*,' she replied unequivocally.

There was no menu, just five price bands – as inflated as Covent Garden opera tickets. This was free-market economics gone Oriental. We asked what the bottom one bought and the waitress rattled off an incomprehensible list ending with 'Quick, please!'

Annie generously offered to treat us to the middle band, and we settled down to a feast of many courses which piled around us faster than we could identify them. It started with shark's fin soup (into which the concubine-waitress grated some buffalo horn: 'To make babies,' she said, pointedly piling a mound on my plate.) Then came 'hundred-year-old' eggs (and they looked the part, but actually they were 1991 vintage, marinated in lime), minced pork stuffed in sesame buns, bird's nest soup (made from boiled up nest of the esculent swallow – and consisting mostly of its spittle), and the Empress Dowager's special weakness, steamed chestnut and honey cakes.

Beneficent Indulgence got the idea for these when she snatched a bun from a peasant during her infamous flight from besieged Peking in

148

1900. Although it was only a boring old steamed corn-bun, dry, yellow and hard, she was famished and thought it was as good as a fairy cake. When she got back to the Forbidden City at the end of the siege she ordered her head cook to find the recipe, but she didn't at all like the result: 'Ugh!' she said to the Chief Eunuch, 'it's as hard as nails. I can't even swallow it. How dare he send me this sort of rubbish! Have that cook killed.' Fearful for their lives, the under-cooks did some quick thinking and substituted macerated *marron* for flour, with a dollop of honey. That did the trick.

I didn't learn much more about the secrets of imperial cuisine that night – the staff were in too much of a hurry to get home – but the smallness of the pieces on each serving dish, combined with their lightness and delicacy, explained how the court survived the monstrous feasts served to them daily. P'u-yi records that Beneficent Indulgence had about a hundred main dishes laid out on six tables for her consumption alone. 'I had about thirty,' he adds modestly. Admittedly a lot of it was for show, part of a ceremony that went on just because it always had, but 'picking', as we had at Fang Shan that night, would have helped the Emperor through a good many of his ritual dinners.

Having seen the colossal gates at the entrance to Pei-hai Park, we took seriously the waitress's warnings about closing time and fled, with our glass slippers intact, two hours clear of midnight. But the cool night air and the moonlight on the lake and the emptiness were too much for Annie, who draped herself on an ornamental bridge below the Chamber for Reading the Classics and demonstrated her 'overtoning'. Concentrating hard for a moment, she produced a deep rumbling note which set up a sympathetic head resonance, creating a series of harmonics, and soon two strong clear dark notes were singing across the water to the Buddhist Temple of Pure Land on the north-western shore. We listened to hear if the wooden walls would throw them back, but it was too far.

'How did you do it?' I asked, impressed.

'You have to put your tongue in a difficult position,' she said, as though she wasn't quite sure herself.

The great gates were, indeed, closed when we got back across the Bridge of Eternal Peace, but inside the gatehouse a park-keeper was asleep with his head on a table. I knocked gently on his window and eventually woke him up. He was a big man and horribly ugly, with a squint and a dent in his forehead, and he wasn't pleased to have been disturbed, but when he caught sight of the pretty Western ladies, his face broke into a lecherous smile. Lumbering over to the gates, this Quasimodo unlocked a trap and released his Esmeraldas, and me, into an unlit street near the back of the Forbidden City.

LOUD Report was all nudges and winks and sly smiles when he came to collect me at the Bamboo Garden the next morning. Flopping into an armchair, he fanned his face with my Panama.

'Excuse me say so, Misiter Socotolan, but I think you dark donkey: you keep secret from Loud Report. Misiter Socotolan, I think you in love with Scottish lady!' He plunged the Panama over his face to cover his delighted embarrassment. Then, talking through the top of my hat, he said:

'When I telephone Bamboo Garden this morning no reply from your room. Why? Because you spend whole night with Scottish lady in China World Hotel. Misiter Socotolan, it's true, it's true!'

The time had come to settle this matter once and for all. But I had to balance the need for honesty against his ability to understand. I had spent the night at the Bamboo Garden – alone – I said, and I wasn't in love with the Scottish lady – or any other lady. Loud Report slid the hat up his face and on to the top of his head, and looked at me with an expression that was part pained and part puzzled.

'You don't love any lady?' he asked.

'I'm not *in* love with any lady.'

'But you like ladies?'

'Oh yes, very much. I couldn't live without them. Some of my best friends . . .'

'But no special lady?'

I shook my head. Loud Report's eyes clouded, his brow creased, as he absorbed this astonishing piece of news. Confused, he removed the hat again and slowly turned it around in his hands.

'You must be so lonely, Misiter Socotolan – living alone with no lady.'

'But I don't live alone. I share my house with a friend, a very close friend. I've known him for a long time and we have a lot of things in common and two dogs, and we used to have hens till the fox got them, and I'm really very happy.'

This simple explanation, which was only a little short of the absolute truth, smoothed away the worry from Loud Report's brow. He leapt to his feet and clapped the hat back on his head.

'I want to meet Scottish lady.'

'I'm afraid she's gone: she flew to Tibet early this morning. But I've got another lady for you.'

O N the first floor of a five-storey brick block in the south-eastern suburb of Ch'ao-yan we knocked on the door of Flat 2 and waited.

Li Shu-hsien – 'Aunt Li' – fifth and last wife of P'u-yi, had telephoned Red Universe out of the blue – whether with or without her 'agent' 's knowledge we never discovered – and invited me for a talk at home. Loud Report was interpreter, and Red Universe was playing duenna.

We waited with some trepidation, for Aunt Li's public reputation rests, to a large extent, on Edward Behr's *The Last Emperor*, which describes her as 'a shrew' with 'a sharp, nagging tongue', a 'misfortune' in P'u-yi's life. So I was expecting a harpy, half spitfire, half Fury, a cross between Beneficent Indulgence and Ena Sharples.

The door was answered by a small, fine-boned, birdlike woman, with a generous mouth and strong sad eyes. She was dressed simply but elegantly in a neat black skirt and an embroidered blouse of cream silk, and her short black hair looked freshly done.

She drew us through a little hall with a tiny, old-fashioned kitchen off it to the left and a bathroom opposite into a bright bed-sitting room, opening on to a small balcony. Loud Report and Red Universe sat on a sofa covered in white lace and I sat beside the narrow bed, which was covered with a blue flowery spread, while Aunt Li fetched some soft drinks from the fridge. Between me and the sofa stood a tall standard fan. By the balcony door was a desk piled with books and papers. And in the corner a table with a vase of plastic flowers and some familiar photographs.

One of the photos showed P'u-yi and Li Shu-hsien as unsmiling newlyweds in 1962 – she a nurse of thirty-seven, serious and responsible, facing the camera head-on; he an official history researcher in a smart Mao suit, nineteen years older, turning in to the camera over her left shoulder, more protected than protective. Another photograph, a happier one, showed the couple in conversation with Premier Chou En-lai, who helped to shield them from the forces of anarchy during the Cultural Revolution.

On a small table near me, inviting attention, was a recent issue of the French magazine *Vendredi, Samedi, Dimanche*, lying open at a double-page spread, a romantic photograph of Aunt Li in the park at Versailles, and the headline '*Moi, la Femme du Dernier Empereur*'.

If only to break the ice, I asked Aunt Li what she'd been doing in France. The ice was more than broken: it melted and the floodgates opened. In all innocence I had touched on her *idée fixe*. She'd been consulting a Paris lawyer, she said, about taking legal action against Edward Behr. Try as I might, I couldn't shift this subject from Aunt Li's mind, so, with her permission, I switched on the tape-recorder and listened to her soft, calm voice delivering its relentless monologue, later translated by Loud Report:

'Nothing Edward Behr wrote about me was true. When I read it I was very, very angry. He didn't understand my life with P'u-yi – he couldn't, because it was private to us. P'u-yi's family was royal and they didn't get on very well together. When he left Fu-shun Prison after ten years' re-education through labour and study, P'u-yi longed for a close and loving family. He had a lot of brothers and sisters but they were not happy together. When he met me in 1962 I understood this, because I had tasted bitterness, too. I lost my mother when I was small. Then my father, who was a bank clerk in Hang-chou, married again and I lived for nine years with my stepmother, who mistreated me. When I was fourteen my father died and for three years things got even worse. In 1941 I couldn't bear it any longer and I came to Peking to live with a cousin. But I did not like having to rely on others for a living, so I enrolled for training as a nurse, and, after a lot of hard work, I finally became independent. With this bond, P'u-yi and I were able to support one another.

'When I married P'u-yi, I found kindness for the first time. For almost six years, until his death, we were inseparable – and never once during all that time did he ever swear at me; everything he did made me happy, because we loved and respected each other. I shall never forget those wonderful days.

'So Edward Behr got it all wrong. I have never spoken to Mr Behr, we have never met. He did write me a letter saying he wanted to meet me, but there was no opportunity. Without meeting me, how could he write about me? He made everything up, and as a result my honour is damaged. In Paris, everyone said: "Is it true, this book?" "No," I said, "I have been slandered."

'During our five-and-a-half years of marriage P'u-yi had to go into hospital on nine separate occasions. When he was there, I was the only person who looked after him. Every day I had to travel on crowded buses to visit him. I'm a very warm-hearted person, but no one appreciated what I was doing for him. When he returned home, I nursed him and gave him his injections and pills. Yet Edward Behr says I never went to the hospital to look after him and that as he lay dying he called for me and I didn't come till too late. All of this is rubbish.

'On October 3rd, 1967, we had some guests to dinner at home. P'u-yi had a lovely time and lots of food – which is what he liked. At ten o'clock, after the guests had left, he was suddenly very ill and I had to take him to the hospital. At that time China was in the grip of the Cultural Revolution, so there was no one there to do anything for him – not even a doctor – I had to do everything, even though I wasn't well myself.

'P'u-yi was in hospital till October 17th. During all that time he had a room by himself, because his condition was so serious [he was suffering from cancer of the kidneys]. The room was tiny – too small even to draw up a chair to his bed. So I pulled two wooden benches along the corridor to his door and catnapped on those at night. I stayed with him like that until his last breath, leaving only to go home once a day to cook some food for us. So much for Mr Behr's accusations.

'In his book Edward Behr says that P'u-yi's body was cremated in hospital. This isn't true. Mr Behr says that no one would accept responsibility for the ashes, so one of P'u-yi's former concubines took them away, at the risk of her own life, and that she delivered them to Chou En-lai. All this is fabrication. When P'u-yi died, I took his body to the hospital mortuary, and the next day I laid him out and dressed him in a suit of cotton-padded clothes for the winter. Because his feet had swollen I bought him a pair of larger-sized shoes. Then I combed his hair, put on his favourite dark blue wool cap and covered his face with a white sheet. The next day I took him out to Eight Treasure Mountain to the masses' cemetery where he was cremated. I did all this by myself.

'When I married P'u-yi, he couldn't do a thing for himself. Because he had been Emperor for so many years, he didn't know how to live like an ordinary person. So I had to do everything, and sometimes, it's true, I did get a bit irritated with him. For example, once I was cooking something in the kitchen and I asked P'u-yi to fetch me some eggs and he dropped them on the floor: everyone saw this, and everyone was annoyed.

'P'u-yi couldn't do anything – he couldn't even dress himself. I had to do all the shopping, the cooking, washing-up, the laundry, the mending, the cleaning. And P'u-yi's wages weren't enough on their own, so I had to go to work. On top of this we had a lot of entertaining to do. P'u-yi was a great believer in Chinese traditional medicines and when he fell ill I had to prepare these for him, too. But I was young and I managed to cope somehow or other.

'Since my marriage I've had to suffer much hardship. And since P'u-yi's death things have been even worse. He didn't leave me any money, only a share of the royalties on his autobiography. So I have to depend on my pension to keep me alive. I'm only a woman, so no one helps me, and even though it's not so bad in China for a single woman, it's not so good either. Please tell the world the truth.'

In his book, *China's Last Emperor as an Ordinary Citizen*, Professor Wang records the background to P'u-yi's fifth and last marriage. In the autumn of 1961, two years after his release from Fu-shun Prison, P'u-yi was invited to dinner by Chairman Mao. It was a 'Hunan-flavoured family banquet' at home, and Mao turned to the former Emperor and said, 'You might get married again.' P'u-yi was advised to give serious consideration to the question of 'choosing a life partner and building a family'. The former Emperor was touched by Chairman Mao's concern, writes Wang, and his friends set about looking for a suitable wife for him. A few months later one of his colleagues on the Literary and Historical Materials Research Committee introduced him to Li Shu-hsien, over a cup of tea at the Cultural Club of the Chinese People's Political Consultative Conference. Through a mutual interest in medicine they took to one another instantly: he felt sorry for her unhappy childhood and, even though he was 'a specially pardoned war criminal, a former Emperor and top leader of the landlord class', she fell for his childlike nature. Four months later they were married. 'Trees may wither, stones may rot, but my mind will never change,' Li Shu-hsien vowed to him. 'Mountains may have tops, rivers may have sources, but the flower of our love will never fall,' P'u-yi vowed in return.

Aunt Li, noticing that our drinks had run dry, that always-hot Loud Report was on the verge of dehydration, left to fetch some more. I was disappointed that none of my questions had been answered. Had Aunt Li not understood them? Don't worry, said Red Universe, it's going very well. Loud Report looked rather glassy-eyed.

This seemed the moment for presents. When Aunt Li had refilled our glasses, I thanked her for seeing me and talking so freely, and presented her with some things from England, including a calligraphic pen set and a pound of coffee. Not to be outdone – for Chinese etiquette requires the matching of like with better – Aunt Li gave me a *cloisonné* seal pendant, which she ceremoniously hung around my neck, like a monarch investing; a Fujian cork picture of a traditional Chinese garden with a pavilion and bridges, clouds, a ravine, a willow tree and a pair of white rabbits; and a packet of prunes. Nor did her generosity stop there. For Red Universe she produced another seal pendant, a mauve blouse and a pair of white shoes; for Loud Report a fan and a white shirt. It was a very happy interlude, with much laughter and posing for snapshots. If giving gave Aunt Li more pleasure than receiving, the company of younger people – especially that of Red Universe, so pretty and intelligent, and of Loud Report, such a 'boy' – bucked her most. I got the impression that her life was not only lonely but even a little haunted. Each time she entered the room, she automatically bolted the connecting door, as though afraid of intruders. And once, when there was a knock at the front door, Aunt Li put a finger to her lips to shush us while she answered it. It can't be easy living with the ghost of a dead Emperor in a China on the verge of a capitalist revolution.

Determined to avoid a return to the subject of Edward Behr, I asked Aunt Li about Yü-yan. I'd heard, I said archly, that he regarded himself as P'u-yi's adopted son and heir – what was her view?

'Huh!' she snorted. 'P'u-yi never meant it seriously; there was nothing official about it. He didn't "appoint" him – he just asked him one day, when they were in the prisoner-of-war camp in Siberia, if he would like to become an adopted son, and, of course, Yü-yan said "Yes". P'u-yi never really regarded Yü-yan as his son and heir. Yü-yan and his family are only saying this now because the success of the film *The Last Emperor* has made imperialism temporarily fashionable. The other day when I was visiting Prince Kung's Palace, where Yü-yan is employed as an historical adviser, I was asked if I was his mother: "Certainly not," I said. "He's six years older than me." In all my time with P'u-yi Yü-yan never called him "Father", only "Uncle". And though they were very close – much closer than anyone else in the Aisin-Gioro family, sometimes, I felt, closer even than P'u-yi and me – it was Yü-yan who informed on P'u-yi at Fu-shun. We mustn't forget that.'

Aunt Li was referring to a key incident in the 're-education' programme, when Yü-yan, having succumbed to his gaolers' remorseless brainwashing, was consciously distancing himself from his former Emperor. Once he'd been what P'u-yi called 'a noble in name but a slave in fact', carrying out, even in prison, a wide range of menial tasks for the helpless P'u-yi, including washing his underclothes and mending his socks. Yü-yan's loyalty had been so unshakeable that P'u-yi had been able to put it to the test. In a passage of his autobiography, he says,

I asked him if he had ever had a disloyal thought, and he confessed that he had once felt that he had been wronged when I made him kneel on the ground for an hour as a punishment. When I told him that I would pardon him, he kowtowed to me, looking as happy as if he had just gone from hell to paradise.

By 1954 – four years into their sentence at Fu-shun – Yü-yan's loyalty had been undermined by Communist ideology. He ignored the dirty clothes piling up in the Emperor's cell, criticized him for his slowness and slovenliness, refused to serve him his food and sometimes cut him when they passed in the exercise yard. Furthermore, it was Yü-yan who forced P'u-yi to hand in to the authorities his suitcase with the false bottom full of 468 pieces of priceless imperial treasure. 'We are all guilty and should confess everything,' wrote Yü-yan in a secret note. 'If you hand them over, the Government will certainly treat you leniently.' And that's exactly what happened. 'As you have a peculiar history,' said the governor, when P'u-yi emptied the jewels on his desk, 'it is only natural that you should have some peculiar ideas. You broke the prison regulations by failing to hand these things over at once, but now that you have confessed, we shall not punish you.' Instead, to P'u-yi's astonishment, he was given a receipt for his property: 'remoulded' men, explained the governor, were of greater value to the state than baubles.

Then, in the spring of 1954, when the Chinese war-crimes investigators were in session at Fu-shun, cross-examining witnesses and extracting written confessions, P'u-yi learned that all his family and former staff in Ch'ang-ch'un had given evidence against him – among them Yü-yan, whose report revealed how P'u-yi had abused his orphan-pages and caused the death of the boy who had tried to escape.

But if Aunt Li was trying to suggest that Yü-yan had betrayed P'u-yi, she was forgetting both the pressure he was under to do so and P'u-yi's subsequent gratitude that he did, because it led eventually to P'u-yi's being successfully 'remoulded' and becoming what he calls in the apotheosis of *From Emperor to Citizen*, 'a new man . . . a real man'. This kind of propaganda may tarnish the honesty of the closing pages of his book, but there is no denying the underlying warmth of feeling they show for Yü-yan.

I didn't want to start a political argument with Aunt Li – it would have been rude, difficult through the medium of Loud Report and Red Universe, who were sharing the interpreting, and impossible without the book itself to back me up – but I needed to press her harder on the relationship between the two men in order to support Professor Wang's theory that the succession lay indisputably with Yü-yan.

Regardless of what went on in the unreal atmosphere of Fu-shun, I put it to Aunt Li, surely there was evidence to show that the bond between the two men transcended mere friendship? Wasn't there something symbolic, for instance, about P'u-yi's having entrusted the ashes of Jade Years, his beloved third wife, to the safe-keeping of Yü-yan? Didn't this imply that he wished the succession to continue there?

Aunt Li laughed – that, she said, was her doing:

'One day, just after I had married P'u-yi, I found a small wooden box in his store-room and I asked what it was. I felt a little frightened when he said it contained the ashes of Jade Years. Then, one night in July 1962, I thought I saw a woman in white creeping towards our bed. As she came nearer I recognized that it was Jade Years and I started screaming. This woke P'u-yi, who asked me what had happened, and I realized that I'd been dreaming – but it was so horribly vivid that my sheets were soaked with sweat. After this P'u-yi decided to move the ashes to Yü-yan's house.'

And were they still there?

Yes, buried under the floor in a ceramic jar, along with some clippings of her nails and a lock of her hair.

If Yü-yan wasn't P'u-yi's heir, then who was? Who had inherited the responsibility of worshipping his spirit and his ancestors' spirits at their tombs?

'I have,' said Aunt Li vehemently. 'I am his wife. We had no children, so I am his heir. China is a new China now. The Ch'ing dynasty has finished – it finished when P'u-yi abdicated in 1912. I never regarded P'u-yi as an Emperor – he was just a commoner, a citizen. Now that China is ruled by the Communist Party, there is no dynasty. So P'u-yi had nothing to pass on.' Aunt Li chuckled at the irony of it all. 'No money, no treasure, no throne, no title, no blood, nothing. It – is – all – finished.'

THE Empire has been longer dead than the last Emperor by half a century, but some of its old philosophies linger on. Eighty years after the dissolution of the Manchus and forty-three years after the proclamation of the People's Republic, ancestor-worship has been so deeply branded into the soul that death is still a potent force in Chinese life.

The Confucian idea was that a Chinese son should care for his parents while they were alive, bury them with the greatest honours when they died and maintain thereafter a steady stream of sacrificial comforts so they wouldn't lose face – or weight – in heaven; and if he failed to meet these basic requirements of filial piety, the son could expect to pay for it when his turn came.

Everything in the old Chinese way of life was retrospective. Take the honours system, for example. A son's disgrace no less disgraced his ancestors than his honours honoured them. So when a man was granted a title by the Emperor, filial devotion required him to seek a title one degree higher for his dead father – which is perfectly logical, after all, for we owe our begetting to our ancestors and not to our descendants.

In an eccentric travel book called *John Chinaman at Home* the Rev. E. J. Hardy (author of *How to be Happy though Married*) points out that 'a dead Chinaman is nearly always more considered than a living one'. So much so that if a man wanted to punish his enemy, he didn't kill him – he killed himself. Murder, according to the imperial Chinese's logic, hurt the enemy only once, but suicide offered the persecutor the chance to haunt the hapless victim till kingdom come.

So great was the Chinese regard for the afterlife, and the ultimate reckoning with the ancestors, that, contrary to our practice in the West, the Chinese reserved their choicest geographical sites not for the living but for the dead. 'In life,' writes Parson Hardy, 'a Chinaman pigs it in a hovel little raised above the level of the surrounding swamp; in death he occupies a breezy hillside spot, commanding often a charming view.'

That might have been all very well at the turn of the century, but burial is a voracious consumer of land – and the Chinese are profligate providers of corpses. Current government statistics show that an average of seven million Chinese people – the equivalent of the entire population of Greater London – die every year. If each dead Chinese were to be interred in a traditional burial mound measuring seventy-two square feet, then the state would need to set aside fifty-four square miles of land for graveyards each year. Given that the birth rate for 1992 – the Year of the Monkey, an auspicious sign for pregnant mothers – is expected to be twenty-four million, it's not difficult to see that burial is antisocial.

Anticipating these trends, Chairman Mao signed a cremation pledge in 1956, in the hope that the people would follow his example. And they did. But the Party didn't: Mao was Mao, after all – one of the greatest figures in the history of China – and when the Chairman's end eventually came, in 1976, the Party couldn't bring itself to honour his wishes. Instead it pickled him in a glass sarcophagus and built a huge granite mausoleum over it, on the most impressive site in T'ien-an-men Square. But the point had been made, and in the thirty-five years since Mao signed the pledge, cremation has gradually replaced interment.

P'u-yi's end in the People's Ashes Hall at Eight Treasure Mountain may have contravened every tenet of the imperial dispatching code, but it was a responsible, public-spirited gesture, which his widow justified to his brothers and sisters at a family meeting after his death. 'P'u-yi loved to go to places bustling with activity,' she reminded them, rather mysteriously. 'Putting his ashes with those of the masses is quite appropriate.'

It's now known that Premier Chou En-lai proposed building a mausoleum for the former Emperor to appease the Manchu minority. But, according to Professor Wang, P'u-chieh, as head of the family, vetoed the idea: 'It would be improper,' he ruled, 'because P'u-yi was just a citizen.'

For a whole month after his death Aunt Li took a bus out to Eight Treasure Mountain every day to be with her late husband's spirit. 'I would hold his ashes to my chest, weeping,' she said, 'and when I'd finished crying, I felt better.'

On May 29th, 1980, with the Gang of Four safely behind bars, the new Chinese leadership held a sort of civil funeral for P'u-yi, who had then been dead for thirteen years, and voted him, perversely – and, in the best Confucian tradition, posthumously – a Hero of the People's Revolution. After the 'memorial meeting', as it was called, Aunt Li went out to Eight Treasure Mountain and moved his ashes from the Masses' Hall to their new and, some might say, inappropriate resting place in the Hall of Revolutionary Heroes.

'I go to see him twice a year now,' she told me. 'Once on the anniversary of his death and once on Clear and Bright [the day in early April when Chinese families get together for a picnic and a bit of annual maintenance at the tombs of their ancestors]. Twenty-four years have passed since he died, and in that time no one else has been to see him except me. Not even his family. No one. Just me.'

Eight Treasure Mountain is, in fact, as flat as a pancake and, despite its fairy-tale name, no more romantic than Golders Green. Expecting a hillock, at least, I didn't realize we'd got there when our chauffeur-driven hired car left the suburban ring road a few miles from the centre of Peking and pulled up outside a red-and-gold pavilion, banked high with potted plants, like an Oriental garden centre.

Without Aunt Li, this pilgrimage would have been impossible, for, alone among the Aisin-Gioro family, she possessed the necessary pass. Although at first she'd refused, she telephoned Red Universe the day after our meeting to say she had changed her mind. To spare her the trouble of accompanying us, I'd suggested that she lend us her pass. Loud Report had been a little shocked at my presumption: 'Not possible, I think, Misiter Socotolan,' he'd judged, with a severe shaking of his head, as though I'd really overstepped the mark this time. But in the event Aunt Li had insisted on coming, too. And, in honour of her, Loud Report had booked the grandest limousine on the Bamboo Garden's books: a big black Nissan Cedric, with air-conditioning and leather upholstery.

Loud Report sat in the front beside the driver; I sat in the back with Aunt Li and Red Universe. 'Driver very nice man,' said Loud Report approvingly.

'Yes,' I agreed – because he was, and a careful and considerate driver, too.

'Yes,' echoed Loud Report, with a stagey nod. 'Very good driver.' If his praise seemed a little excessive, the reason soon became clear: 'Did you know, Misiter Socotolan, this man was driver for Teng Hsiao-p'ing?'

The delicious irony of being driven to see the last Emperor's ashes by one so close to the Communist seat of power quite took the sting out of the cost of the car. I longed to ask if China's senior leader were as bossy and short-tempered as his reputation suggested; and did he really hawk and spit as vigorously as a tubercular peasant – or was that a party trick he reserved for Mrs Thatcher? But I held my peace, and imagined instead.

It was baking hot and dazzling in the midday sun, and Aunt Li put on her sunglasses as she climbed out of the car. She had dressed for the occasion in a brilliant silk top of imperial yellow and a black skirt with smart black shoes sporting silver roses on their toes. She wore a gold necklace, a gold watch and on her right hand a gold ring engraved with what looked like a little crown.

At the crematorium office she handed over her pass, which two women officials examined with much chatter and gesticulation before giving up two sets of keys. Aunt Li, after a quarter of a century of regular visits, knew the ropes. With an encouraging wave, she led us along a covered walkway, through a garden and across a paved courtyard, planted with flowering shrubs and a pair of guardian ginkgos, to a dusty red building with a traditional tiled roof and a verandah supported by thin columns.

We were alone in the hot silence. Loud Report – fanning, mopping and puffing in the airless heat – looked around with wide eyes; he'd never been to a crematorium before and he wasn't used to the stillness.

Aunt Li turned the key in the padlock, released the chain and pushed open the heavy rust-red doors. We stumbled into the cool darkness of the Hall of Revolutionary Heroes. Once our eyes had adjusted to the gloom, we saw rows and rows of identical chocolate-coloured cabinets with glass doors, stacked four high and a dozen across, like display cases in an old-fashioned museum. Each cabinet was about two feet high by one-and-a-half across and a foot deep; most contained a photograph of the deceased with an identifying text, a casket of ashes and some plastic flowers.

Aunt Li's hero was in Cabinet 26, two down from the top at the end of the row, near a window. She unlocked the glass door and stood back to show us the contents: in the centre, a delicately carved wooden casket bearing a circular photograph of Citizen P'u-yi in spectacles and Mao suit; on the right, a little wicker basket of plastic flowers; on the left, an empty orange vase.

With tender efficiency, like the nurse she once was, Aunt Li removed each object and dusted it with a flannel she'd brought in her handbag. She was a wife doing the housework, but she was also a widow at her husband's shrine and, ashamed to be watching so private a rite, I turned away and waited with Loud Report and Red Universe in the shade of the verandah.

At length Aunt Li joined us, carrying the casket. It looked heavy and Loud Report, always the gentleman, ran forward to help her, bewilderment clouding his face as he remembered he was carrying the ashes of the last Manchu Emperor. Aunt Li asked if I would like to photograph the casket outside in the sun. That was just what I had wanted, but now I felt shy. Nevertheless, I snapped away at it and her and the Hall of Revolutionary Heroes in as many permutations as my roll of thirty-six would allow. Then Aunt Li suggested that I might like to be photographed holding the box myself. Curiously embarrassed, I handled the relic as gingerly as a time bomb and, standing over the Emperor's ashes in the burning sun, posing, eyes screwed up against the dazzle, for Loud Report's camera (which turned out to be broken again), I suddenly noticed a sweet scent rising like incense from the hot wooden box; for one mad moment I imagined the heat had rekindled the imperial cinders and that the Son of Heaven was about to manifest, like the genie in Aladdin's lamp. Loud Report read the panic in my face and rushed forward to rescue our hostess's husband from my trembling hands.

'All present and correct, Misiter Socotolan?' (Loud Report's English primer had given him a cliché for every occasion.)

'Yes, thank you, Loud Report. Just a bit hot, that's all. Shall we put him back now?'

'Hmmm!' said Loud Report, catching a whiff of the Emperor as he relieved me of the casket. 'He smell nice, like hotel men's room.'

'The box is made of scented cedarwood,' explained Aunt Li proudly, as she tucked it back in its hero's cabinet.

The orange vase beside it looked so pathetic without anything in it that I wished I'd had the foresight to bring some flowers with me. Impulsively, I ran back to the office in search of a stall. Some hope. The women officials, puzzled by the primitive daisies I tried to sketch in my notebook, giggled politely behind their hands.

Suddenly I remembered the camellia bush we'd passed on the way to the Hall of Revolutionary Heroes. Checking that I was alone, and feeling as nervously guilty as a grave-robber, I stole three scarlet blooms and some stalks of shiny leaves. Aunt Li, ignorant of their provenance, accepted them gracefully and arranged them in the vase, but the orange and scarlet clashed so violently that one bloom disintegrated in protest. Unperturbed, Aunt Li brushed the petals on to the floor and closed the glass door.

'My ambition,' she confided, through Loud Report, on the way back to the waiting car, 'is to build a proper tomb for P'u-yi at the Mausoleum of Abundant Peace in the Fragrant Hills – but I have not enough money. Do you speak French?' Caught off balance by this *non sequitur*, I nodded more enthusiastically than the truth warranted. 'Good. Perhaps you can help me with a very important matter.'

MONSIEUR, [I wrote to Aunt Li's Paris lawyer, M. Raymond Dohet, in a fax from Red Universe's office that afternoon] '*Permettez-moi à me présenter: je suis un ami anglais de Li Shu-hsien, la veuve de P'u-yi, le dernier Empereur mandchou. Mme Li m'a démandé pour découvrir, si possible, où est sa monnaie qui le journal* Vendredi, Samedi, Dimanche *lui a donné pour l'histoire de sa vie dans l'édition de* VSD *de la derniere semaine de mai 1991. Mme Li m'a dit que vous et la traducteuse chinoise Mlle Chang Wen-jou et M. Tang Chin-shih avez visité la Banque de Chine à Paris le 30 mai pour envoyer F10,000 à Mme Li au Pékin, mais jusqu'à ce moment Mme Li n'a pas reçu cette monnaie. Pouvez-vous me dire, s'il vous plaît, où est cette monnaie maintenant? C'est très important pour Mme Li. Merci mille fois, et pardonnez-mois pour le français si mauvais. Avec tous mes compliments, Tony Scotland.*'*

The French was so bad that even Red Universe winced. 'You wish to send this?' she asked, holding the letter at arm's length.

---

* Sir, Please allow me to introduce myself: I am an English friend of Li Shu-hsien, the widow of P'u-yi, the last Manchu Emperor. Mme Li has asked me to discover, if possible, where is the money that the paper *Vendredi, Samedi, Dimanche* has given her for her life-story in the *VSD* issue that came out in the last week of May 1991. Mme Li has told me that you and the Chinese translator Miss Chang Wen-jou and M. Tang Chin-shih went to the Bank of China in Paris on May 30th to send 10,000 francs to Mme Li in Peking, but until now Mme Li has not received the money. Could you please tell me where is the money now? This is very important to Mme Li. A thousand thanks, and forgive my terrible French. With my very best regards, T. S.

'Of course, I do,' I said irritably. 'There's nothing wrong with it. It's just business French.'

In fact, I doubted whether M. Dohet would be able to read my writing, let alone understand my execrable French; and even if he achieved both, it did occur to me that an Ancien Conseiller de Paris might think it odd that an Englishman called Scotland was faxing him from Peking on behalf of the ex-Emperor's widow's privy purse. But there wasn't time to do anything about it: I was leaving China in three days, and anyway Red Universe hadn't got a *Larousse*. The spirit of the thing was what counted, I persuaded myself. And, talking of spirits, wasn't Aunt Li banking on me, in a roundabout way, to lay her late husband to rest in the Fragrant Hills? Hadn't I a duty to the eleven imperial ancestors to lend a hand in the provision of a proper tomb for the last of the Manchus?

With one eye on Parnassus and the other on the Toshiba, I fed in my letter and dialled up Paris.

L OUD Report, on the instructions of Principal Chang, was delivering my list of twenty-eight questions to Yü-yan for his preliminary consideration, so that he would know what was expected of him when – if – we met again.

With the expert assistance of his father, Sun Hsüeh-ch'en (a professor at the Chinese Institute of Scientific and Technical Information), Loud Report had written out all the questions in Chinese. They began with 'Are you the "nephew" P'u-yi called "Little Jui"?' and ended with 'Do you regard yourself as the rightful ruler of China?' In between were questions about Yü-yan's ancestors, his wives, sons and grandsons; about court life in Ch'ang-ch'un, his commitment to the restoration cause and his attitude to the Japanese; prison life in Siberia and Fu-shun; his life and work since then; the whereabouts of Jade Years' ashes; and, of course, the circumstances of his appointment to the succession.

Loud Report had taken with him a camera, a tape-recorder and, for the third time, all my little gifts. Just on the off chance.

W ITH only three days left in China I deeply resented having to waste one of them sitting in my room at the Bamboo Garden, with the balcony doors closed and the curtains drawn against the sun, breathing in the fetid smell of drains and listening to the interminable clanking of the air-conditioning, as I waited for the telephone to bring me news – from Loud Report about his meeting with the Pretender, from Principal Chang about my next meeting with Yü-yan and from Paris or Aunt Li about her missing francs.

Throughout the day I'd been fending off the straw-hatted, cotton-trousered, barefooted cleaning women with their besoms and buckets. It infuriated me that they wouldn't accept that I didn't want my room cleaned. I was paying for it, after all, and if I chose to lock them out, well, that was my prerogative. Besides, they never did clean it anyway: they simply swabbed the used glasses with a grimy rag, refilled the Thermos with more undrinkable water, made the bed with half the sheet tucked under the mattress, wiped out the bath with the towels (which they then re-hung on the rail, as new), replaced the 'sanitized' band, with its supposedly reassuring red cross, on the broken lavatory seat and folded the exposed sheet of loo paper into the arrow-head that hotels all over the world think we're daft enough to mistake for the start of a new roll.

It was late afternoon and, in a state of depression, frustration and gloom, I was cooling down in a bath scented with Armani aftershave, sucking a juicy baby pineapple. Bits of rind floated in the water around me; my penknife, sticky with pineapple juice, lay on the lavatory seat; my freshly washed pants and shirts were dripping on my head from the makeshift line above. The radio, by my bed next door, was playing the Ping-chu opera *Eliminating the Spies in the Ancient City*.

Serious music is available on no fewer than four radio stations in Peking, two of them in stereo. Their programmes start at about 6 a.m. and close down at 12 a.m. And the range of music they broadcast is remarkably eclectic: from Chinese opera to Wagner and even Tippett, from *pipa* solos to guitar transcriptions of hits from Western musicals, from the ballet *The Red Detachment of Women* to Bach played on authentic instruments; Turkish love songs, French accordion music, traditional court music of Japan, Romanian dances and Sir Arnold Bax's Symphony Number 1. Full details in the indispensable *China Daily*. It would have been fine if the hotel radio worked properly, but there was a fault on the volume control which meant that it only received anything at full blast, which was why I couldn't listen unless I was in the bathroom with the door closed.

All might have been well if it hadn't been for the radio. But *Eliminating the Spies* had worked itself up to such a lather of passion that I didn't hear the bell or the front door opening or the raised voice or the banging on the bathroom door. And suddenly there was a woman on the bath-mat. Waving a brown envelope in the air, she released a volley of agitated Chinese which sent me reeling back in the bath, poleaxed. As my ears attuned to her speech, I began to recognize a leitmotiv: whatever her message was it had something to do with 'Wang'.

'Professor Wang?' I ventured cautiously.

The effect was electric: she closed her eyes and sighed ecstatically, as though I'd come to the relief of Mafeking. Unable to get out of the bath, because my visitor was blocking the path to the towel rail, and aware that she wasn't going to leave till she'd explained her mission, I asked her if she would mind opening the brown envelope. I reached across to the lavatory seat for my penknife, rinsing the sticky blade in the bath, and handed it over, to help her to understand. Puzzled – but not alarmed, as I suppose she might have been – she hesitated for a moment. Then, with a laugh, she slipped the blade under the envelope flap and withdrew a dozen photographs of miscellaneous Wangs – Professor Wang, Mrs Wang, the boy Wangs and Mr Interpreter Wang, with Loud Report and me. She looked triumphant.

'Aren't they nice!' I exclaimed. 'How very kind of the professor! If you'd just give me a minute I'll put something on and perhaps you'd like to stay and have a drink?'

She understood no more English than I Chinese, but I hoped my tone and the general context of our meeting might convey something of my meaning. This was China, however – the land of topsy-turvydom, where a man shakes his own hand when he meets you, laughs when he announces the death of a relative, wears white at a funeral, plays badminton with his feet, calls North-East East-North, rows a boat facing the wrong direction, mounts a horse from the wrong side, knits his socks from the toe upwards, stacks his books in piles and not rows, eats his fruit unripe, paints the soles of his shoes white and goes to sleep with his neck on a block of wood. Mistaking my wave in the direction of the bedroom for a wave of dismissal, the lady left, crestfallen. By the time I'd got out of the bath and wrapped myself in a towel she'd disappeared down the corridor.

The cleaning women, who'd been lurking in their cupboard with jam jars of cold green tea waiting for just this chance, pushed through my open door. Naked man or no, they were determined to do my room. All right, I thought, if that's the way they want to play it, I'll show them. Grabbing one of their besoms and pushing aside the two beds, I attacked the dusty carpet and its accumulated litter of overnight detritus with such manic ferocity that the women, fearing that the northern spirits had got me, dropped their cleaning things and fled in the wake of the Wangs' messenger.

The telephone rang.

'Hello!' said a pleasant Chinese voice in English, 'Do I speak with Mr Scotland, scholar of Manchu history? I am university professor – friend of colleague of Red Universe – and I wish to discuss comparative cultures of early Chinese civilizations . . .'

'This isn't a frightfully convenient moment, actually,' I said, grabbing the towel which was slipping from my waist, 'I'm having a bath.' I might have announced I was having a baby for all the effect it had.

'I am very interested in this subject,' the caller continued, regardless. 'Did you know that there is a writing of Confucius which foretells the Gulf War?'

My towel fell off. As I bent to retrieve it, the telephone slipped from my hand. From somewhere under my bed the professor droned on about Chinese civilization. Bare, baffled and beaten, I banged my head on the pillow.

'Hrr-hmm.'

Looking up, I saw the boy from reception, bearing a tray of fruit.

'With vice-manager's compliments,' he said.

IT used to be thought that the pavilion-topped Prospect Hill which dominates the northern end of the Forbidden City was a gigantic coal heap in disguise, a secret store of fuel in case of siege – hence its nickname, Coal Hill. Man-made it certainly is – the five symmetrical peaks, each supporting an open-framed, white-painted, blue-and-yellow-tiled pavilion, are too perfect to be natural – but coal isn't the material: in fact, it's built of the earth excavated from the moats and ornamental lakes around the Forbidden City.

The original purpose was threefold: to protect the Son of Heaven from the evil influences believed to haunt the gloomy and unpropitious north – it was for this reason that all imperial architecture always turned its back on the north and faced instead the sunny and auspicious south; to screen him from the cold winds which blew down from the Mongolian Steppes; and to provide him with a pretty backdrop.

The Mings, who built it in the Middle Ages, called it the Protecting Hill of the Great Within. When the Manchus came they planted its slopes with orchards and changed its name to Hundred Fruits Hill. Latterly it was stocked with hares and pheasants and other small country creatures to lend authenticity to the impression of *rus in urbe*. Today Coal Hill is a public park separated from the purple walls of the Forbidden City and its northern entrance, the Gate of Spiritual Valour, by a wide and busy street which runs across what used to be a huge parade ground.

From my first-floor balcony at the Bamboo Garden, if I leaned right over and pushed aside the thick pine branches, I could just see the top of Coal Hill. Frustrated and caged as I then felt, it represented the same spirit of freedom as the emperors must have experienced when they gazed up at it from the Forbidden City. I might have only two days left in Peking, but what was the point of wasting time waiting for the telephone to ring? If I didn't get to talk to the Pretender what did it matter? I'd established who he was and that was the main thing. A second day's telephone-watching in my Bamboo Garden cell and I'd go mad.

Grabbing one of the vice-manager's complimentary bananas and my Panama, I set off for an outing to Coal Hill.

Seeing might be believing, but it isn't reaching. I made the mistake, common enough in vast, sprawling, organic Peking, of thinking that my destination was closer than it actually was. Sodden and breathless, I reached the bottom of Coal Hill as exhausted as though I'd run all the way from Ulan Bator. Like a schoolboy I bought myself an ice, and like a pensioner I rested on a bench in the cooling shade of a plane tree. Having got my breath back, I bought a ticket at the eastern gate and, convinced, despite the wretched evidence to the contrary, that I was still a stripling, I hurled myself up the almost sheer path to the summit and collapsed in a box hedge within a hundred yards. At least I thought it was a box hedge – till it kicked and screamed. I was sitting, it seemed, on a courting couple, their limbs locked together in kissless, maidenly embrace, and the neighbouring shrub I grabbed hold of to hoist myself up was another – no less virginal – courting couple, and the bushes and trees beyond were alive with more of the same. I apologized and dusted myself down and tried not to notice the electric susurration of decorous petting that radiated from the foliage all the way to the top.

At the top itself, in the central Pavilion of Ten Thousand Springs, a party of brightly dressed schoolchildren, oblivious of the spectacular views around them, were concentrating intently on a bristly-headed boy delivering what seemed to be some kind of political testimony with such sinuous physicality that one of the girls was moaning gently, like a vestal jive-bunny.

Down below us, to the south, lay the boxlike outlines of the Forbidden City, with its tiled roofs glinting in the sun; while all around spread the chaotic asymmetry of the capital city of China, all 7,000 square miles of it, the home of ten million people.

I descended on the western side, following the voice of a tenor singing an Italian opera aria. I never found the tenor, but, at the bottom under a great cedar, I stumbled on a group of working women doing their T'ai-chi-ch'uan exercises, arms outstretched, bodies swinging low in smooth slow rhythm, eyes glazed in quiet concentration. I watched for some minutes, admiring their unselfconsciousness as much as their discipline and coordination. Suddenly it was all over, and to my amazement the women broke into couples and waltzed sedately around the cedar trunk to the tune of 'Edelweiss' which one of the women sang in Chinese to the accompaniment of a cassette hanging in the branches.

THERE were two notes waiting for me at the Bamboo Garden. 'The money has come from Paris,' said one, from Red Universe. 'Aunt Li invites us all to dinner tonight. Please telephone my office.'

The other was from Loud Report: 'Success-full.'

'THE money has been paid,' confirmed Aunt Li, beaming, as she welcomed us for dinner. 'Thank you for arranging it.'

I wasn't at all convinced that I'd arranged anything. Certainly, I hadn't received and still, to this day, haven't received, any reply to my illiterate fax. But it hardly mattered who had secured the transfer of funds: the main thing was that Aunt Li had got her francs and could now proceed with her plan to build a proper tomb for P'u-yi.

I had bought our hostess some French chocolates at the hard currency shop, the Friendship Store, next door to Red Universe's office and, despite Loud Report's snort of disapproval – 'You can't give chocolates to a woman' – Aunt Li seemed pleased. In return – for giving never works one way in China – she presented me with some wicker bowls.

Unlike the practice in the West where the guests sit around drinking for an hour first, working up an appetite and playing social placing games, at Aunt Li's that night dinner was waiting on the table in the bed-sitting room as we entered, and we were encouraged to plunge right in. The question was where to begin, for the table was heaped with dishes: a dozen varieties of edible fungus, cold fish cutlets, hot sea cucumbers, tomatoes in sugar, omelettes, dried meats, soup, sweet-and-sour carp. All had been prepared by Aunt Li in her little kitchen, and now she hovered over us, assiduously replenishing our plates like an Oriental *Hausfrau*, with an enigmatic smile, half solicitous, half wilful.

My Western response was to eat – or try to eat – all she piled on my plate, but, when my capacity reached its absolute limit, Loud Report, observing a certain clandestine loosening of the belt, whispered that if I stopped eating Aunt Li would stop piling: Chinese manners, he explained, require a hostess to continue offering more so long as her guest continues to eat.

It reminded me of what Professor Wang had told of P'u-yi's obsession with food. There was nothing the former Emperor enjoyed more, he'd said, than communal dining. In Ch'ang-ch'un he used to gather his brothers, sisters, nephews and their spouses at the great U-shaped table in the formal dining room of the Salt Tax Palace. 'He loved to see everyone grabbing at plates of food, all at once,' the professor said. 'And P'u-yi himself was the main grabber.'

Presumably it was a reaction against the lonely feasts of his childhood, when, as the infant Son of Heaven in his schoolroom in the Palace of the Nurture of the Mind, he'd had to eat his way, single-handedly, through twenty or more main dishes three times a day, watched by dozens of kneeling eunuchs. The operation was called 'using the viands', and when each meal was over, the senior Eunuch-of-the-Presence had to give a full and detailed report to the three High Consort mothers, ending with the formula, 'and the Lord of Ten Thousand Years consumed it with relish'. Actually, he'd done nothing of the kind, but in imperial China facts were always subservient to the rituals of tradition.

Much later, after his pardon and release from prison and his marriage to Li Shu-hsien (by which time the former Emperor's appetite had waned to a weakness for steamed gold-and-silver cake – made of corn and wheat flour – and the occasional outing to a local restaurant for fried fish and crispy chicken), P'u-yi found another outlet for his gregariousness: he used to invite the neighbours' children round for tea parties, with lots of sweets and cakes and dressing up. This was in 1963, when he was working for the Party's Literary and Historical Materials Research Committee and he and Aunt Li were living in a spacious courtyard dwelling in Tung-kuan-yin Lane in West Peking, with two bedrooms, two sitting rooms, a dining room, bathroom, store-room (where Jade Years' ashes were kept), and pine, pear and banyan trees.

Professor Wang makes the point again and again that P'u-yi was fond of children. He especially enjoyed telling stories and playing games – and joining them for nursery food. Fatherless himself, he did consider adopting a child, but Aunt Li felt that her health wasn't up to it, and he didn't insist.

When Aunt Li was satisfied that I really didn't want more to eat, she asked how many children I had. She seemed rather disappointed that I wasn't even married and gratifyingly disbelieving that I was as middle-aged as I promised I was. A little embarrassed, she switched her attention to my shoes. 'They are like Chinese shoes,' she said. Since I rather prided myself on their being distinctly, and expensively, English, I was faintly miffed; Loud Report, who knew this, smiled to himself.

At last even Loud Report had to surrender to saturation and, with a burp – and a rueful look on his face – he stretched his legs out straight to give his stomach more room to expand. For some minutes he and I found it actually painful to breathe, we were so full. I felt ashamed and envied Red Universe her self-control – and better manners. Aunt Li sat smugly with her hands in her lap: two bloated men was proof that she'd acquitted herself beyond the call of duty.

After a brief rest we helped to clear the dishes. Then, having brushed the tablecloth and washed our hands and faces, we returned to the attack with hunks of water melon.

Aunt Li saw us down the unlit stairs with a little torch. Outside it was raining and the peasants who'd come up from the country to sell their melons were sheltering in lamp-lit tents on the pavement – the men, shirtless, playing cards beside mounds of fruit; the women, in striped pyjamas, asleep on straw pallets.

LOUD Report's 'Success-full' meant that his meeting with Yü-yan had gone well: the Pretender had approved my twenty-eight questions and was looking forward to giving me the answers in person. But the Pretender was only a puppet. The strings were pulled by Principal Chang – whether for ideological or financial reasons, I still wasn't sure – and the next move was up to him.

We met, at the principal's request, in the Ch'ien-men Hotel, in a shadowy alcove of the lobby, by the long curving glass counter of the crafts shop, under the gaze of a hundred brightly coloured Peking Opera masks – and three young sales people, standing, bored, sleepy and silent, their ears quivering like radio aerials.

I had no idea why Principal Chang seemed to spend so much time at the Ch'ien-men. Perhaps he used it as a sort of Bond Street gallery-cum-office, where his better students could produce, display and sell their calligraphic works for a week at a time. But I didn't understand why this couldn't be done, more conveniently, more cheaply, less furtively, in the Calligraphic Institute itself. Today though, it was mine not to reason why: Loud Report and Red Universe had begged me to sit quietly and smile sweetly while they did the talking. The object was to persuade Principal Chang to give me unlimited access to Yü-yan for the lowest possible price.

The meeting began with an examination of my questions. Never mind that the Pretender himself had already approved all twenty-eight, the principal was distinctly unhappy about a number of them, particularly those relating to Manchukuo and the Japanese, the succession, Siberia, Fu-shun and Jade Years. Mr Scotland must understand, he said, that Yü-yan was an old man who'd had a hard life and didn't want to be reminded of the bad times. Quite, my advocates countered, but Mr Scotland would be very sensitive in his questioning and Yü-yan wouldn't have to answer if he didn't want to – though he had already given a clear indication that he was happy to answer them all. OK, said the principal, tell you what: Mr Scotland can put all twenty-eight questions to me tomorrow and I'll answer every one of them. That, I replied, would be acceptable if I could attribute the principal's answers to Yü-yan himself, but I would want to hear from Yü-yan's own lips that he approved of the arrangement. The principal looked uneasy. Finally, and with none too good a grace, he grabbed the list again and ticked off five questions – all easy genealogical ones – and at Red Universe's wise insistence, for she guessed that five could probably be pushed to twenty-eight once we'd got the Pretender talking, I agreed.

There remained only the matter of money and, between them, the negotiating parties reached an elegant arrangement, whereby I would purchase for the equivalent of £100 a piece of Yü-yan's calligraphic work, which would give me the right to take and publish photographs and to ask the five approved questions.

The principal narrowed his black eyes and watched me warily as I considered the proposal. Catching a surreptitious wink from Loud Report, I assented. The principal leaned forward and patted my knee with a beautifully manicured hand.

Upstairs, in the same bedroom as last time, wearing a white open-necked shirt with the sleeves rolled up and grey flannels tightly belted around his slim waist, the Pretender was working on a calligraphic poem, while his wife lay on one of the beds, wreathed in cigarette smoke.

When Yü-yan had finished his poem, we all shook hands again. At last, after three foiled attempts, I was able to hand over the presents I'd chosen so carefully in London: a calligraphic pen with a range of specialist nibs and ink, a book about English calligraphy, a pound of Whittard's coffee, 200 American cigarettes and, in an envelope with his name on it (lest there be any doubt when it came to the reckoning with the principal), the cash. The Pretender then invited me to choose a piece of calligraphy. Ignorant of the art, unable even to understand what the characters represented, I selected the one he had just finished: at least, I thought meanly, there could be no doubt that Yü-yan had done it.

The painting – for that is how it's described – measures just under three feet high by just over one wide, and comprises four large, thick, brush-painted characters in black ink, one on top of the other, with Yü-yan's full name and seal (in red ink) at the bottom left, and the place and date of execution balancing that at the top right. I asked the meaning of the four characters and was told the first (*Mo*) meant Chinese ink, the second (*Hai*) meant Sea, the third (*Ch'ien*) was One

Fig. C: Yü-yan's calligraphic poem, 'The Eternal Ocean of the Art of Calligraphy', bought by the author in Peking, in June 1991. On the left are the Pretender's signature and seals; the four characters of the text are in the middle; and on the right are the date and place of execution.

Thousand and the last (*Ch'iu*) represented Autumn. Together they could be read as something like: 'The Eternal Ocean of the Art of Calligraphy'.

Yü-yan laughed as I gazed at his work, charmed but somewhat bewildered. 'Mr Scotland,' he told Loud Report, 'looks as blank when he "reads" my Chinese calligraphy as I feel when I "read" his book of English calligraphy!'

Fig. D: The Pretender's signature and seal.

Ever since Professor Wang had identified Yü-yan as the Pretender, the man who would be Emperor, I had pursued him with a single-minded determination. Now, at last, I'd run him to ground – and all of a sudden I wondered why. I already knew the answers to my questions, thanks to the co-operation of Professor Wang and Aunt Li; repeating them to Yü-yan himself was really no more than a journalistic tidiness. He was an old man who had been badly buffeted about by life without ever really understanding why; years of brainwashing and hard labour must have taken their toll. He was unlikely to want to tell me very much I didn't already know; and he would be especially guarded in the presence of Principal Chang, his work-unit director. So I didn't expect his answers would reveal very much. Nor did I mind if they didn't, for all I wanted was corroboration of what I already knew – from the horse's mouth.

I switched on the tape-recorder and a silence fell on the hotel bedroom as we all waited for my first question. Suddenly exposed, I felt my self-confidence ebbing away. What right had I to disturb so many lives in order to satisfy a silly whim? They none of them knew the real purpose of my quest, and I really had no idea of the consequences for them of their agreeing to help me. I was encouraging them to step out of line in a society where any errant act is regarded with grave suspicion. It's true that they'd all volunteered their assistance and that they all stood to gain something by it: Professor Wang wanted wider academic kudos; Mr Interpreter Wang was glad of the opportunity to practise his English and to earn some foreign currency; Aunt Li hoped I would restore her reputation as a good wife; Principal Chang was after the money; Red Universe was motivated by loyalty to her boss, who had asked her to help a friend of his niece; Loud Report was having a jolly jape, expenses paid; and the Pretender had sold another piece of calligraphy. But they couldn't know how I would interpret their roles in my book: they'd trusted me to represent them honestly, and perhaps their real reward lay in my honouring that trust. Perhaps, in other words, the chances of my being able actually to help them were greater than the potential risk their contact with me exposed them to. So it was up to me. Daunted by the responsibility, but glad it was mine, I felt strengthened for this finishing straight.

I studied the faces around me. Loud Report and Red Universe looked apprehensive, the principal was suspicious, Yü-yan's wife amused and the Pretender, sitting, erect and collected, in a lace-draped armchair, was waiting expectantly.

'Are you "Little Jui"?' I asked.

Red Universe translated the question and Loud Report translated the reply.

'Yes.'

'How did the name originate?'

'We used to have many names in old China. My family name is Aisin-Gioro. Yü-yan is my given name. My court name was Yan-jui. When P'u-yi summoned me to Ch'ang-ch'un, he gave me the familiar name "Little Jui".'

'What was your father's full name, and whom did he marry?'

'Beitzu Aisin-Gioro P'u-ch'eng. My mother's name was Ching-kuei, of the Manchu clan of Fu-ch'a.'

'Where and when were you born?'

'In 1918, in the Tun Wang-fu, the palace of my grandfather, Beileh Tsai-lien, son of Prince Tun. It was a large palace with several hundred rooms, and it occupied a site measuring 70,000 *mu* [about 11.5 acres] on Tung-hsieh Street in the west of Peking. But there's nothing left now. It's disappeared without trace – you can't even find a single roof tile.'

And now the fifth and last permitted question. It wasn't an interesting one. Was I wise to waste what might be my only opportunity to ask Yü-yan if he regarded himself as the last Emperor's son and heir? Things seemed to be going smoothly – surely the principal wouldn't stop me now? I took a chance and pressed on, as planned.

'Whom did Prince Tun marry, and when?'

Yü-yan chuckled. 'I don't know. I wasn't born.' The tension was broken and, if only from relief, we laughed, too. The principal showed no sign of intervening, so I continued with my questions and asked the Pretender about his sons.

The eldest of the three – the man poised to succeed Yü-yan as Pretender – is Hêng-chen, known as Yüan-yüan, who was born in 1944, the elder of two sons by Yü-yan's first wife, Ching-lan of the Manchu clan of Ma-chia (she died in T'ien-ching while Yü-yan was a prisoner-of-war in Siberia). Yüan-yüan broke his hand in an accident at work some years ago, which prevented his earning his living through manual labour (the implication being that this was the only honest way to work in Communist China); he is now a film projectionist with the Crop Production Unit of the People's Liberation Army in the city of Shihezi in the mainly Muslim Hsin-chiang Uighur Autonomous Region in the far North-West of China. His wife, Tu Yan-ling, is a ticket seller at the local public baths and they have three children: two girls (by Tu Yan-ling's first marriage) and a teenage boy, Hêng-hsin – all of whom have chosen to abandon the surname of Aisin-Gioro in favour of Hêng, the first character of their given names.

Yü-yan's second son is Aisin-Gioro Hêng-k'ai, known as Li-li, who was born in 1945, the younger son of Yü-yan's Manchu first wife. Li-li is an electrician at an agricultural hospital in Ho-pei Province, not far from T'ien-ching, where he was born. His wife, Liu Hsiu-chüan, is a teacher and they have one son, a twelve-year-old called Ying-hui, who, like so many other members of the Aisin-Gioro family, uses the common Chinese surname, Chin – which gives them some protection from persecution whenever the tide of political opinion turns anti-imperial.

The third son – Yü-yan's only child by his second wife, Chang Yün-fang – is the banker Tung-tung, born in Shan-hsi Province in 1966; and he, as we know, has no scruples about his Manchu origins: his full name is Chia-pin Aisin-Gioro Hêng-chün. P'u-yi took a shine to this boy, gave him the name Hêng-t'ao and proposed to adopt him. But Chang Yün-fang objected, and after P'u-yi's death she changed back the boy's name to Hêng-chün.

So far so good. I glanced at Principal Chang, who still showed no sign of wanting to bring the interview to a close. So I went on.

'When did you leave home in Peking and go north-east to Ch'ang-ch'un?'

'In 1936. I went with my elder brother Yü-t'ai; he died about ten years later.'

'What were your duties in P'u-yi's court?'

'I didn't have any – I just studied with the other imperial "nephews" at court. We had excellent wages and living conditions.'

Without looking at Principal Chang, I slipped in a banned question: 'P'u-yi believed the Japanese would restore him to the Dragon Throne – did you believe this, too?'

'At that time,' the Pretender replied, 'my brother and I were very poor. We threw in our lot with the Emperor just to earn a living. It never occurred to me to ask the Japanese whether they planned to help the restoration.' The principal didn't bat an eyelid.

'You were very close to P'u-yi during the Manchukuo years – perhaps closer than anyone else – but later, in the War Criminals' Prison in Fu-shun, you drifted apart. Why?'

'In Ch'ang-ch'un I used to help P'u-yi with his daily chores. That was why my relations with him were better than anyone else's. At Fu-shun this relationship continued – but only for a time.'

'Did you remain friends afterwards?'

'Yes. I used to call on him till he died. We were friends to the end. In fact, Li Shu-hsien used to complain that P'u-yi was nicer to me than to her!'

Still no signal from the principal.

'What did you do after leaving Fu-shun in 1957?' I asked.

'At first I was given a job teaching Chinese at a workers' further education centre in Peking. But when Chairman Mao launched the Great Leap Forward in 1958, I had to switch to washing and pressing work at a haberdashery factory in Peking. [Although he had been pardoned for his role as a collaborator with the Japanese in Manchukuo, he was still politically out of favour.] In 1959 I was suddenly arrested and sent for hard labour at the T'ien-t'ang-ho Farm [a Public Security detention centre in the suburbs of Peking]. During this time I was allowed to return home several times a month to visit my family – and P'u-yi, who had just been released from Fu-shun.'

I longed to ask Yü-yan what these experiences had meant to him. Didn't he feel any resentment towards P'u-yi for all that he'd been through, since allying himself to the imperial cause in 1936? Or towards the Republic for the persecutions which had continued long after his official pardon? What had 'hard labour' actually involved? Was he frightened that the tide might turn again? What were his real feelings about anything? But I knew I couldn't broaden our discussion; I was lucky enough to be able to conduct even this formal interview.

'In 1966 the great storm of the Cultural Revolution broke over China – how did this affect you personally?'

'I was arrested again and sent to Shan-hsi Province for thirteen years of re-education through labour.'

'Were you separated from your family for all this time?'

'My two eldest sons had left home. My wife and our third son moved to Shun-yi County in the outer suburbs of Peking, so that Tung-tung could continue his education undisturbed.'

He hadn't answered my question; perhaps he didn't want to, and to press him might have brought the interview to a close, so I left it.

'And what happened after the Cultural Revolution in 1979?'

'We returned to Peking and found work as road sweepers.'

'You've had a hard life.'

'Yes,' he replied, without any rancour, 'my life has been hard. But the recent political reforms have made things easier. I was able to retire from street cleaning, and now I can devote more time to my calligraphy. And since 1987 [and a revival of interest in the imperial past] I have been working as a consultant to the state on the restoration of Prince Kung's Palace in Peking.'

From princeling to road sweeper and now, at the end of an

extraordinary life, his Dragon's blood had brought him back to the beginning again – as an outsider with insider information.

I plucked up my courage for the big question:

'In his autobiography, *From Emperor to Citizen*, P'u-yi records that when you were both prisoners of the Russians in Siberia, he adopted you as his son and heir – is this true?'

'Yes, it is true. It happened in the summer of 1950, just before we were handed over to the Chinese.'

'So you are the chosen heir of the last Emperor?'

'Yes.'

'And do you regard yourself, now that P'u-yi is dead, as the rightful ruler of all China?'

It was a preposterous question: no one can be Emperor ever again. For as long as Communism survives – and it may outlive the present elderly leadership longer than the Western world cares to believe – no amount of reforms to its substance will threaten its structure. It's that which keeps China whole. When eventually the structure collapses, it won't be an Emperor who pulls it down, but dozens of petty tyrants in dozens of petty nation-states. And China will be China no more.

So how was Yü-yan going to answer? This one really broke the rules. He turned to Principal Chang – perhaps for political clearance, perhaps for an overtime fee.

Principal Chang was nothing if not acquisitive, but he was also an *apparatchik*. With an inscrutable smile, he leaned towards my tape-recorder and pressed the off button.

LOUD Report had booked our favourite Nissan Cedric – with Teng Hsiao-p'ing's driver at the wheel again – for the run out to the airport.

Sitting in the back with me, he spent most of the journey leaning forward in such close conversation with the driver that his chin occasionally came to rest on the man's shoulder. Once or twice I caught the driver's eye in the mirror, as he listened to Loud Report's account of our Ch'ang-ch'un adventures, and he smiled sympathetically.

'Driver very shocked about Professor Wang,' said Loud Report.

'Make sure he doesn't tell Mr Teng,' I said. 'Or the professor may be sent away for re-education.' Loud Report passed the message on and both men laughed, politely.

After further animated conversation in Chinese, with frequent nods and glances in my direction, Loud Report said: 'Driver ask why you come to China, Misiter Socotolan.'

What the hell, I thought, I'm leaving now – there's nothing to lose by spilling the beans. 'Tell him I came to find an Emperor.'

Loud Report turned back to the driver, whose raised eyebrows I could see in the mirror. 'Driver want to know, "Did you find Emperor?"'

'I did. He's a retired road sweeper and he lives in a hut with a mud floor near the Drum Tower with his second wife, his third son and the nail-clippings of the last Emperor's favourite concubine.'

Teng Hsiao-p'ing's driver giggled all the way to the airport – where I paid him to wait for Loud Report and then drive him home to his parents.

Parting may be such sweet sorrow if it's bedtime and you're Juliet and Romeo's expected back in the morning. But for the rest of us, at foreign airports, it's just plain bewildering. I was fretful and anxious, not knowing which door to go through or when, anticipating problems with my luggage and notebooks in Customs and, worst of all, filled with a growing sense of unease about the effect of my visit on all those who had played a part in it: Mr Hsü, the Ch'ang-ch'un Wangs, Winter Stone, Aunt Li, the Pretender, Red Universe, Teng Hsiao-p'ing's driver, Loud Report's parents, his girlfriend Morning Mist and specially Loud Report himself. The Public Security were sure to cross-examine them all, probably had done already; would there be trouble? There couldn't be trouble, I told myself, because no one had done anything wrong. But I wasn't entirely persuaded that the Public Security would be swayed by simple Western logic. Nor was I convinced that the Public Security were the only threat: had Loud Report and Red Universe seen the last of Professor Wang and Principal Chang, or had I condemned my friends to a sentence of further harassment?

Loud Report was ominously silent. He stood beside me, pale and trembly, his eyes cast down, his arms hanging limp; he looked as shrivelled as a burst balloon. It was goodbye time. Taking his hand in both of mine, I tried to deliver the farewell speech I'd been practising all morning – expressing my gratitude, admiration, concern and fondness. But I couldn't do it: the words didn't come out right, it was a hopeless, inadequate fudge.

Loud Report's natural spontaneity and simpleness put my stumbling, stilted sentences to shame. 'Goodbye, Misiter Socotolan,' he said. 'Boss, English spee, my buddy. I will miss you.'

At the Bamboo Garden that morning I'd given him some presents and keepsakes, but I'd kept one back for now: a battered old penknife, each blade and gadget of which he'd explored and marvelled at many times during our month together.

'Hawghgh!' he exclaimed, his mouth open and his eyes wide, as he slowly opened his fingers and saw what I'd slipped into his hand. Suddenly he pressed his cheek to mine, buried his head in my shoulder and cried.

'I have classmate who is pilot,' he said, when we had both pulled ourselves together. 'He drink white spirit and smoke like volcano.'

'And what's he like as a pilot?' I asked.

'Pffff! I never flied with him, thank you.' He shuddered at the thought. 'My friend very frightened boy. When he land and take off he shut eyes and hold head.'

It was vintage Loud Report, but his heart wasn't in it any more; he was putting on a brave show.

From the Customs hall I looked back and waved. Loud Report was still standing at the place behind the glass partition where we'd parted. He didn't wave and he didn't smile; he was motionless, expressionless, a waxwork of Loud Report reproaching Misiter Socotolan for abandoning him. I'd flown into his life, turned it upside-down for a month on a wild and whimsical goose chase, and now I was flying away again. But if Loud Report thought I was going to forget him, he was wrong. With him, because of him, I'd got my story – I'd found the Manchu Pretender – but the empty throne of China, at the approach of the third millennium, belonged not to Duke Aisin-Gioro Yü-yan or any of his noble Manchu cousins, not to the venerable scion of a decadent dynasty, not to the past: it belonged to the future, the hopeful, the young, the newly democratic – it belonged to Loud Report and his generation.

GLOSSARY

Aisin-Gioro: clan name of the Manchu Emperors and their descendants.

Beileh: Manchu title equivalent to Prince of the third degree, borne by sons of Princes.

Chia-pin: Manchu courtesy title akin to 'the Hon', revived by Yü-yan's third son, Tung-tung.

Ch'ing, Ta (Great Pure): Chinese name of the Manchu dynasty, which ruled China from 1644–1912.

Ch'i-pao: Chinese dress, long, high-necked, slit-skirted.

Erh-hu: Chinese two-stringed fiddle.

Hu-t'ung: one of a network of narrow lanes which were such a distinctive feature of imperial Peking.

Lü-ch'a: green tea.

Pipa: Chinese lute.

Ta-a-ko: a title meaning literally Great Elder Brother, given to Beileh P'u-chün on his appointment as heir apparent in 1908.

Tuan-hsiu (Cut Sleeve): an ancient Chinese term for homosexuality.

Tung-pei: literally East-North, i.e. Manchuria.

Wei-ch'i: chess.

Yuan: the basic unit of Chinese currency, subdivided into 10 *jiao* and 100 *fen*. Ten *yuan* was, at the time of writing, equivalent to £1.

BIBLIOGRAPHY

Aishin-Kakuda, Hiro [née Saga], *Ruten No Ohi* (The Wandering Princess), Bungei Shunji, Tokyo, 1959.

Aisin-Gioro Pu Yi (translated by W. J. F. Jenner), *From Emperor to Citizen: The Autobiography of Aisin-Gioro Pu Yi*, Foreign Languages Press, Beijing, 1989.

Aisin-Gioro Pu Yi (edited by Paul Kramer, translated by Kuo Ying Paul Tsai), *The Last Manchu – The Autobiography of Henry Pu Yi*, Weidenfeld & Nicolson, London, 1987.

Behr, Edward, *The Last Emperor*, Macdonald, London, 1987.

Bishop, George, *Travels in Imperial China – The Exploration and Discoveries of Père David*, Cassell, London, 1990.

Bland, J. O. P. and Backhouse, E., *China under the Empress Dowager – Being the History of the Life and Times of Tzu Hsi*, William Heinemann, London, 1912.

Bridge, Ann, *Peking Picnic*, Triad/Granada, London, 1981.

Carl, Katherine A., *With the Empress Dowager of China*, 2nd edition, Société Française de Librairie et d' Edition, Tientsin, 1926.

Chan, Charis, *Imperial China*, Viking, London, 1991.

Cotterell, Arthur, *China – A Concise Cultural History*, John Murray, London, 1988.

Der Ling, Princess, *Old Buddha*, Dodd, Mead & Co., New York, 1930.

Dingle, Edwin J., *Across China on Foot: Life in the Interior and the Reform Movement*, J. W. Arrowsmith, Bristol, 1911.

Dingle, Edwin J., *China's Revolution 1911–1912*, T. Fisher Unwin, London and Leipzig, 1912.

Fleming, Peter, *One's Company – A Journey to China*, Jonathan Cape, London, 1934.

Fu Hu (translated by George Meng), *Tales of the Qing Court*, Hai Feng Publishing Co. Ltd., Hong Kong, 1990.

Giles, Herbert A., *China and the Manchus*, Cambridge at the University Press, 1912.

Hardy E. J., Rev., *John Chinaman at Home*, T. Fisher Unwin, London, 1912.

Harris, Audrey, *Eastern Visas*, Collins, London, 1939.

Hosie, Alexander, *Manchuria*, Methuen, London, 1904.

Hummel, Arthur W., ed., *Eminent Chinese of the Ch'ing Period (1644–1912)*,

United States Government Printing Office, Washington, 2 volumes, 1943 and 1944.

Johnston, Reginald F., *Twilight in the Forbidden City*, Victor Gollancz, London, 1934.

Jung Chang, *Wild Swans – Three Daughters of China*, Harper Collins, London, 1991.

Li Lu, *Moving the Mountain – My Life in China from the Cultural Revolution to Tiananmen Square*, Macmillan, London, 1990.

Li Wen-da, ed., *Pictorial Biography of the Last Emperor of China*, Dragon Publication Co., Hong Kong, 1987.

Lum, (Bettina) Peter, *Peking, 1950–53*, Robert Hale, London, 1958.

Mackerras, Colin P., *The Rise of the Peking Opera 1770–1870*, Clarendon Press, Oxford, 1977.

Martin, W. A. P., *The Siege in Peking*, New York, 1900.

Maugham, W. Somerset, *On a Chinese Screen*, Mandarin, London, 1990.

Maugham, W. Somerset, *The Painted Veil*, Mandarin, London, 1991.

Paludan, Ann, *The Chinese Spirit Road: The Classical Tradition of Stone Tomb Statuary*, Yale University Press, 1991.

Parker, Edward Harper, *John Chinaman and a few others*, John Murray, London, 1901.

Power, Brian, *The Puppet Emperor – The Life of Pu Yi, Last Emperor of China*, Corgi Books, London, 1987.

Priest, Alan, *Portraits of the Court of China*, Metropolitan Museum of Art, New York, 1942.

Saga Hiro *see* Aishin-Kakuda, Hiro.

Salisbury, Harrison T., *The New Emperors: Mao and Deng*, Harper Collins, London, 1992.

Scidmore, Eliza Ruhamah, *China – The Long-Lived Empire*, The Century Co., New York, 1900.

Seagrave, Sterling, *Dragon Lady: The Life and Legend of the Last Empress of China*, Macmillan, London, 1992.

Spender, Stephen and Hockney, David, *China Diary*, Thames and Hudson, London, 1982.

Taisuke, Mitamura (translated by C. A. Pomeroy), *Chinese Eunuchs*, Chas. E. Tuttle, Rutland, Vermont, 1970.

Terzani, Tiziano, *Behind the Forbidden Door – Travels in China*, Allen & Unwin, London, 1984.

Trevor-Roper, Hugh, *A Hidden Life: The Enigma of Sir Edmund Backhouse*, Macmillan, London, 1976.

Tsui Chi, *A Short History of Chinese Civilisation*, Victor Gollancz, London, 1942.

Varè, Daniele, *The Last Empress*, Doubleday, Doran & Co., New York, 1936. *Laughing Diplomat*, John Murray, London, 1938.

Vespa, Amleto, *Secret Agent of Japan*, Little, Brown & Co., New York, 1938.

Waln, Norah, *The House of Exile*, The Cresset Press Ltd., London, 1934.

Wang Qingxiang, *A Pictorial Biography of Aisin-Gioro P'u-yi*, Shanghai People's Publishing House, 1990. *China's Last Emperor as an Ordinary Citizen*, China Reconstructs (Great Wall Books), Beijing, 1986.

Wan Yi, Wang Shuqing and Lu Yanzhen, eds. (translated by Rosemary Scott and Erica Shipley), *Daily Life in the Forbidden City – The Qing Dynasty 1644–1912*, Viking, London, 1988.

Warner, Marina, *The Dragon Empress*, Weidenfeld & Nicolson, London, 1971.

Welch, Denton, *Maiden Voyage*, Penguin, London, 1983.